Sun Struck

**NEW
HORIZON
PRESS**

Dear Reader,

We proudly present the newest addition to our internationally acclaimed true crime series of *Real People/Incredible Stories*. These riveting thrillers spotlight men and women who perform extraordinary deeds against tremendous odds: to fight for justice, track down elusive killers, protect the innocent or exonerate the wrongly accused. Their stories, told in their own voices, reveal the untold drama and anguish behind the headlines of those who face horrific realities and find the resiliency to fight back...

Florida is well-known for its beautiful weather, picturesque beaches and exciting nightlife. Yet it is also a deadly place where killers run loose and child abductions occur often. *Sun Struck: 16 Infamous Murders in the Sunshine State* by Robert A. Waters and John T. Waters, Jr., gives you the inside stories of the most shocking and savage murders ever committed in the Sunshine State. With in-depth analysis the authors attempt to answer the question of why so many crimes and murders occur in Florida.

The next time you want to read a crackling, suspenseful page-turner, which is also a true account of a real-life hero illustrating the resiliency of the human spirit, look for the New Horizon Press logo.

Sincerely,

Dr. Joan S. Dunphy
Publisher & Editor-in-Chief
Real People/Incredible Stories

Sun Struck

16 Infamous Murders in the Sunshine State

by Robert A. Waters and John T. Waters, Jr.

New Horizon Press
Far Hills, NJ

Waters, Robert A. and Waters, Jr., John T.
Sun Struck: 16 Infamous Murders in the Sunshine State

Cover design: Wendy Bass
Interior design: Susan Sanderson

Library of Congress Control Number: 2009922797

ISBN 13: 978-0-88282-312-6
New Horizon Press

Manufactured in the U.S.A.

2013   2012   2011   2010   2009 / 5   4   3   2   1

"He sits in the lurking places of the villages;
In the secret places he murders the innocent;
His eyes are secretly fixed on the helpless.
He lies in wait secretly, as a lion in his den;
He lies in wait to catch the poor;
He catches the poor when he draws them into his net.
So he crouches, he lies low,
That the helpless may fall by his strength.
He has said in his heart,
'God has forgotten;
He hides his face;
He will never see it.'"

Psalm 10: 8-11 (New King James Version)

Dedicated to our father,
John T. Waters, Sr.

Authors' Note

The information, conversations and other events portrayed within these stories have been taken from court documents, police records, press accounts, media research and interviews.

In an effort to safeguard the privacy of certain people, some individuals' names and identifying characteristics have been changed. Events involving characters happened as described. Only minor details may have been altered.

Table of Contents

Preface

There must be something in the water.

Florida, the land of enchantment and tourist mecca to millions, is also home to the strangest killers in the nation.

It's the home of the Gainesville Ripper, the Tamiami Strangler, the Hog Trail Killer, the Vampire Rapist and the Soldier of Fortune Killer. It's the land of homegrown serial murderers such as Bobbie Joe Long, Gerard Schaefer and the final killing ground of notorious fugitives like Ted Bundy, Aileen Wuornos and Andrew Cunanan.

Sun Struck: 16 Infamous Murders in the Sunshine State is more than a true crime book. Within the framework of sixteen murders, the authors, both native Floridians, explore the unique culture of the state, including how its ecology, topography and institutions can sometimes facilitate murder.

In Florida, the overriding backdrop is growth. Unending growth. Unhealthy growth. In just a few years, the state's population has increased from three million to twenty million and shows no sign of slowing.

Although Florida's climate is generally mild, hurricanes, tornadoes, sinkholes and wildfires regularly destroy homes, businesses and lives. In the swamps, there are thirty-foot-long snakes and fifteen-foot-long alligators.

Killers sometimes dump the bodies in those swamps, leaving nature to dispose of the evidence.

The state is surrounded on three sides by the Atlantic Ocean and the Gulf of Mexico. Locals and visitors alike enjoy fishing the many rivers, lakes and ponds in the state. But water can also hide evidence of murder.

For instance, there's the fisherman who placed his seven-year-old victim in a crab trap and dumped her into Tampa Bay. Although the body was never found, Willie Crain was convicted of murdering Amanda Brown. He currently sits on death row.

Florida is a land of contrasts. Cuban refugees live next door to descendents of Confederates. Many African-Americans live in suburbia—yet others fight to survive in drug-scarred ghettoes. Major cities have a high percentage of Asians and Mexicans. In restaurants, it's not uncommon for a Spanish-speaking family to order their meal from a waitress with a Mississippi drawl. And while the ever-present tourists are a source of income for millions of Floridians, the many criminals who inhabit these lands view them as easy targets. Retirees make up nearly 20 percent of the population and are routinely victimized.

Here, diverse cultures compete, creating tensions and conflict. There are cowboys and crackheads, Christians and hustlers, farmers and urbanites, rednecks and retirees, street kids and snowbirds.

Put together, this cauldron cooks up a bitter stew of crime.

Even though Florida has more than twenty million residents, vast chunks of wilderness still defy development. People can, and do, disappear without a trace.

On February 9, 1989, Tiffany Sessions, a student at the University of Florida, left her apartment to go jogging. The pretty co-ed was never seen again. Over the years, the Gainesville Police Department tracked down thousands of leads. Her father, wealthy real estate developer Patrick Sessions, spent a fortune in an attempt to find his daughter. Ten years after her disappearance, investigators thought they had a break when a convicted rapist and murderer with the unlikely name of Michael Knickerbocker confessed to killing and burying her. But when cops dug up the area he specified, they found nothing.

Tiffany Sessions is still missing.

On July 22, 1976, twelve-year-old Dorothy "Dee" Scofield walked into a department store in Ocala. Her mother, who was next door at the Florida Highway Patrol Office, never saw her again. That afternoon, witnesses claimed they saw a car with two men and a frightened child speeding through the Ocala National Forest. The men, if they existed, were never found. Investigators privately speculated that the child may have been sexually assaulted then fed to the monster-sized alligators that inhabit the dark swamp. To this day, Scofield's photograph is occasionally seen on milk cartons and missing children's Web sites and her family still wonders what happened to her.

While disappearances are common, unidentified bodies also turn up on occasion. On April 21, 1996, workers in Tropicana, Florida, found a corpse inside a refrigerated boxcar. Nicknamed "Boxcar Jane Doe," the young victim had been wrapped in pillow cases and trash bags and tied with chains. An autopsy revealed that she'd been suffocated. After years of dogged police work, the girl was identified as a fifteen-year-old runaway from a Philadelphia foster home. In a sad ending to a sad life, it was determined the girl had been strangled. Her killer has never been found.

State officials estimate that 800 people move to Florida each day. While most are law-abiding, some are predators. In 1984, John Crutchley, a transplant from Virginia, moved to Merritt Island to work for NASA. It wasn't long before women began to disappear. In 1985, the college-educated engineer kidnapped a young woman off the streets. He took her to his home, tied her wrists and feet, then secured her upside down to a hoist in his ceiling. As she dangled helplessly, Crutchley used needles with tubing to drain her blood into a jar, which he then drank like lemonade. For two days, the victim endured rape, torture and humiliation from her insatiable attacker. The following day, while he was at work, she was able to escape. A passerby took her to the hospital where it was determined that half the blood had been drained from her body. This earned Crutchley the moniker "Vampire Rapist" and the undying hatred of millions of Floridians.

The woman barely survived and testified against him. Crutchley was charged with kidnapping, sexual battery and possession of marijuana, along with the unusual charge of "theft of blood." He was sentenced to twenty-five years in prison. Ten years later the Vampire Rapist was paroled (against massive public protests), but was imprisoned again when he failed a drug test.

On March 30, 2002, the madman accidently asphyxiated himself in his jail cell while experimenting with autoerotic masturbatory techniques.

Crutchley is suspected of killing a dozen women from Virginia to Florida, but investigators never found the hard evidence needed to tie him to the murders and disappearances.

For pure weirdness, the case of the so-called "Apopka Stalker" stands out. In early 2001, letters from a stalker began appearing outside the home of a twelve-year-old girl. They were all written in red ink and many described contacts the writer had had with the victim. "My how nice you look, baby doll," one read. "You were right next to me the other night. I bumped into you."

The letters described explicit sex acts the writer wished to perform on the girl and told of how he had molested other adolescent girls. Police did everything they could think of to catch him. Even though they staked out the girl's home, new letters continued to appear, as if a ghost had left them. Cops tracked down all registered sex offenders in the area and obtained handwriting samples. None matched. They published samples of the writing in local newspapers. No one came forward to identify the writer.

After nine months, the letters stopped. But by then the child had become psychologically traumatized. "She's twelve," the girl's mother said. "And she's gone back to sucking her thumb. She's terrorized."

The Apopka Stalker has never been identified.

In 2008, there were 581 homicides in Florida. Though statistically a small number, because of an abundance of sensational cases and the perception that crime is rampant, Floridians generally favor tough legal sanctions for those convicted of violent crimes.

During the late 1980s, after the courts had ordered the release of many inmates due to overcrowding, legislators provided funding to build new prisons. And because of a perception that judges were "soft on crime," the legislature passed laws mandating lengthy sentences for certain violent acts. In addition, new laws aimed at reducing gain time began to take effect. In 1990, for instance, most prisoners served only 33 percent of their sentences. By 2003, time served was 85 percent.

These and other anti-crime legislation have played significant roles in the reduction of violent crime rates since the early 1990s.

Polls consistently show that 75 to 80 percent of residents favor the death penalty. For sixty years the preferred method of execution was the electric chair.

Old Sparky, as the chair is called, has had a long and checkered history. It was first used in Florida in 1926. Then, in 2000, after several botched executions, the Florida Supreme Court ordered legislators to give murderers the right to choose between electrocution and lethal injection.

Two female serial killers, Aileen Wuornos and "Black Widow" Judy Buenoano, have been executed in recent years.

Wuornos, glamorized in books and film, was in reality an unattractive man-hater who murdered seven strangers simply to steal their possessions.

In addition to poisoning two husbands for insurance money, Buenoano committed one of the most atrocious murders in Florida's history. Her nineteen-year-old son, Michael Goodyear, was in the Air Force. He made the mistake of naming his mother as the beneficiary on his life insurance policy. When he came home on leave, Buenoano fed the airman massive doses of arsenic. Although it didn't kill him, the poison paralyzed him from the waist down. After he received a medical discharge from the Air Force, his mother took it as her mission to "nurse" him back to health. However, she made sure his policy was paid. Instead of improving under Buenoano's care, Goodyear's condition deteriorated until he became bedridden.

By May 13, 1980, Buenoano was desperate for money. On that day, she strapped her son into a wheelchair and took him for a canoe ride in the East River near Pensacola. Once out of the sight of other boaters, Buenoano capsized the canoe. Strapped to his wheelchair and wearing heavy leg braces, Goodyear was helpless. He quickly sank to the bottom and drowned. Buenoano swam to shore where she was "rescued" by passing boaters. The drowning was ruled an accident and within a few weeks, she cashed a check for $100,000.

It was only after she was caught attempting to dynamite her third husband that suspicion fell on Buenoano. Authorities exhumed the corpses of her two previous husbands and her son. They found lethal levels of arsenic in all the bodies. She'd collected large insurance premiums on each victim. There were few protests when she met her fate in the electric chair.

After Buenoano's execution, Old Sparky began misfiring. In 1997, onlookers watched in horror as Pedro Medina's head exploded in flames during his execution. But the ordeal of Medina, who had been convicted of murdering an Orlando schoolteacher, elicited little sympathy from the public. In fact, one politician exclaimed, "Maybe this will deter others from coming to Florida and committing murder."

Once lethal injection became the state's method of execution, many residents contended that it was too easy a way to die, like simply going to sleep.

A case in point is the December 10, 2002, execution of a career criminal named Linroy Bottoson. In 1979, he kidnapped seventy-four-year-old postmistress Catherine Alexander after robbing her of $18,000 in money orders. Then he held his victim captive in the trunk of her own car for more than three days. Eventually, he decided to kill her. He drove Alexander to an orange grove, stabbed her a dozen times, then ran her over. When he noticed that she was still twitching, he ran over her again, finally completing the murder. Bottoson was captured when his wife tried to cash the money orders. While a small group demonstrated in front of Florida State Prison at Raiford to protest his execution, many observers noted that it took the murderer less than five minutes to die. On the other hand, Alexander was tortured for eighty-three hours before succumbing to a horrible, prolonged death.

These tales told in *Sun Struck* aren't warm cozies. In fact, here are the inside stories of the most atrocious murders in the annals of crime.

Wild and strange, crazed and brutal, Florida murderers have distinct styles of their own. They've made criminal history again and again. Theirs is part of the legacy of the Sunshine State.

Maybe it's the weather. Maybe it's the lifestyle. Maybe it's the mix of cultures. In any case, life in the tropics can be murder.

Part One
Strangers in Paradise

Introduction

Families who've had a son, daughter, husband or wife kidnapped never forget. While the case may go cold, the horrendous events are never far from the minds of the victims' loved ones.

"Part One: Strangers in Paradise" describes five stranger abductions that took place in the Sunshine State.

"A Murder of Innocence" examines the Jessica Lunsford case. On February 25, 2005, the nine-year-old vanished from her own home in the middle of the night. By this time, the era of true crime "talk shows" had arrived. Night after night, television viewers across the country were bombarded with a startling question: If we're not safe in our own beds, are we truly safe at all?

Carlie Brucia, eleven years old, was the first known person to have their abduction caught on videotape. "The Video" recreates her kidnapping and the desperate manhunt for the person responsible. The bone-chilling images of the young girl being led away were played and replayed thousands of times as a horrified nation remained riveted to their television sets.

"The Crab Fisherman" delves into one of the few cases in the state where prosecutors obtained a conviction even though the victim's remains were never found.

"Murder in the Redlands" tells the sad story of a boy with a near-genius IQ who was snatched after he got off his school bus. It was only through a lucky chain of events that his whereabouts were discovered.

"An American Monster" reveals the complete story of a nationally publicized case which went unsolved for over twenty-five years. With the possible exception of the Lindbergh abduction, the Adam Walsh disappearance is the most well-known kidnapping case in America.

In each of these cases the authors will focus on children taken by sexual predators.

FBI statistics reveal that stranger abductions are rare, maybe 300 a year. But they are among the most devastating of crimes. Parents, relatives, friends and communities are often paralyzed with fear and grief. Additionally, because of the mystery and the primordial human loss caused by a child abduction, the media tends to overhype these stories.

The randomness of the attacks makes stranger abductions among the most difficult of cases to solve. In the paragraphs below, the authors have listed a few cold cases from the Sunshine State.

Sixteen years after she went missing and was found murdered, Jennifer Renee Odom's killer still walks the streets.

On the afternoon of February 19, 1993, the pretty twelve-year-old stepped off her school bus near Dade City and began walking the 100 yards to her home. Within eyesight of the double-wide she lived in with her parents and sister, Jennifer vanished.

Students on the bus told investigators they saw a faded blue pickup truck slowly following her.

A week later, Jennifer's nude body was discovered in an abandoned orange grove twenty miles away. Heavy rain and scavenging animals had destroyed any evidence that the killer might have left. Two years later, her book bag and clarinet were located near Weeki Wachee, fifteen miles away from where her body was found. Although her killer has never been caught, an unidentified fingerprint was located inside her clarinet case. Investigators think it could belong to Jennifer's killer.

Jennifer Odom was killed by a massive blow to the head and was likely sexually assaulted.

Her family still lives in the home they shared with Jennifer. There is no closure, only a tearing of the heart that never ends. "We talk about her every day," her mother, Renee Converse, said.

In the authors' hometown of Ocala, a mystery—forgotten by most—still remains. The case is so cold that on the thirtieth anniversary of the abduction of Dorothy "Dee" Scofield, the local newspaper didn't even run an article about it. A week before Independence Day 1976, while Dee's mother visited the Florida Highway Patrol Office to renew her driver's license, Dee walked about 100 yards to a department store. Within minutes, the twelve-year-old vanished and was never seen again.

The store went out of business many years ago and is now the site of the Marion County Public Library. Few visitors to the artsy, slick-tiled building now remember the mysterious events that occurred there so many years ago.

Dee's mother lives on and remembers. She still recalls the alleged sighting and the desperate searches in the alligator-infested Ocala National Forest. There was the grief, the guilt, the lives torn apart. The family eventually moved to another state to try to numb the pain, but it never let up.

Dee's father died many years ago, some say of a broken spirit. An unknown monster destroyed a loving family, and unless he's still alive and confesses, this mystery is unlikely to ever have an answer.

In the heart of the Magic Kingdom, on January 24, 2006, a twenty-four-year-old woman went missing without a trace. Jennifer Kesse walked out of her condominium apartment and into oblivion. She was beautiful, college-educated and had a well-paying job that she loved.

Unbeknownst to the tourists who flock there, Orlando, where she lived, festers with a criminal underbelly that belies the glitter of Disney World. Jennifer was aware of this—she always carried a cell phone and pepper spray.

Three days after her disappearance, Jennifer's car was found in a parking lot about a half-mile from her condominium. Film from surveillance videos in nearby businesses showed a man (or woman) dressed in a painter's uniform exiting the vehicle and walking away. The suspect was five foot three to five foot five inches tall. He, or she, has never been identified.

Her father, Drew Kesse, commented during an interview on *KidnappingMurderandMayhem.Blogspot.com*: "Jennifer was well known for her 'safe calls.' If she was out and did not feel she was in a safe place, she would get someone on the phone. In that way, she would have help if she needed it. She would call mostly at night, coming and going from stores in Orlando or even from a night out. If we [her parents] got the safe call, we used to tease her and say, 'What's up, none of your friends around? Had to go down the list?'"

Despite all her efforts to stay safe, Jennifer Kesse joined the sad ranks of the missing.

On January 16, 1981, eighteen-year-old Mary Opitz walked out of a mall in Fort Myers and vanished. A package containing items she'd purchased was found lying near her locked car. Incredibly, police initially treated the case as if Opitz was a runaway. Then, a month later, Mary Hare, also eighteen, disappeared from the same mall. A few weeks later, her body was found in Lehigh Acres. She'd been stabbed to death. Opitz has never been found, and neither case was solved.

These cases, as well as that of Colleen Orsborn, have been attributed to serial killer Christopher Wilder. On March 15, 1984, Colleen, fifteen years old, headed out the door to school in Daytona Beach and simply vanished. She has never been found.

According to investigators, Wilder was seen in the areas of each disappearance.

Dead serial killers always make convenient suspects in unsolved murders. A confirmed rapist and serial murderer, Wilder's method of operation was to approach attractive girls and women at shopping malls and pose as a fashion photographer. A smooth talker with an Australian accent, he convinced his victims to follow him to his car. There he forcibly abducted them. Wilder enjoyed torturing his victims and seeing the fear in their eyes just before snuffing out their last breaths.

His confirmed Florida victims were twenty-year-old Rosario Gonzalez of Miami, twenty-three-year-old Elizabeth Kenyon of Coral Gables and twenty-one-year-old Terry Ferguson of Indian Harbor.

In 2007, an apparent dumping ground for an unknown serial killer was discovered near Fort Myers. The skeletal remains of eight men ranging in age from eighteen to forty-nine were found in a remote, swampy forest. No clothing or other personal items were found. Forensic scientists think that some of the bodies may have been there for as long as twenty years.

Two victims have been identified: Erik D. Kohler, twenty-one years old, and John C. Blevins, thirty-eight years old. Each had minor criminal backgrounds, mostly related to drug and alcohol abuse.

Daniel Conahan, the infamous Hog Trail Killer who now sits on death row, has been mentioned as a possible suspect. He liked to pick up drifters and men who were down on their luck. He offered them money to pose for photographs, then raped and murdered them. Many of his victims were murdered in Punta Gorda, just a few miles from Fort Myers.

Florida is known for its sun and surf.

But it also has serial murderers and blood-thirsty maniacs who stalk the cities, beaches and forests of paradise.

Chapter 1
A Murder of Innocence

"I want to talk to a lawyer, because, I mean, if people [are] trying to accuse [me] of something I didn't do. I didn't do it."

John Evander Couey, questioned by authorities
about the disappearance of his nine-year-old neighbor.

The old home shook and rattled as flames roared through it. The blaze quickly ate the tin siding and plywood frame, then began licking at the two-by-fours holding the home together. An observer at the scene said the rows of planks looked like cracking ribs as they wilted in the heat.

The fire department was slow getting to the home, but by the time they did arrive, only a blackened hulk remained.

The fire had been set on purpose. An unknown arsonist, it seemed, had made a desperate attempt to burn away the stain that infected the house. It didn't work.

Jessica Marie Lunsford was still dead.

It was early Wednesday morning, February 24, 2005, when Mark Lunsford heard his daughter's alarm clock beeping. Jessica was always prompt about getting up. She loved school and rarely missed, so the continued braying of the alarm worried Lunsford.

His job was a grind. He worked sixty to eighty hours a week and was always bone-tired. He'd been married twice, but was now divorced. At forty-two, he lived with his parents, Ruth and Archie, and Jessica in a home in Homosassa, Florida. When he wasn't working, Lunsford's favorite pastime was to ride his motorcycle along the rural back roads. Sometimes Jessica climbed up on the back and went with him.

On the previous night, Jessica had attended church. She'd memorized a Bible verse, Philippians 4:13. "I can do all things through Christ who strengthens me," she repeated to her class.

Plastered across her bedroom door was a crepe paper sign that she'd written by hand. "Knock before you enter," it read.

Mark Lunsford opened the door and called Jessica's name. The room had a night-light near the bed and a flashlight on the nightstand. Jessica was afraid of the dark.

In the half-light, Mark couldn't see his daughter, so he switched on the overhead bulb. She wasn't in her bed. Stuffed animals were everywhere, including the huge toy tiger she slept with—but Lunsford noticed her purple dolphin was missing.

Less than a week before, on Sunday, Mark had taken his daughter to the Tampa State Fair. Jessica rode the Ferris wheel, mounted a mechanical bull, climbed a rock wall and enjoyed the excitement of the evening. At the fair, Mark bought her a pink felt hat. She pulled it onto her head and smiled innocently into the camera as her father snapped a picture.

Mark also won the purple stuffed dolphin. He later joked that it took about $35.00 to get it.

He was puzzled. Where could his daughter be? He walked back to his parents' bedroom. They slept with the door open and Mark peered in. Still no Jessica. After calling her name and checking the other rooms, he awoke Ruth and Archie. Mark asked if they knew where she had gone. The grandparents were as perplexed as Mark himself.

By now a cold fear had enveloped the occupants of the house.

After another quick check around the place, Mark's mother called 911. It was 6:08 A.M. Her voice shook with emotion as she spoke with the dispatcher.

"My granddaughter is missing," she said.

"What's her name?"

"Jessica Lunsford. L–U–N–S–F–O–R–D."

"What is her date of birth, ma'am?"

"October the..." Ruth's voice trailed off into a series of sobs.

"That's okay, ma'am, you're doing good," the operator said. "October what?"

"October 6, 1995."

"In '95?"

"Yes ma'am," she said.

"Okay, ma'am, we're getting you some help."

Since Homosassa had no police force, the Citrus County Sheriff's Office had jurisdiction over the disappearance of Jessica Lunsford. Almost immediately, the first deputies on the scene realized that this was an unusual case. They contacted the Crimes Against Children Unit (CACU). A child was missing under suspicious circumstances from her home near the fishing village of Homosassa, they reported.

The deputies were mystified.

Had she run away? Had she walked outside and become lost? Had she met someone she knew after everyone else went to bed? Or had some human predator come into the home and snatched her? At the time, that seemed to be the least likely scenario, but it was the job of the CACU to find out.

In his book, *Nature's Masterpiece at Homosassa*, Pulitzer Prize-winning journalist W. Horace Carter wrote: "Eight miles of winding river carry water as clear as Russian vodka from a deep, rocky spring to the shallow mouth of the Homosassa where it joins the Gulf of Mexico."

Times and the environment changed. By 2005, man had encroached into that wilderness, establishing a chaotic assortment of ranch-style homes, house trailers, RVs and campers. Newcomers nested in the swamps while visiting fishermen caught speckled trout, mango snappers, tarpon and giant sheepshead in the river and the channels along the coast.

Still, there was plenty of natural beauty left. The homes where Mark Lunsford lived were surrounded by forests. Raccoons, deer and even an occasional wild turkey could be seen rummaging in the undergrowth.

After being called by the responding deputies, investigators arrived. Almost immediately, they transported Mark and his father to the Sheriff's department, while his mother remained at home in case Jessica returned. Mark Lunsford later said he refused to leave his home until he was promised by detectives that a thorough, door-to-door search of the homes in the area would be conducted.

As Mark entered the interrogation room at the Sheriff's department, he received a decidedly frigid reception from the investigators. He was surprised. Instead of being treated as a sympathetic father, he soon realized that he was a prime suspect. Mark had a few skeletons in his closet and he'd moved down to Homosassa in order to put his past behind him, he said. A former girlfriend had accused him of domestic violence, but he'd never been charged.

At the Lunsford house, the search was slow in getting started. Many investigators initially thought the girl would be found within hours. They contacted the local elementary school to find out if Jessica had shown up. She hadn't. Finally, in the late afternoon, they called in search dogs.

Investigators originally thought that Mark himself or his father had done something to the girl.

In the early hours of the investigation, detectives came up with an unusual strategy designed to break the case. They told Mark they'd found blood on his father's underwear. DNA tests, they said, confirmed that it was Jessica's blood. It was a lie, of course, but he didn't know it at the time.

Cops arranged for Mark to meet Archie in an interview room and recorded the confrontation between father and son. Angry words were exchanged, but Archie emphatically denied the accusation. Investigators' hopes for a quick confession were dashed, but the tension between Mark and his father lasted for weeks.

The suspects were brought back into separate interrogation rooms and grilled some more. Throughout the day, detectives took turns trying to wring a confession from one or the other.

After they failed, and with no evidence to hold the two, they were released.

About a hundred-and-fifty yards away from the Lunsford residence, a home sat rusting in the sun. Several decades-old cars littered the yard.

Late in the afternoon, detectives approached the house. Dorothy Marie Dixon opened the creaky door and identified herself as the owner. When asked if she knew anything about the disappearance of her neighbor, Dixon denied it.

Two others in the house were also questioned. The owner's daughter, Madie Dixon Secord, murmured that she knew nothing and stormed back inside. Her boyfriend, Matthew Dittrich, also brushed off the cops.

The detectives never went inside the house.

By the next day, the media had descended on the once-quiet community. Greta Van Susteren, Nancy Grace and Geraldo Rivera were a few of the cable network stars who focused their television broadcasts on issues involving crime. The disappearance of a pretty little girl was the type of case that kept their viewers enthralled.

Just a day earlier, Jessica Marie Lunsford had been an anonymous nine-year-old living in a little-known town. Now she had *become* the news.

While researching evidence about the case, a reporter from the *St. Petersburg Times* interviewed the pastor of the church Jessie attended. Jessica was a "quiet girl with a radiant smile," William LaVerle Coats said. "She was outgoing and friendly, but shy in some respects." She was a member of a Bible study group at the church.

Her family and friends stated that Jessica and her father were very close. She enjoyed having him read to her and loved to sing for him. She had a karaoke machine and memorized country songs. Country musician Toby Keith's "Let's Talk About Me" was one of her favorites. She also liked pop singer Celine Dion.

The family gave the Citrus County Sheriff's Office dozens of photographs to use in trying to locate Jessica. One, the picture of her wearing the pink felt hat, struck a chord with the public. The image depicted the beauty and wholesomeness of youth. The photograph was sent by the sheriff's office to the National Center for Exploited Children and placed on missing persons posters. Reflecting on the effect the photograph had on people, Bob Thompson, a professor of Communications at Syracuse University, said, "It made you like that kid. It's that great American toothy innocent smile that evokes so many utopian ideas of childhood."

Although the sheriff's department had gotten off to a slow start, they quickly made up for lost time. They still suspected someone in the family, but by now Mark and his father had taken and passed polygraph tests. According to the FBI polygrapher, Ruth's answers were inconclusive, probably because of stress.

Sheriff's deputies, FBI agents, Florida Department of Law Enforcement officials, neighboring police agencies and hundreds of volunteers launched a massive search for the missing girl.

The unthinkable was beginning to creep into the thoughts of some veteran investigators: Could a stranger have entered the house and snatched Jessica? The family admitted that the front door may have been left unlocked, but Jessica's little dog hadn't barked. Investigators were unable to explain exactly why the dog remained silent if an intruder had entered the home.

While the search continued, reporters learned more about the missing girl. She loved to eat at a local Italian restaurant, but she didn't like pizza. Jessica enjoyed shopping with her grandmother at department stores and collected assorted dolls, mostly of the porcelain variety. Her favorite colors were pink and purple.

And she had her grandfather wrapped around her finger. Anytime they went to the store, she came back home toting a bag of caramel candy and wearing a big grin.

Jessica was just beginning to wear makeup. "I gave her an old box of cosmetics that she would play with," Ruth said. "Well, one Sunday we were getting ready to go to church and she came out with all this makeup on. I said, 'Jessie, that's too much for church.'" She smiled at the memory.

After two days, there were no leads. Searchers labored though swamps looking for any clues. Old-time fishing guides stood up their paying customers to search the river and waterways. Helicopters swooped over the landscape.

Detectives continued to pressure Mark and Archie.

Meanwhile, at the home of Dorothy Dixon, the owner's half-brother John Evander Couey had barricaded himself in his room.

"People don't like me for some reason," Couey once said. He never figured out that his obsession with little girls and drugs turned off most people.

John Couey was five feet four inches tall and weighed about 125 pounds. Even though he was only forty-seven years old, drug and alcohol use had aged him so badly that most people thought he was twenty years older. He'd been arrested at least twenty-four times in his life. The less serious charges included disorderly intoxication, carrying a concealed weapon, burglary, driving while under the influence of alcohol, fraud and larceny. Because of a long history of DUI charges, Couey's driver's license had been suspended for ninety-nine years.

But there was more.

In 1978, while burglarizing a neighbor's home, Couey molested a five-year-old girl who was asleep in her bed. He was convicted of attempted rape and sentenced to ten years in prison. The judge, however, placed him on probation. In a recurring theme in his life, however, he never reported to his probation officer. Couey was arrested again and sent to prison to serve his time. In another recurring theme, after only two years, he was released.

An article in the *Tampa Tribune* reported that he was "paroled in 1980 [but] became a fugitive within a month. He moved and failed to tell authorities. They caught up with him the next year, after he broke into another home. He received [another] ten year sentence but was released in 1984."

He continued to commit petty crimes. By now, he'd become addicted to crack cocaine and many of his arrests were drug-related.

Couey was arrested for indecent exposure three years later.

Shortly after that, he was arrested for fondling a child. He admitted to the crime, but told arresting officers that he didn't think prison would help him. "I want to get help for myself so I will never do this again," he said. He was sent to prison for the third time, but was again released early. After once again violating his probation, Couey was sent to prison for two more years.

At the time of Jessica's disappearance, he was on probation for drunk driving and marijuana possession. A registered sex offender, he was required to notify local law enforcement agencies of any change of address. As usual, he failed to contact the Citrus County Sheriff's Office when he moved in with his half-sister. When a probation officer couldn't locate him at his former address, a warrant was issued for his twenty-fifth arrest.

It was later learned that Couey had been dismissed from several jobs for making inappropriate comments to young girls. In at least one instance, he told a co-worker to "look at that good-looking woman." When the co-worker saw that Couey was referring to a preteen girl, he said he got chills up and down his spine. Couey was quickly fired from that job as well.

After the third day of searching, there were still no leads. The Lunsford home had been searched several times. The only item missing was the purple stuffed dolphin.

Search dogs, including cadaver dogs, continued to scour the neighborhood. They walked by the home of the disinterested neighbors and never alerted. Investigators again interviewed the occupants. This time, police asked about John Couey. Dixon and the others denied knowing his whereabouts.

Ground searches in the woods surrounding the neighborhood continued. It was frustrating to the cops. The longer the search went on, the less likely that Jessica would be found alive. They knew that for every kidnapped victim who is recovered alive, there are hundreds of children who never return. Many are found dead—others are never located.

The Lunsford family had withstood days of scrutiny and heavy-handed interrogations by police, as well as nasty speculation by the media. It seemed obvious to all but the most biased investigators that Jessica was adored by her father and grandparents and that she loved them in return. In fact, she seemed to bring a certain intimate warmth to the household that none of the other family members could match. Yet until the case was solved, the family would remain suspects.

Jessica's mother, Angela Bryant, was interviewed by detectives in Morrow, Ohio, where she lived. "She is not a suspect," Sheriff Dawsy told the media. "At this point," he continued, "we're looking for anything, including a body. [But] I don't like what I see. It makes me extremely nervous."

Mark had begun to hold impromptu press conferences, many times wearing his motorcycle jacket and dark sunglasses. Reporters liked his folksy style. "I want my daughter home," he said. "If there is anything anybody knows, there are a lot of numbers you can call. Help me find my daughter and bring her home."

Atlanta Braves pitcher Mike Hampton and his wife offered a $25,000 reward for information leading to an arrest. Hampton, who had won 141 games as a major league pitcher, was a Florida native who had lived in Homosassa for most of his life.

By the following week, the reward had grown to $115,000. This was the best indication that Dixon and her family had no knowledge of the abduction. Had they known he'd kidnapped Jessica, there's no doubt that they would have turned him in immediately.

John Evander Couey used a bus ticket to flee the area.

Citrus County Sheriff Dawsy stood at a bank of microphones near the Lunsford home. Dawsy had been in law enforcement for twenty-five years, yet he'd never seen a case like this. So far, every lead had dried up. But now he had a solid suspect.

As the media hung on every word, the sheriff announced that authorities were seeking a person of interest. While searching through databases of convicted sex offenders in Citrus County, detectives learned that John Evander Couey had lived near the Lunsford home at the time Jessica disappeared. He'd been convicted of several sex crimes, Dawsy said, all involving young girls.

Investigators had interviewed the occupants of the home where Couey lived three times. They finally learned that he was the half-brother of Dorothy Dixon. It was only after detectives searched the house and found evidence of someone staying in the spare bedroom that Dixon admitted that Couey had already left.

Couey had recently been picked up by police at a Salvation Army shelter in Savannah. However, he'd been questioned and released.

Detectives Gary Atchison and Scott Grace were en route to Georgia, Dawsy said. They hoped to be able to locate and interview the "person of interest" of which they were in search.

The suspect had watery blue eyes. The wrinkles ridging his eyes were permanently etched into his face. As he sat at the table chain-smoking, John Evander Couey was so small he had to look up at the two detectives interviewing him.

The room was tiny, slate-gray, with no windows. A tape recorder sat on the table.

Atchison and Grace had first traveled to Savannah, but learned that Couey was no longer there. Television coverage of the case was at a fever pitch, however, and with his face all over the news, there was no place to hide. On March 17, a worker at a Salvation Army shelter in Augusta, Georgia, recognized him and called 911. Deputies from the Richland County Sheriff's Office arrested Couey for violation of probation and for leaving the state of Florida without notifying probation officers. They held him until Citrus County authorities arrived.

When Atchison and Grace interviewed Couey, he steadfastly denied any knowledge about the disappearance of Jessica Lunsford.

Finally, about three hours into the interview, Detective Grace said, "John, would you take a lie detector test for us?"

Couey looked rattled, as if he wasn't expecting the question.

"I guess," he said. "I'm just—I want a lawyer, you know."

The United States Supreme Court had interpreted the Fifth Amendment of the Bill of Rights to mean that a detective must immediately stop questioning any suspect who requests an attorney.

The detectives continued their interrogation. They later claimed that they were unclear as to what Couey was asking or what he really wanted them to do.

Time was passing quickly. Atchison and Grace knew they were in a predicament. Jessica might still be alive, awaiting rescue from some cage or bunker or locked room. They were steadfastly focused on the business of finding the little girl.

After several more requests for an attorney, the detectives ended the interview for the day.

The following day they again spoke to Couey. He was much more cooperative and now said he had no objection to taking a polygraph. "This is the way I'll be able to clear my name," he said.

FBI Special Agent John Whitmore was assigned to conduct the examination. It went badly for Couey. After it was over, he told Whitmore, "I done it. I want to tell Gary and Scott about it."

Before re-interviewing Couey, Atchison rushed to a telephone and called Sheriff Dawsy. He told the sheriff that the department needed to "secure that residence."

A few minutes later, Couey confessed to kidnapping, raping and murdering Jessica Lunsford. The body, he said, could be found buried in the backyard of where he lived.

Sheriff Dawsy drove to the Lunsford home. As the yellow crime scene tape was being circled around Dixon's home, Dawsy relayed the news to Mark and his parents.

For three weeks, Jessica had lain in a makeshift grave just yards away from her own home. The family was devastated.

As investigators dug for Jessica's body, Grace and Atchison again interviewed Couey. By now, he'd been transported to the Citrus County jail. What he told them would send shockwaves across the nation.

"I did it," Couey said, sobbing. "I sexually assaulted her...I buried her alive...I hate myself. I'm sorry. It hurts me. You don't realize how much it hurts me."

He described watching Jessica from the front porch of his home. She was "cute," he said. As he watched her ride her bicycle and play with her dog, he thought about having a "relationship" with her.

Sometime in the early morning of February 24, Couey entered the house through an unlocked front door. He wasn't sure of the time, because he'd been smoking crack and drinking beer. He wore gloves so he wouldn't leave fingerprints. He never saw a dog, he said, but he could see Ruth and Archie sleeping, because they kept their bedroom door open.

He stole into Jessie's bedroom, Couey said, and told her to get up. She was wearing a pink nightgown. He led her outside and they walked across the street to the trailer where he was staying. He claimed that she followed him willingly.

(Authorities later disputed much of Couey's confession. In response to critic Bill O'Reilly, State Attorney Brad King said in the June 26, 2005, edition of the *St. Petersburg Times*: "In his prior crimes against children, Couey had used his hand across their mouth to prevent the victims from saying anything. The best evidence is that Couey used a combination of force, threats and promises to move Jessica from her home to his room, to sexually assault her and then murder her.")

Couey forced Jessica to climb a ladder he'd placed at his window so they wouldn't disturb the others in the house. He then followed her into his bedroom. Almost immediately, Couey sexually molested the child. Afterwards, he claimed they slept together the rest of the night.

Pedophiles routinely think their victims are willing participants in their sex crimes. Couey was no exception. During the interview, even though he admitted that what he'd done was wrong, he minimized his own participation and tried to convince detectives that "he and Jessica developed a relationship."

Couey claimed that when they awoke, they again "had sex." He then placed her in his closet, he said, and told her to keep quiet. He claimed that he fed her hamburgers, chicken nuggets and pizza. Couey also said Jessica urinated on the floor of the closet.

The evidence shows that these statements were lies. "As reported by Jessica's family, she did not like pizza," Brad King wrote. "Further, her stomach did not contain any food at the time of her death. Couey also claimed that in order to prevent the other occupants of the house from knowing of Jessica's presence, she did not use the bathroom in the home, but instead urinated on the floor in the closet. The FDLE's analysis of evidence taken from the closet has not identified any urine..."

Couey stated that he intended to release her on the following day, but then he saw deputies searching for Jessica. "I usually would watch out the window," Couey said. "[I'd] watch y'all that whole time, during the day...[I'd] sit in there in the bedroom, and popped a piece of my blind up...and I could see everything going on out there." People were going back and forth through the house, but Couey claimed that Jessica never made any noise to alert them. According to Couey's statement, Matthew Dittrich even came into his room. Secord's boyfriend was "flipping out," he said, and Jessica never made a sound. He never noticed the kidnapped girl.

On the third night, Couey went outside and dug a hole. He claimed that it only took him fifteen minutes because the ground was sandy. He said he could see the news media in the distance, but no one noticed him. Then he went back inside and raped Jessica for the last time.

After it was over, Couey tied her wrists with speaker wire and ordered her to climb into a black plastic trash bag. "I told her to get inside one bag, and she did," he said. "I told her to sit down and I tied the first bag and I had the other bag and I tied it. Then I just carried her out there."

As he tried to put her into the hole he'd dug, Jessica struggled. "She pushed her head up...because the bag tried to stretch," he said.

Couey continued, "I pushed the sand on top of her and [patted] the sand down."

Detective Grace asked, "John, after you put her in the hole and you covered her up, what did you do next?"

"Went back in the house and went to bed."

Incredulous, Grace asked, "[Were] you able to go back to bed?"

"Yeah, I just laid back down and went to sleep," Couey said.

Dr. Steven Cogswell, Medical Examiner for the Fifth Judicial District, arrived at the house where Couey lived. The wind was blowing and a chill was in the air. Television crews, having been alerted by the crime scene tape surrounding the trailer and the high-powered lamps that lighted the scene, attempted to film the excavation of Jessica's body. However, cops circled their cars around the grave.

"At the time I arrived," Cogswell said in a court deposition, "most of the excavation of her body had been accomplished—that is, the area around the grave site had been cleared. The excavation or the removal of dirt down to the top of her head had been accomplished."

Cogswell ordered his investigator, Nadine Baez, to take photos of the scene as Jessica's remains were uncovered. Like archaeologists, forensic technicians from the Florida Department of Law Enforcement scraped away the sand. When that was done, they lifted the body from the hole. After Jessica was transported to his laboratory in Leesburg, Cogswell examined the trash bags that held the child. He made a startling discovery. "The right index and middle fingers were [poking] through the bag," he said. "Actually through both bags, I should say, through both the inner and the outer bags."

As he removed the bags so that he could analyze Jessie's body, he was once again stopped in his tracks: Even with her hands tied, Jessica was clinging to the purple stuffed dolphin that had been missing from her room.

It was an appalling scene. The dolphin appeared to have been her last ray of comfort before she gasped her life away.

Cogswell removed the speaker wire from Jessica's wrists.

The autopsy revealed that the child had suffocated. Her death probably took three to five minutes, Cogswell said.

Vaginal lacerations indicated that Jessica Lunsford had been raped.

When the results of the autopsy were released, the nation was repulsed by the monstrous crime that suddenly became everyone's worst nightmare.

The Lunsford family was devastated.

"I hope you rot in hell," Mark Lunsford exclaimed in an interview, speaking directly to Couey. "I hope you get the death penalty."

Angela Bryant said, "He will pay for hurting those children out there and my daughter. He deserves everything that's coming to him."

Mark's mother could not be interviewed. "I'm in no condition to talk right now," she said.

At the church Jessica attended, her minister, William LaVerle Coats, offered a prayer. "Lord, we don't always understand your ways," he said. "We accept what has taken place here and ask that you would give us some peace."

A few days later the local Presbyterian Church (which could hold more people than Jessica's church) was filled to capacity as more than 1,000 mourners paid their respects. Many were strangers to the Lunsfords. A montage of photographs depicted Jessica's short life in sequence, from birth to the day before she was abducted.

A sobbing Sheriff Dawsy spoke. "I'm so sorry I didn't bring her back home to you alive," he said, addressing the Lunsford family.

Looking toward heaven, Mark Lunsford said, "I always said she would come home, and she did."

On April 1, John Evander Couey was indicted by a Citrus County grand jury. He was charged with first degree murder, burglary, kidnapping and sexual battery. Since his arrest, he'd been placed in isolation at the Citrus County Jail due to threats from other inmates.

Couey spent much of his time reading tracts about the Bible. During his confession, detectives had asked about his religious beliefs. "I know the Bible pretty good," he said. "I don't live it, but I know it. [But] I don't have the right to talk about the holy word when I'm sitting over here doing the Devil's work."

He also told investigators that he could be forgiven for murdering Jessica Lunsford, because the apostle Paul had been forgiven for murdering Christians.

But he stated emphatically that he deserved the death penalty.

Mark Lunsford now had a national audience when he spoke. He soon became an effective advocate for children's issues, established the Jessica Marie Lunsford Foundation and began working with legislators to pass the Jessica Lunsford Act. The Act, signed by then-Florida Governor Jeb Bush, provided electronic monitoring of sex offenders, mandatory background checks of contract workers who work at schools and additional money for prisons.

Lunsford also lobbied legislators from other states, as well as national politicians. More than thirty states and the federal government eventually passed some version of "Jessica's Law." The innocent child's death had impacted millions of Americans.

As the trial date approached, Couey's defense attorneys moved to throw out his confessions and all evidence recovered after those confessions. The suspect, they said, had requested an attorney seven times. His request was ignored each time. Had the motion been granted, Couey would have been a free man.

Circuit Judge Ric Howard, who would be trying the case, threw out his initial confessions but allowed the evidence to be used. Rick Ridgeway, Chief Assistant State Attorney, and Pete Magrio, Assistant State Attorney, were chosen to try the case for the prosecution. Dan Lewin and Alan Fanter, both Assistant Public Defenders, had the unenviable job of representing Couey.

Because of pretrial publicity, Judge Howard accepted a change of venue request by the defense and began calling potential jurors from nearby Lake County. Such was the notoriety of the case that twelve impartial jurors could not be found. Finally, the case was moved to Miami where a jury was finally seated.

The trial began on February 12, 2007.

Even though Couey's initial confessions would not be heard, evidence against him was overwhelming.

Jessica's left thumb print as well as prints from Couey's two index fingers were located on a pizza box found in his room. Her DNA was discovered in his closet. Blood found on his mattress matched Jessica's DNA and another spot tested positive for her blood and his semen.

Prison guards testified that Couey admitted to murdering Jessica.

More evidence included the fact that Jessica's body was found buried underneath the window of the room Couey occupied.

Prosecutors showed jurors photographs of Jessica's body. Several refused to look at the pictures, while others sobbed.

The defense's strategy was to convince the jury that Couey was mentally ill. Defense Attorney Fanter spoke on his client's behalf. "[As a child, Couey] suffered from neglect, an unstable home life, a violent home life," he said. "He didn't choose to be a pedophile. He didn't choose to have a mental illness."

The jury didn't agree. They took just four hours to find John Evander Couey guilty of all charges.

Outside the courthouse, reporters asked Mark Lunsford if the verdict brought closure. "I haven't figured out closure yet," he responded. "Losing a child to a sexual predator is a horror that you go through alone."

A week later, the jury recommended that Couey receive the death penalty.

In August, Couey was sentenced to death.

Jessica Lunsford, the girl in the pink hat, had at last received a measure of justice.

Twisted metal, melted plastic and charred, broken beams were all that was left of the home where one of the most notorious crimes in American history was committed. Couey's last residence, which had sat empty for several years, burned down two years later.

Several neighbors said they saw it burning and never called the fire department. Instead, they stood on their porches or in their yards and thought about a child who went missing. A beautiful child. An innocent child whose murder changed America.

Child predators roam Florida with impunity. John Evander Couey was a three-time convicted child molester who had consistently received long prison sentences, yet served short terms. Floating through the criminal justice system, his dangerousness went unrecognized for years. In Florida, this happens time after time. Rapists, child molesters and pedophiles consistently go unrecognized, untreated and unpunished. The Jessica Lunsford Act and other laws have been passed with the objective of locking up offenders for longer periods. Whether these new laws will work remains to be seen.

Chapter 2
The Video

"We were just stunned. I wasn't really expecting to see what I saw. It was chilling."

> Car wash owner Mike Evanoff, reviewing video of an abducted child caught on his surveillance camera.

On the evening of February 1, 2004, 150 million television sets across America were tuned to the Super Bowl. The New England Patriots and Carolina Panthers were playing what sports writer Peter King later described as "the greatest Super Bowl [football game] of all time." Streets in most cities were deserted as fans were glued to their sets. Sarasota was no exception.

While blizzards roared across much of the northeast, it was balmy in south Florida.

Sarasota, with about 350,000 residents, was known for its beautiful beaches and its "*artiste* mantra." Violent crime was rare.

Along Bee Ridge Road, just east of the city, a young girl walked alone. Eleven-year-old Carlie Brucia wore a red short-sleeve shirt, blue jeans and carried a pink backpack. The sixth-grader was five feet tall and weighed 120 pounds. She had dark blonde hair, glistening blue eyes and a ready smile.

As she made her way home from a sleepover with friends, she jogged for a few moments, slowed to a walk, then repeated the sequence over and over. From a distance she looked older.

A few blocks from her home, Carlie decided to take a shortcut behind the local car wash. The car wash was part of a complex of businesses that included a driving range, a video arcade, an ice cream parlor and a mini-golf course. Carlie and her friends hung out there sometimes, so she knew the area well. Once she crossed a small patch of grass behind the car wash, she would come to McIntosh Lane. Then, it was just a short walk to McIntosh Road and on to her house.

As Carlie walked around the building to the rear of the car wash, a yellow station wagon drove by. It slowed, then circled back. The car parked about twenty feet in front of Carlie, blocking her route.

Several hundred feet away, a few golfing enthusiasts, undaunted by the Superbowl, chipped balls on the green of the nearby putting range. They were oblivious to the horror that was unfolding within viewing distance.

Carlie made it to the car wash tracks that guided vehicles into the washing machines.

Then, just that quick, she was gone.

At 7:30 that evening, Susan Schorpen called 911 to report her daughter missing. She lived about a mile from the home where Carlie had spent Saturday night. An hour earlier, Susan had received a call from Connie Arnold, the mother of the girl Carlie was visiting, telling her that her daughter had begun walking home. Since it was against Susan's rules for Carlie to walk the streets alone, she sent her husband, Steven Kansler, to pick up the young girl. He drove the route she usually took, including several shortcuts he knew about. He even drove all the way back to the home of Carlie's friend looking for his stepdaughter.

After a half hour of fruitless searching, Kansler was stumped. Where was Carlie?

The deserted streets frightened him. He drove home and told his wife to call the police.

Within hours, a bloodhound was tracking the missing girl. The dog started at Carlie's friend's home and headed directly to Bee Ridge Road.

After several blocks, the dog turned into the car wash. In the parking area behind the business, it stopped and lost the scent.

Detectives assumed that a car had picked up the girl. Although Carlie could have left with a friend, many of the cops felt from the beginning that this case had a bad smell to it.

By now, it was pitch-dark. While detectives interviewed Carlie's parents, more than two hundred searchers began scouring the area. Nearby businesses were checked and police knocked on neighborhood doors. As residents learned a child was missing, many offered to help in the search.

Investigators checked the mother and father. They found neighbors had complained of turmoil in the household. Detectives interrogated Schorpen and Kansler for much of the night. Neither parent seemed capable of harming their daughter. In fact, they appeared to be genuinely upset and perplexed. Cops began to focus on the theory that an unknown person may have kidnapped the child.

Susan and Joseph Brucia, Carlie's father, had married in New York. Almost immediately after Carlie was born, they divorced and Susan moved to Florida. Joseph maintained a good relationship with Carlie and she visited him at least twice a year. When police called to inform him about Carlie's disappearance, he immediately booked a flight to Sarasota.

After Schorpen moved to Florida, she married Steven Kansler, who had a son.

At school, Carlie was well-liked and respected among both teachers and students. She excelled in her studies at middle school, particularly math. At the time of her disappearance, she was learning French.

"She'd come up to me and speak these words I didn't even know," said one friend, laughing at the memory.

Carlie loved singer/actress Jennifer Lopez and had memorized many of her most popular songs. But she would occasionally sing off-key on purpose, just to make her mom laugh.

When new kids enrolled in school, Carlie was always one of the first students to greet them and try to make them feel welcome.

Investigators learned that Carlie was intelligent, well-adjusted and mischievous. In short, police didn't think she'd run away.

They knew that, while rare, stranger abductions were among the most difficult to solve.

In an odd twist, investigators found that Carlie loved to watch true crime shows. *America's Most Wanted* and *Forensic Files* were two of her favorites. As Carlie followed the recreations of kidnappings and murders on the screen, Kansler told police that she was confident in her own ability to avoid such violence. "She was always saying, 'That wouldn't happen to me,'" he said.

By early Monday morning, investigators weren't so sure.

It was just after daybreak when Mike Evanoff pulled into work. He was surprised to find yellow crime scene tape surrounding his business. He and his father had opened the car wash just a couple of years earlier as a complement to the other businesses in the complex.

As he unlocked the door to his office, a uniformed deputy approached. "What's going on?" Evanoff asked.

"You can't open up yet," the cop said.

"How come?"

"We're investigating a missing girl."

Evanoff couldn't believe it. The cop pulled out a picture.

"Have you ever seen this girl?" he asked.

Evanoff studied the photo. Kids hung out all the time at the ice cream parlor and the miniature golf course, but he usually worked at the car wash and didn't recognize her.

The cop pointed to a video monitor and asked the owner to check it.

A series of eight security cameras had been set up in different sections of the car wash, because customers sometimes accused workers of stealing items from their cars. While many video recorders used by businesses took only black and white film, Evanoff had spent a little more money so the images would be in color. After installing the monitors, he noticed that accusations of theft had dropped significantly.

Evanoff went into his office and clicked on the video. It was a time-motion system, so it only recorded when there was movement in front of the sensors.

As soon as he turned it on, a dramatic scene began to unfold on the monitor. In broad daylight, a young girl walked into the parking area behind the car wash. Suddenly, a man strode purposely toward her. He reached out and grabbed her right arm, spoke to her for a moment, then pulled her away.

Within seconds, she was out of camera range.

The car wash manager, who was watching the video with Evanoff, ran out of the room, sick to his stomach.

The cop stepped outside and informed the deputy of his find. Within minutes, it seemed that every investigator in Sarasota County had gathered at the car wash.

Detectives knew they'd copped a break. They picked up the videotape and rushed it back to headquarters.

Sarasota detectives and FBI agents gathered in a conference room to watch the video—they were shocked by what they saw.

At 6:21 P.M., a girl was seen walking onto the asphalt parking area behind the car wash. She wore a red shirt, blue jeans and a backpack. It was Carlie Brucia.

Suddenly, a man appeared in the frame. He was dressed in a gray uniform, similar to the clothing worn by many automobile mechanics. The man walked toward the girl, his back to the video camera.

At first, she didn't seem to notice him. Then, as he drew closer, she turned slightly to the left, as if to try to maneuver around the man who had suddenly violated her space.

They both stopped. With his left hand, the man firmly grasped her right wrist. He spoke to her for a few seconds. His profile was visible—the man looked threatening, the cops sitting in that dead-still room probably thought. Now the camera had a straight-on view of the girl's face—she looked frightened, confused. Then the man turned to walk back the way he came, pulling Carlie's arm. At that point, the monitor captured a full frontal view of the man. He was short, just a few inches taller than Carlie. He had a burr cut and wore short sleeves. The shadows of several tattoos were seen on each arm. He wore a white name tag on the right side of his shirt, near the breast.

The final image was of a pale and bewildered girl fading off the screen.

Just that quickly, the man and child were gone.

The camera switched back to the still mode and waited for another movement to activate it.

"Run it back," somebody said.

The tape was rewound all the way to the beginning. Exactly three minutes before the scene that had just played out before their eyes, investigators saw a different image appear.

As the girl entered the rear of the car wash, a yellow or cream-colored station wagon drove slowly by. In a minute, it appeared again, going in the opposite direction. The car looked to be an American model.

It appeared that somebody may have been stalking the girl.

Detectives needed to act fast. They called Schorpen and Kansler to the Sheriff's office. After viewing the video, each parent confirmed that the girl was indeed Carlie. Sobbing and hysterical, both denied having ever seen the man who led her away.

Investigators issued an Amber Alert. The description of Carlie and her abductor were broadcast throughout Florida and the nation.

Even though investigators could make out general characteristics of the man seen in the video, they couldn't read his name tag or distinguish the shadowy tattoos on his arms. Copies of the videotape were sent to NASA. The aerospace engineers had been successful in the past in enhancing the quality of videos. Speaking of the name on the tag, FBI agent Carl Whitehead told the media that "it appears to be a short name, maybe three or four letters."

In fact, since there were no other leads in the case, Sarasota County sheriff's detectives and the FBI decided to release the entire video to the media. Local television stations picked it up first. But the images were so startling and so graphic that the video was soon being shown almost non-stop on national cable news networks. Suddenly, more people were watching the abduction of a young girl than had watched the Super Bowl a day earlier.

Within minutes of the release of the tape, calls began flooding the hotline that police had set up just for that purpose. Investigators would eventually track down 771 tips based on the video. For instance, a caller from Ohio thought he'd seen Carlie at a grocery store. Another tipster from Wisconsin said she saw a "homeless-looking" girl who looked like Carlie freezing in the snow. Psychics came out in force. Some asserted that the child was dead, probably in a pond or a canal. Others claimed to see the spirit of the girl alive, waiting for police to storm in and rescue her. The psychics were long on generalities and short on substance.

While police discounted many calls, they couldn't ignore others. Sixty local callers told police to check out an automobile mechanic named Joseph P. Smith. "It looks just like him," they all said.

One call in particular needed to be investigated. Ed Dinyes called and said he recognized his former business partner. A few months before, they had started an automobile repair shop together. Smith lasted only a few weeks before going on a cocaine binge and leaving Dinyes stranded with too many customers and not enough mechanics. The partnership was over almost as soon as it began.

Dinyes told investigators he was absolutely sure that Joe Smith was the person seen on the video.

"I've seen Joe with the uniform on from the back side and the front side," he said. "I worked with him in the shop. I know what he looks like. His sneakers. His haircut. His gait. It's just the way he walked in the shop. I watched him reach for the girl. I've seen him pick up tools like that."

Dinyes's wife also recognized their former friend and called the hotline.

Detective Toby Davis of the Sarasota County Sheriff's Office was assigned to interview Smith. A quick check of police records showed that he was currently on probation for drug offenses. Davis noticed that the suspect had been arrested thirteen times—two of the charges were for violent crimes against women.

Two days later, Davis met with Smith. The suspect was about five feet eight inches tall. He was chunky, like the man in the video. He was currently renting a room from his friend, Jeff Pincus. Smith said it was because his wife had kicked him out of their home. He admitted that his continuing drug use was the cause. His drugs of choice, he said, were heroin and cocaine. He'd tried many times to kick the habit, but was unable to do so.

When asked how he'd spent the previous Sunday, Smith said that he'd spent most of the day salvaging parts from cars in a junkyard. He claimed that at about six o'clock he'd visited his brother and stayed there until six-thirty. Then he drove to a local boat dock where he sat looking out over the bay. He stayed until midnight and returned home. His friend Jeff would back him up, he said.

The detective asked Smith to roll up his sleeves. When the suspect complied, Davis observed that each arm was decorated with multiple tattoos. There were skulls, dragons, panthers, half-naked women and hearts inscribed on his forearms and biceps. The tattoos, Davis probably thought, seemed to match those of the mystery man in the video.

Up to that point, Smith had been passive and not the least bit curious. Finally, he asked, "What's this all about?"

Davis showed him a picture of the abductor grabbing Carlie's arm.

"That looks like me," Smith said. "But it's not me."

If Smith thought that his brother, John, and Pincus would support his alibi, that notion was quickly dispelled. Jeff said that Smith had borrowed his yellow station wagon at about three o'clock on Saturday afternoon. He said he'd be back in an hour but didn't return until around 7:30 Monday morning. Jeff was angry and asked where he'd been. "I don't think it's [any of] your business," Smith said. Then he huffed into his room and slammed the door.

Before Smith took the car, Jeff said he had rolled the odometer back to zero. When Smith returned, he had driven more than 300 miles.

Detective Davis impounded the station wagon.

He also spoke with Smith's brother. John told the investigator that Joe had indeed stopped by his house, but that they didn't speak since they'd quarreled recently. He complained that Smith was always stealing from him.

Investigators learned that Smith had violated his parole and could have been locked up since he hadn't paid his court costs in a timely manner. In August 2003, his probation officer notified Judge Harry M. Rapkin that Smith was behind on his payments. This was considered to be a serious violation, but no action was taken. Months later, the probation officer again notified the judge that Smith wasn't making the payments. The officer recommended that he be taken into custody. Judge Rapkin refused to return the multi-convicted felon to jail. He later defended his actions. "In the USA," he said, "we don't put debtors who can't pay in prison."

Just one month later, Carlie was abducted.

On Tuesday, Detective Davis arrested Smith for violating his probation. At about 1:30 P.M., he was booked into the Sarasota County Jail.

Investigators were sure they had the kidnapper. But, being an ex-con, Smith knew enough to keep his mouth shut. After the initial statement to Davis, he'd invoked his right to an attorney. Smith was assigned veteran public defender Adam Tebrugge.

The suspect's silence placed law enforcement officials in a dilemma. Carlie could still be alive somewhere, but Smith wouldn't tell them where he'd taken her. Later that day, frustration boiled over at a news conference.

Sarasota County Sheriff William Balkwill told reporters that Joe Smith was the only suspect. "We have made it clear to Joseph and his counsel that we want to know where Carlie is," he said.

On Wednesday, Carlie's family held a press conference calling for her return. "Help me bring my baby home," Susan Schorpen pled.

Because of the dramatic video, the case had created a nationwide buzz storm. Reporters swarmed to Sarasota. Viewers couldn't seem to get enough of the real-live abduction caught on tape.

Meanwhile, hundreds of searchers scoured the city. Police helicopters circled rural areas. Cadaver dogs sniffed in remote places. Abandoned houses were searched. Still, there was no sign of the missing child.

However, a break would soon come and from an unlikely source.

While the media was sensationalizing every facet of the case, and while cops were quietly knocking on doors, John and Patricia Davis, John and Joe's mother, arranged to meet with Smith in the Sarasota County jail.

Despite their past differences, John knew that his brother needed someone. He was also curious. Could Joe actually have kidnapped a child? After all, Smith had two children of his own and seemed to love them.

The man in the video certainly looked like Smith, but John and his mother wanted to be sure.

"Did you do it?" John asked, cutting to the chase. "Did you take that little girl?"

Smith looked pale, his eyes swollen and red. As his brother and mother spoke, he sobbed. He would barely look at them.

"Tell us what happened, Joe," Patricia said.

"I'm sorry," Smith said. He spoke low and mumbled so that they could barely understand him.

"What did you do?" his brother asked.

Smith murmured that he'd had sex with the girl.

"Oral sex," he said. "Rough sex."

"Oh God," his mother screamed and fled the room.

"What does that mean?" John asked.

Smith wouldn't answer. His brother moved over in the chair and hugged Joe. Together, in the small room, they held each other and wept. They'd once been close, but the years and the drugs had separated them. While Joseph Smith was a thief who would do almost anything for the narcotic, his brother never would have guessed that he would kidnap and murder a little girl.

But now he knew.

"Where's she at?" he asked.

He could barely hear the response. Something about a church. Somewhere near Proctor Road or Cattleman Road. There was a concrete "thing" on the property. And there was a tree line behind the building.

There was only one more question to ask: "Is she dead?"

Smith stared at the floor. "I don't know," he said. "She could be."

As his brother went to leave, Smith said, "I'm sorry. I just got carried away."

John was repulsed, but he was also afraid. He feared what other inmates did to child molesters.

As his brother walked out of the meeting, investigators were standing in the hallway. He sheepishly told the cops that Joe hadn't admitted anything. They knew the brother was trying to protect Joe. They were sure of it when their mother had burst out of the room wailing and ran straight to the bathroom.

After leaving, Joe's brother and mother drove along Proctor Road. They stared at every church building they saw, but were unable to find one that matched all the details of Smith's confession.

Before they even got home, Joseph Smith called John. This time they spoke in a coded language the two had developed when they were children. For instance, Proctor Road became "Avenue P." Smith had now become very paranoid. He thought police were monitoring his calls. Inexplicably, however, they weren't.

Smith told his brother to go to the church on Proctor Road.

That evening, John had second thoughts about keeping this vital information from police. He knew he could be held as an accessory. In a hot case like this, cops would throw the book at him. He talked it over with his mother. Patricia was devastated. She'd forgiven Joe so many times, even when he stole from her. But this time, he'd gone too far. He'd kidnapped a child—a child who might still be alive.

At about 9:00 that night, John called the FBI.

Agents David Street and Leo Martinez, as well as Sarasota County Sheriff's Detective Toby Davis, met Joe's brother and his mother at their house. After hearing the story of Smith's confession, they all traveled to the church. It was about three miles from where Carlie had been abducted.

A front was moving in and heavy rain was expected.

In the darkness, the church looked massive. Palm trees and lush vegetation surrounded it. An oasis for the soul, the cops may have thought. And maybe a graveyard for an innocent child. Behind the building, the dark silhouette of a tree line sent chills through them all. Everything was exactly as Smith had described it to his brother.

Inside the church, Pastor Rod Myers was meeting with the elders of his congregation. Via communication with the authors of this book, he wrote, "When we exited the building, we noticed two to three cars in our parking lot, and I walked over to see who was there. An officer—I believe he was [with the] FBI—met me and told me we needed to leave the property. I pressed him on why and he told me they suspected that Carlie had been left in a wooded area of our property."

Jail officials were instructed to allow Smith access to a telephone. John called him again. Smith, unaware that John was cooperating with police, verified each landmark. Sobbing, Smith explained that they were at the right place. Patricia was shaking so hard that she was barely able to stand.

It was beginning to rain, but Detective Davis, who didn't want to disturb the crime scene, felt they needed a forensic specialist. At 12:40 A.M.,

Sarasota Sheriff's Sergeant Sheila Sullivan, a crime scene technician, arrived. After being briefed by Davis and the FBI agents, she slowly walked along the wooded area holding a high-beam flashlight.

"I figured the most likely place to find Carlie would be in a wooded area," she later said. "I walked a little farther along the chain-link fence and near there I began to smell the odor of a decaying body, which I'm familiar with. I walked in no more than five feet and saw a red shirt."

Sullivan's heart sank. "Carlie's head pointed to the north," she said, switching to the present tense as her mind relived that day and that moment. "Her right leg is extended. Her left leg is bent. I see the spaghetti straps of her blouse and she's wearing no pants or panties."

Sullivan walked back to the investigators and informed them of her find. She didn't have anything to cover the body with, so she drove to a nearby store and purchased a drop cloth.

After she placed it on the body, the skies opened up and the rain poured down.

Before Carlie's remains were even moved, Detective Chris Hallisey and Sergeant Paul Richard prepared a probable cause affidavit to arrest Joseph P. Smith for kidnapping and first degree murder. It read:

"On February 1, 2004, an eleven-year-old female named Carlie Brucia was reported missing to the Sarasota [County] Sheriff's Office.

"Through investigative efforts, a surveillance video was obtained from the car wash located in Sarasota. As depicted on the video, at 1821 hours Carlie was seen walking along the rear of the car wash. This was a reasonable route to walk from her friend's home. As Carlie was walking, a man approached her. The subject was a white male, five-foot-six to five-foot-eight with medium build, dark hair, tattoos on both forearms, wearing a dark-colored shirt (commonly worn by mechanics), dark pants and white sneakers. It was apparent that Carlie did not recognize this subject and she attempted to pass by him when he stopped her and forcibly walked her out of camera view.

"Witnesses provided information that the Defendant was in fact wearing the clothing depicted in the video.

"Two days later, the Defendant was interviewed and provided a statement as to his activities on February 1, 2004.

"Through investigation, and interview of various witnesses, Affiant was able to establish unequivocally that the Defendant provided misleading and false information during the statement.

"On February 5, 2004, the Defendant told a witness that he abducted and murdered Carlie Brucia. Based upon specific information provided to the witness by the Defendant, this witness was able to lead investigators to the body of Carlie Brucia. A preliminary forensic examination of the body indicates Carlie Brucia died as a result of homicidal violence.

"Based upon the above facts, Affiant has probable cause to believe the Defendant observed Carlie Brucia walking home through the parking lot of the car wash on February 1, 2004.

"The Defendant then maneuvered the vehicle he was operating to a location, in a premeditated manner, to conceal his actions, where he was able to approach Carlie. The Defendant then forcibly abducted Carlie from the parking lot of the car wash and drove her from this location. Through the means of homicidal violence, the Defendant then murdered Carlie Brucia. Affiant believes the Defendant was solely responsible for these actions..."

Pastor Myers arrived at the church the next morning just as Carlie's body was being removed. He later said, "The entire ten-acre piece of property was a crime scene. I was let in and was immediately inundated with media calling (they were not allowed on the property until the next day). The area where Carlie was discovered was a wetland area overgrown with Brazilian pepper trees and undergrowth. It was on the north side of our property."

Later, the site where the child had been found became a permanent memorial as members of the church started a garden in her name. In the days following the discovery of Carlie's body, hundreds of strangers brought flowers, teddy bears and cards to show their grief.

On Friday, Dr. Russell Vega, the medical examiner, performed the autopsy. He later testified that Carlie had died from ligature strangulation.

"The ligature was something like a narrow shoe string," he said, "and the mark crisscrossed in the back; the killer would have been behind Carlie and slightly higher, using continuous manual pressure for several minutes before she died."

Carlie's brassiere had been pulled up over her right shoulder. It had been unclasped. There were bruises on various parts of the body, but the medical examiner determined that they could have been caused by drag marks or "animal activity."

By now, the media had dug deep into Joe Smith's background. "Violence and drugs litter kidnap suspect's history," read one headline from the *St. Petersburg Times*. Other lead captions read: "Outrage and tears" and "One chance too many?"

It soon became apparent that the suspect should have been locked away when the kidnapping and murder of Carlie occurred. The crime didn't have to happen.

Smith's lengthy rap sheet left people shaking their heads.

In 1993, he had been charged with aggravated battery, loitering and prowling after he attacked a woman with a motorcycle helmet. She suffered a broken nose. The strange thing, she said, was that she'd never seen her assailant before and had not said or done anything to provoke the attack. Smith was sentenced to sixty days in jail and two years of probation.

In April of the following year, officers spotted Smith buying drugs from a known dealer. When they attempted to apprehend him, he sped away. He was eventually arrested, but was acquitted at trial.

In November 1997, he was charged with battery after his wife called police to tell them he was tearing down the house. He'd punched holes in some of the walls and broken windows. He never stood trial for that incident.

In September 1996, a former business partner accused Smith of stealing tools. But, again, he was never tried.

In July of the following year, at 1:30 A.M., Smith attempted to lure a woman into his car in a nearly-deserted grocery store parking lot. When police arrived, they found a serrated knife in his pocket. He was convicted of carrying a concealed weapon and sentenced to one year of probation.

Another crime Smith was accused of committing mirrored the Carlie Brucia case.

The following year in November, a twenty-year-old female named Teri Stinson was walking along U.S. 41 in Bradenton. She was going to see her cousin, who lived only a few blocks away. In an interview with a reporter from the February 14, 2004, edition of the *St. Petersburg Times*, Stinson said that Smith, who wore a shirt with his name tag on it, "came out from behind the bushes and tried to pull me over [to him]."

Stinson grappled with her assailant, but he seized her wrists so that she couldn't move. At some point during the struggle, she slipped and fell to the ground. He dropped on top of her. She begged him to leave her alone, even offering to give him fifty dollars if he'd go away. He ignored her plea and said, "If you don't stop screaming, I'll cut you."

Several people passing by in an automobile saw the struggle and stopped. It was only when they jumped out of their car armed with golf clubs that Smith fled. Cops were called and he was quickly located and arrested.

When he went to trial, Smith was clean-shaven and articulate. He took the stand and said that he'd been attempting to pull Stinson from oncoming traffic. "It's all just a big mistake," he said. Surprising both the prosecution and his own attorney, the jury acquitted him.

Two years later, Smith was arrested when police found six bundles of white powder in his car. It turned out to be heroin.

In addition, he had a forged prescription for painkillers in his possession. He was convicted of prescription fraud and possession of heroin and could have been sentenced to five years in prison. However, once again, he received probation.

In April 2000, Smith tested positive for opiates, a violation of his probation and was referred to an outpatient treatment center.

That next month, he was arrested for fraudulently trying to obtain prescription drugs and violating his probation. He was sentenced to six months of house arrest. Again, Smith was ordered to enter a drug treatment program.

In September 2001, he was arrested again while attempting to purchase hydromorphone with a forged prescription. When police searched his car, they found dozens of blank prescription pads stolen from a local doctor. Smith was charged with prescription fraud and violation of probation. This time, he could have received ten years, but got off with seventeen months in state prison.

He got out of prison after two years, but was rearrested a week later for possession of cocaine. Smith got a three year probation for this offense.

Months afterwards, he spent two weeks in yet another treatment center after he attempted to overdose on drugs.

It was two months before Carlie's abduction and murder when Smith's probation officer informed Judge Rapkin for the second time that the offender had not made any recent payments on his court costs. The judge received the recommendation that Smith be picked up and put back in jail. But Judge Rapkin refused, writing, "I need evidence [that] this is willful." No further action was taken.

Two days after Carlie's disappearance, Smith finally was arrested for violation of his parole.

But by then, Carlie Brucia already had died.

With such a lengthy arrest record, Sarasotans were outraged that Smith was still on the streets. Many turned their fury on Judge Rapkin, who began receiving death threats. In fairness, the judge had a difficult task. If he locked up every doper who came before him, the jails couldn't hold them all. And he was right—debtors' prisons, at least in America, had long since gone the way of many other bad ideas.

However, it seemed that something should have been done to keep Smith locked up.

Carlie's jeans, underwear, one sock and backpack were missing, but Sarasota County investigators sent her shirt and bra to the FBI lab. A semen stain was found on her shirt. When checked against Smith's DNA profile, it was a match.

While processing the station wagon, investigators found two head hairs consistent with Carlie's. They were on the floor mat in the back. Seven fibers from the car were "consistent with Carlie's shirt."

Smith, who still wouldn't speak with police, showed no reticence in opening up to his brother about the crime. By now, officials were recording and monitoring all his telephone conversations. But he continued to call his brother to talk about the case.

He said that he had noticed Carlie running along the street and decided to abduct her. He also claimed that he thought she was older, maybe fifteen or sixteen. Smith told his mother that the murder was an accident and that it occurred because he was high on drugs. In fact, he later claimed that he had ingested a "pure" strain of heroin that "blew my mind" and that he didn't remember what he'd done after that.

Smith also wrote a coded letter to his brother. Daniel Olson, an FBI cryptoanalyst, translated the letter. In it, Smith admitted that he threw the girl's clothes and backpack into four different dumpsters.

Joseph Smith's trial was a media circus. News agencies from around the world crowded the courthouse. Reporters who couldn't get in waited outside, attempting to interview anyone who passed their way.

The evidence was so overwhelming against Smith that the verdict was never in doubt. According to FBI scientist Jennifer Luttman, the genetic profile on Carlie's red shirt matched Smith's by "1 in 92 quintillion."

Assistant State Attorney Debra Riva asserted that Smith had seen Carlie jogging home and drove the station wagon around behind the car wash. When she was forced into the car, he bound her hands with shoelaces. Once she was incapacitated, Smith drove his victim to an undetermined location and sexually assaulted her. After the rape, he used the shoelaces to strangle Carlie.

According to the prosecution, Smith drove to the church, pulled Carlie's body out of the station wagon and dragged her into the tree line. He discarded any incriminating evidence by throwing her clothing and backpack in separate dumpsters.

Defense attorney Adam Tebrugge was a forceful advocate for his client. Even though he had little to work with, he did hammer home the fact that a technician in the FBI forensic laboratory had been convicted of falsifying reports several years prior. Many of the cases she'd handled were thrown out on appeal—therefore, he concluded, the jury couldn't be sure that the lab got it right this time. Tebrugge also implied that Smith's brother could have been the contributor of the semen found on Carlie's shirt.

On November 17, 2005, the jury returned a verdict of guilty on all counts: first-degree murder, kidnapping and sexual battery.

In the sentencing phase of the trial, Carlie's parents described her as a straight-A student, a bubbly child who loved to sing. Joseph Brucia testified that he thought about committing suicide after his daughter's death. "When Carlie was taken away from my family and me, it hurt us to the core," he said. "I would think, surely this cannot be real...there were many times I no longer wanted to go on and contemplated taking my own life. My life will never be the same."

Susan Schorpen, Carlie's mother, stated that "[Carlie] was so full of life, such a happy-go-lucky little girl. [She was an] all-American girl. She was, and still is, very special to me. Carlie was the light of my life, my best friend."

Surprisingly, sixteen witnesses testified to Smith's sterling character. He was good to his children, they said, and he worked hard when he wasn't high on dope. But in rebuttal, the state produced a letter he'd written to another inmate that contradicted that assessment.

The letter, written to his friend, Blaine Ross, who was accused of murdering his parents, complained about Smith's brother cooperating with the FBI. "If John ever comes to [the] prison to visit," he wrote, "I'll break his jaw."

Then he gave Ross some advice on beating up another inmate. "When you kick [his] ass," Smith wrote, "punch him first in the throat. It will incapacitate him and then you can really go to work on him. Give him a couple for me, okay?"

In the penalty phase of the trial, the jury ignored Smith's character witnesses and recommended that the child-killer be put to death. The vote was ten to two.

As Judge Andrew Owen prepared to deliver his sentence, Smith begged the court for mercy. "I take responsibility for these crimes," he said. "I don't understand how it all happened. I was very angry at myself and very high. I knew it was wrong, but I could not stop."

He said that on Super Bowl Sunday his wife had informed him that she never wanted to see him again, because of his continued drug use. "I lost my business, my family, my self-control," he said, reading from a prepared statement. "I just wanted to die that day. I copped a bunch of heroin, cocaine and began injecting, hoping I would overdose. It was different than any other time. I think it was mixed with something."

Like the jury, Judge Owens was not impressed. "Joseph Smith," he said, "based upon your actions, you have forfeited your right to live freely among us. For the murder of Carlie Jane Brucia, you are hereby sentenced to death. May God have mercy on your soul."

One of the frightening things about the case is how close Smith came to getting away with murder. Without the video, police would have had few clues. The DNA on Carlie's shirt would almost certainly have been washed away by the rain and when the body was finally discovered, there would have been little or no evidence.

Behind the church in the beautiful wooded area where Carlie Brucia's body was found, the members of that church established a memorial garden to honor the innocent eleven-year-old. The pastoral setting draws visitors who contemplate the good that enhances life and the evil that sometimes destroys it.

Carlie Brucia is gone but not forgotten.

The signs were everywhere in the Carlie Brucia case—Joseph Smith was in and out of the criminal justice system for at least ten years. While many of his crimes were drug-related, others were violent sexual attacks. There's little doubt that Florida's lenient criminal justice system allowed him to wander the streets until he exploded. The frightening thing is that Smith might never have been caught had the car wash videotape not been running. Florida has attempted to tighten up their sex offender laws, but it's probable that there will be more attacks by already convicted predators.

Chapter 3
The Crab Fisherman

"It's everybody's excuse: 'I had a bad childhood.' [But] he knew what he was doing."

Roy Brown, the father of murder victim Amanda Brown.

Just before dawn, on September 11, 1998, a white pickup towing a twenty-foot fiberglass boat pulled onto the boat ramp next to Courtney Campbell Bridge in Tampa, Florida. With tires screeching, the driver backed down the ramp. The truck was going too fast, however, and stopped only when water sloshed all the way onto the front tires. The sudden stop knocked the boat loose. It floated free and the driver had to jump out and grab an anchor line to keep it from drifting out into the bay.

Four crabbers, standing on the dock, shook their heads. Old Willie Crain was one crazy dude, but they'd never seen him acting so weird as that day.

Nathan Richardson called out, but Crain ignored him. He tied the boat to the dock, then drove his truck back up to the parking lot.

When Crain got out and raced back down to the ramp to get into his boat, Richardson noticed he wasn't wearing "slickers." Crabbers who were going fishing always wore the rain gear to protect their clothing. Instead, Crain wore a maroon shirt and dark blue slacks. The fishermen noticed that he cradled a bundle of clothes under his arm.

"Fool thinks we wanna steal his traps," someone said and they all snick-ered. "I hear the bastard threatened to kill anyone he caught in his zone..."

Out on the water the boat engine roared, drowning out their conver-sation. The crabbers looked on in confused silence as they watched Willie Crain speed off down the Double Branch area of Tampa Bay.

Crain was shaking.

He'd made a decent life for himself—at least for a second grade dropout. He owned his own home free and clear, a spit-new pickup truck, a high powered boat and, because of his crab fishing business, always had plenty of spending cash. Sure, he had a past, had even done hard time. The last few years, however, he'd managed to avoid the law.

But he'd done something during the night that threatened to put him back in prison.

Wind blasted his face as the boat raced through the darkness.

Crain kept more than a hundred traps in the bay. Many were in secret locations, places he could get to only at high tide—the more difficult they were to find, the less chance that a rival crabber would stumble on them.

He felt lucky, because he had a ready buyer for anything he could catch—a seafood restaurant owned by his daughter, Patricia, and her husband. In addition to being a popular restaurant, the business sold seafood to retail chains.

Crain stopped the boat in the middle of the bay. He didn't need maps or one of those newfangled Global Positioning Systems (GPS) that the other crabbers used. He'd been crabbing since he was eleven years old and knew these waters by memory.

He glanced around. The water was black and still.

Seeing no one else, he let out a grappling line. Crain pulled up a trap, a wire mesh enclosure about two feet square and a foot high. Water streamed from it as he brought it on board and he reeled from the stink of the bait—chicken livers. The trap had an inverted funnel, so that once a crab entered, it couldn't get out.

He opened the lid and glanced around again to see if any other crabbers were on the water. He was alone, so he picked up the bundle he'd brought. He struggled for several minutes to make it fit, but finally stuffed it into the cage. Then he replaced the lid, latched it shut and dropped the trap back into the water.

Crain took a deep breath as the case slowly sank out of sight and the ripples on the water spread into the darkness.

The city of Tampa has a deeply stained past. Home to more than two million people, it is surrounded by St. Petersburg, Clearwater and the Gulf of Mexico. Tampa Bay, the biggest body of water in the area, provides a fishery unsurpassed in Florida.

In the 1880s, Cubans began to arrive in increasing numbers. They settled in Ybor City, established world-famous cigar factories and brought the first lottery games to Florida. Bolita, or "little balls," was wildly popular in the Cuban community. (To play the game, one hundred ivory balls, each with a number written in black, were dumped into a bag. Then each player reached into the bag and pulled out a ball hoping for the one winning number.) By the late 1920s, the Mafia arrived and took over the profitable pastime. In time, bookmaking, gambling, prostitution, liquor and drugs were added to the bolita rackets.

Underworld figures with names like George "Saturday" Zarate, Salvatore "Silent Sam" Lorenzo (so named because he refused to break under police torture) and the Trafficante family roamed Tampa's streets, extorting local businesses and collecting huge payoffs. Between 1930 and 1960, there were dozens of gangland murders. Local reporters named this the "era of blood."

Another era of blood began in 1984. A serial killer named Bobby Joe Long prowled the notorious Nebraska Avenue, home to pimps, pushers and predators. On that sad street, hookers openly plied their trade. They're the debris of society—addicted, diseased, tired, dispirited. They sleepwalked through sad lives, rarely surviving past forty. Bobby Joe Long murdered at least eleven women in the red light district before he was captured. He currently sits on death row.

Other notorious Tampa murderers were Lawrence Singleton and Oba Chandler. Singleton kidnapped a fifteen-year-old girl, raped her, then used a hatchet to chop off her arms. Because she survived, he only served eight years in prison. Shortly after his release, he murdered Roxanne Hays, a prostitute. Sentenced to death, the much-despised murderer cheated the executioner when he died in 2001.

Chandler abducted three tourists—a mother and her two teenage daughters. After raping them, he tied them to cinderblocks, then dumped them alive into the dark waters of Tampa Bay where they drowned. He currently awaits execution.

Kathryn Hartman never thought about the past. She lived minute-to-minute, hour-to-hour, day-to-day. On the night of September 10, she left her home and drove to a local lounge.

Hartman's seven-year-old daughter, Amanda Brown, was spending the night with her father and stepmother in Lakeland. With a free night, the divorced mother had told an acquaintance that she intended to "party hearty."

As Hartman entered the lounge, honky-tonk music blasted from the high-powered sound system. A poster advertised a karaoke shindig each Wednesday. The place was packed and couples line-danced on the open floor in front of the bar.

As soon as Hartman sat down, the bartender brought a man over to her table. The man trailing her was rail-thin. His face seemed too small for his body and his watery-blue eyes blinked incessantly. Sunken lips made it obvious that he needed dentures.

"This is my dad," the bartender said.

"W-W-Willie C-C-Crain," the man introduced himself.

The noise in the background made it difficult to hear. And the man's stutter didn't help things. But Hartman had no money and was hoping to find someone to buy her a few drinks.

Willie Crain did just that.

"Two screwdrivers," he said to his bartending daughter. When she returned with the drinks, Crain pulled out a roll of cash and peeled off a fifty dollar bill. His daughter gave him his change and he handed her a ten-dollar tip.

Even if Crain wasn't the best-looking guy in the world, the cash got Hartman's attention.

They sipped their drinks for an hour.

Then Billy Ray Cyrus' "Achy Breaky Heart" suddenly erupted from the speakers. Crain asked, "W-w-wanna dance?"

Hartman climbed out of her seat and onto the floor. She was unsteady on her feet so Crain held her, guiding her through the steps.

They sat down again and Crain bought her another drink. He began to talk, but Hartman was only half-listening. Crain told her he was lonely, that he needed a good woman and that his two daughters were all that kept him going. He asked about her family and when Hartman told him about her own daughter, Amanda, Crain's eyes lit up.

"What's she like?" he asked.

"She's seven years old and about, uh, maybe this tall," Hartman said, holding her hand up to waist level. "Amanda weighs maybe forty, forty-five pounds. Goes to elementary school. She's pretty as a picture and an A student."

"What color hair's she got?"

"Brown."

Crain's odd curiosity about her daughter didn't arouse her suspicions.

After more drinks, someone yelled, "Last call for alcohol." It was 2:00 A.M.

"You wanna go home with me?" Hartman asked.

"Y-y-yeah," Crain said. "But first I gotta stop at my daughter's house."

After the bar closed, Crain drove to his daughter's home. Hartman followed. They went inside and his daughter fixed the couple breakfast. Then Crain followed Hartman to her home.

They crashed on the sofa. It wasn't long before Crain began groping Hartman. When she didn't resist, he began French-kissing her. Hartman just wanted to go to sleep.

In the middle of a sloppy kiss, Crain sat up and said, "I c-c-can eat you out and make you come."

Hartman rolled her eyes, but made sure Crain didn't see her.

"No way," she said. She paused, thought again of his money, then said, "At least not tonight."

Crain seemed used to rejection. He shrugged, but Hartman noticed him staring at a photograph of Amanda.

After an hour, Crain suddenly got up and left.

Kathryn Hartman was in the kitchen at 2:30 P.M. on Thursday, when Amanda came home from school. Her father, Roy Brown, had dropped her off at school that morning. After school, she caught the bus home. Now she emptied her book bag onto the table and began to do her homework.

Someone knocked on the door.

It was Willie Crain.

Hartman invited him in, and he sat at the kitchen table beside Amanda.

"What ya doing?" he asked. Hartman noticed that even though he was drunk, he didn't stutter around the child.

"Math."

"Yeah? Lemme show you how to do it," Crain said and moved closer to the little girl with brown flowing hair.

After trying to explain it to her, he said, "I'll give you a dollar if you get it right."

She did and he gave her two dollars.

Hartman was making spaghetti.

"So you got a loose tooth, huh?" Crain said to Amanda. Hartman figured he must have seen Amanda using her tongue to push at the tooth.

Her daughter nodded and Crain said, "I'll give you five dollars to let me pull it."

"Uh-uh," Amanda said.

She completed her homework, then went outside to play. Hartman asked Crain if she could borrow twenty bucks and he responded by giving her two hundred.

"Y-y-you don't have to pay me back," he said.

Crain said he had to go somewhere. Hartman invited him to come back for supper.

As Crain got into his white pickup, Hartman noticed him staring at Amanda as she did cartwheels outside with a friend.

When supper was ready, Hartman called Crain. He showed up a few minutes later, smelling of beer.

After eating, Crain called Amanda to come over to him. They sat at the table and played tic-tac-toe. Then they traced their hands on a notepad. Hartman leaned over Amanda and wrote, "I love my Amanda." Then Crain wrote, "I like Willie."

"I got a big video collection at my house," Crain said. "Wanna go see it?"

"Yeah," Amanda said. "Do you have *Titanic*?"

"Got it," Crain said. "It's one of my favorites."

"Can we go, Mama?" Amanda begged. "Please?"

Hartman was tired and didn't want to leave. "You've got school tomorrow," she said. "The movie lasts three hours and you can't stay up that late."

"She can miss school one day," Crain said. "Let her watch the movie, then she can sleep in tomorrow."

Hartman hesitated, then nodded.

"Okay," she said.

The three got into Crain's pickup truck and headed over to his home.

They sat on a couch in the living room and began watching the movie. A few minutes later, Crain suggested they move into his bedroom, because it was air conditioned. By now, he was so drunk that Hartman could barely understand him.

The phone in the kitchen rang. Crain went to answer it, then called Hartman to him. It was his daughter and Crain wanted Hartman to speak to her. The conversation lasted twenty minutes.

When Hartman returned to Crain's bedroom, the door was closed. She entered and saw him sitting on the bed with Amanda between his knees. Hartman didn't say anything, but she picked Amanda up and placed her daughter next to her on the other side of the bed.

After watching a few minutes more of *Titanic*, Crain turned it off. He said he wanted to show them all the channels he could get with his satellite dish.

As he was switching through the channels, Amanda said she needed to use the bathroom.

Crain stated that she could use his toilet and Hartman took her to the bathroom.

When they came back out, Hartman was rubbing her forehead. "You got anything for pain?" she asked.

"Sure," he said.

"Wanna little weed to top it off?" Crain asked.

Hartman shook her head.

Hartman went to the bathroom, but made sure she left the bedroom door open. When she returned, it was closed again.

By now, she could barely keep her eyes open and asked Crain to take her home.

After they arrived back at Hartman's house, she told Amanda to take a bath. When her daughter got out of the tub, Hartman helped her rinse the shampoo from her hair, blow-dried it, then put a nightgown on Amanda.

Amanda's hair was still damp when she entered the kitchen. Crain insisted on helping her to blow-dry it again. Hartman noticed that his hands were all over Amanda. She told her daughter that she could sleep with her. Sometime around 2:00 A.M., Amanda lay down on Hartman's bed and dozed off.

Crain was drunk and Hartman told him he could sleep it off at her house, then changed into a nightgown and went to bed. She lay beside Amanda, who was sound asleep.

A few minutes later, Crain appeared in the bedroom. He was still dressed. The pain pill had made Hartman so sleepy that she didn't object when he climbed in between Amanda and the wall.

At 6:12 A.M., Hartman awoke.

Crain and Amanda were gone.

The search for seven-year-old Amanda Brown was one of the most extensive in the history of Hillsborough County. She became everybody's child. Police officers with bloodhounds searched the immediate neighborhood around Hartman's home. They collected trash from dumpsters and yards. Then they spread out to surrounding areas, using members of the Florida National Guard and hundreds of citizen volunteers.

As the search for Amanda Brown got underway, detectives initially targeted three possible suspects: her mother, her father and Willie Crain. Detective Dorothy Flair obtained Hartman's permission to search the trailer. Investigators collected fifty items of evidence, including the dress Amanda had worn home from school, her panties and the *Titanic* video. Hartman told Flair that Crain had let Amanda borrow the video. Investigators also collected Amanda's toothbrush in order to obtain the girl's DNA.

Detectives learned that Hartman had no life insurance on Amanda. They quickly eliminated her as a suspect.

Within hours of the disappearance, Detective Ron Noland brought Amanda's father, Roy Brown, and his wife, Sylvia, in for questioning. The couple denied that they had taken Amanda and gave samples of their blood. They both took lie detector tests and passed. Neither had taken out insurance on Amanda, and they seemed to have no reason to abduct or murder the child.

Noland learned that Amanda visited the Brown home several times a week.

It didn't take long for investigators to conclude that the Browns had nothing to do with the disappearance.

Willie Crain was another matter.

When detectives looked into his background, they found a man with a long history of sexually abusing young girls.

In 1985, Crain pled guilty to five counts of sexual battery on a child. His victims were between seven and ten years old. In one case, investigators learned that a nine-year-old girl had gone to school with bruises on her legs. When questioned by her physical education teacher, she stated that her mother's boyfriend had beaten her. Police were called and they determined that the child had been sexually and physically assaulted. The mother's boyfriend was Willie Crain.

Crain confessed and stated that he had beaten the girl, because she had "worn shorts to an amusement park." He'd been "having sex" with her for months and considered her to be his "girlfriend." Crain felt that the shorts were provocative and that other men would be sexually attracted to her. Further investigation turned up four additional young victims, each of whom had been sexually molested by Crain over a five-year period.

Crain was convicted and sentenced to twenty years in prison. He served only six years before he was released.

Investigators knew now that one of the last two persons to see Amanda Brown alive was a convicted pedophile whose preference in victims were young girls of the same age.

Detective Michael Hurley obtained written consent to search Crain's house, boat and trucks. While Hurley was coordinating the search, investigator Albert Brackett interviewed the suspect.

Crain stated that he was the tenth of twenty-one children sired by his father. A brother, Linwood, was serving time in a Florida prison for murder. Crain said that he'd been sexually abused by his father. He also claimed that when he was a child, an aunt often tied him to a chair and beat him with a leather belt. She "got off" on it, Crain said. Because of her alleged abuse, he had a hard time relating to adult women.

However, he denied any knowledge of Amanda's disappearance. He stated that he'd spent the night before with a woman and her daughter whose first name began with an "A," but said he couldn't remember her full name. He generally corroborated Hartman's account of the events of Wednesday night and Thursday, but continued to deny that he had kidnapped the girl.

Hurley noticed scratches on Crain's back and arms and had them photographed. Crain said that he was always getting scratched when he was out crabbing. Hurley asked him to demonstrate how he could get long scratches on the backs of his arms. Crain sat in a sullen silence, then stated that he didn't care whether the detective believed him or not. (Expert witnesses later testified that the scratches could have come from fingernails. But other experts said they might have been caused by the wire mesh of a crab trap.) During a search of Crain's trailer, investigators noticed a strong odor of bleach in the bathroom. The walls and floor had been recently cleaned. Opening the lid of the toilet, they found a small spot of blood underneath. Officers confiscated the lid. In the washing machine, detectives found blue jeans, a shirt and boxer shorts. Even though they'd been washed, the shorts had a blood spot on them. All the clothes taken from the washer were placed into evidence.

They also collected a rolled up wad of toilet tissue from a trash can in the bathroom.

The forensics unit sprayed luminol (a chemical used to detect trace amounts of blood) in the darkened bathroom and, according to police reports, "the whole area lit up." This indicated the presence of blood or bleach on the floor and walls.

Searches of Crain's trucks and boat yielded nothing.

As investigators focused on their prime suspect, they searched the area surrounding the Courtney Campbell Causeway, including the shoreline, trash cans and even garbage trucks they found hauling trash.

Overnight, posters showing the pretty girl with the impish smile seemed to sprout up all over the area.

A few days into the search, detectives set up a roadblock at the intersection of Williams Road and Old Hillsborough Highway. They interviewed 156 people who regularly traveled the area between midnight and dawn. They learned nothing of value.

Aerial searches also proved disappointing. Helicopters equipped with Forward Looking Infrared (FLIR) devices were used extensively, but no trace of the missing child was found. Dive teams spent weeks searching the waters of Tampa Bay. Divers waded through shallow areas and dove in the deeper channels. They scoured the causeway, nearby mangrove islands and the shoreline all the way down to the Howard Frankland Bridge.

Police enlisted the aid of local crab fishermen and pulled hundreds of traps. They sent divers into the waters of Tampa Bay in hard-to-find areas that crabbers suggested. Again, all their efforts were futile. In order to get a DNA sample from Amanda's biological parents, Detective Hurley obtained additional samples of blood from Kathryn Hartman and Roy Brown. In addition, items used by the child were sent to the lab for testing.

Once the DNA profiles were obtained, officers sent the items collected from Crain's house to the lab. According to a court document, "the bloodstain found on the toilet seat in Willie Crain's home...has the same DNA profile found on the items represented as belonging to Amanda Brown...[In addition], the bloodstain found on the boxer shorts...has the same DNA profile found on two items represented as belonging to Amanda Brown." Finally, a small stain found on the toilet tissue contained a combination of both Amanda's and Crain's DNA.

After the tests came back positive, Willie Crain was arrested and charged with the kidnapping and murder of Amanda Brown, even though her body had not been located. If convicted, he faced the death penalty.

In a surprise move, Crain called a Tampa television station to deny his guilt. However, during the interview, he admitted that he had sexually abused his own daughters when they were young. His protestations of innocence seemed less than convincing after this confession.

"I don't think Willie Crain is smart enough to hide a body where nobody could find it," said one of his attorneys. Amanda Brown was not dead, the defense claimed—she had simply run away from a dysfunctional home. Kathryn Hartman, he asserted, was a horrible mother and no one could blame the child for leaving. Indeed, there was no proof that Willie Crain had murdered her.

At the trial, Crain's defense team claimed that the bloodstains found in his house had come from Amanda's loose tooth. The prosecution countered by calling several people who had seen Amanda shortly before she disappeared, including Kathryn Hartman, Roy Brown and his wife. Each stated that although the tooth was loose, it was not bleeding. Nathan Richardson, who had seen Crain rushing to his boat on the morning Amanda disappeared stated under oath that Crain had once bragged about being able to "get rid of a body where nobody will ever find it." At the time, Richardson had thought Crain was talking about other crabbers with whom he'd been feuding. He stated that on the day Amanda went missing, Crain had gunned his boat and charged down the river. When he returned less than twenty minutes later, the bundle he'd carried with him was nowhere to be seen. The crab fishermen had never known Crain to take a "joy ride" in his boat. For that reason, they were surprised that he was not wearing slickers and that he didn't go crabbing that morning.

The prosecution's case consisted entirely of circumstantial evidence. According to prosecutors, Crain waited until the pain pills took effect and Kathryn Hartman was fast asleep. Then he took Amanda from her mother's bed. The state's theory was that Crain was the only suspect with both opportunity and motive.

Amanda may have been asleep when Crain placed her in his truck. Then, according to the prosecution, he drove her to his house where he sexually assaulted her. Her blood on his shorts, the toilet and the tissue connected Amanda to him.

They surmised that after murdering her, Crain used bleach to clean up the blood. Then he placed his bloodstained clothes in the washing machine. Even though he washed them, one spot remained.

Early that morning, prosecutors contended, Crain wrapped Amanda in some old clothes and drove to the boat ramp. He got there before dawn. Even though he hoped to avoid being seen, he was recognized by other crabbers. Crain ignored them and hurriedly motored out to one of his traps where he "buried" the girl's body.

Crain knew that within a few days crabs would strip all the flesh from the corpse, leaving nothing but a pile of bones. The clothes and bones would eventually decay and there would be no sign of the crime.

After three days of testimony, Willie Crain was found guilty of the abduction and murder of Amanda Brown.

At sentencing, his attorneys claimed that he'd had a "terrible" childhood, that he was a borderline alcoholic and that his IQ score of eighty-two indicated that he was mentally retarded. Because of these circumstances, the defense argued that life in prison would be the appropriate penalty. The prosecution countered that while he may have had a rotten childhood, was an alcoholic and had a moderate-to-low IQ, it didn't exculpate his guilt.

Jurors agreed with the prosecution.

On September 17, 1999, Crain was sentenced to death.

Willie Crain currently awaits his fate on Florida's death row at Union Correctional Institution in Raiford. He continues to proclaim his innocence. Every so often, he makes the local news with claims of having been "railroaded." His appeals, however, are winding down and he could be executed within a few years.

Roy Brown now works tirelessly on behalf of missing children. After another child, Jessica Lunsford, was abducted and murdered in 2004, he met with legislators and helped get Jessica's Law passed.

The body of seven-year-old Amanda Brown was never found.

The terrain of the state of Florida is ideal for permanently disposing of bodies. Willie Crain had fished the waters around Tampa Bay for many years. After kidnapping and molesting little Amanda Brown, Crain thought that by getting rid of her remains he could escape justice. Fortunately, DNA placed Amanda at his home. In the past, Florida killers have disposed of bodies in some of the bottomless sinkholes that dot the state, in rivers, the surrounding oceans and countless lakes and ponds. Many times the corpses are found, but in others, as in the Brown case, the remains never turn up.

Chapter 4
Murder in the Redlands

"If you can guarantee that I'll get the death penalty, I'll tell you what really happened."

> Juan Carlos Chavez, responding to questions by authorities concerning the whereabouts of a missing child.

Dade County is known for Miami, Coral Gables, Hialeah and the nightlife glitter of its beaches. In fact, South Beach, home of lithe partiers from all points of the globe, even has a diet named after it.

However, a few miles south of the action lies the only tract of undeveloped land left in Dade County. It's called "the Redlands," named for the region's red clay soil. "Original clapboard homes of early settlers, u-pick'em fields, coral rock walls and abundant farms dot the tropical landscape," writes local author Karen Allison on her Web site. From the sky, the 100,000 or so acres bathe the landscape in a sea of green.

Like fugitives, proprietors of farms in the Redlands are always looking over their shoulders. They know that when Dade County developers look at south Dade, they see a different kind of green. In fact, fierce political battles regularly take place between farmers and urbanites who would dump Miami's sprawl onto the Redlands.

Brent Probinsky, who grows exotic plants on his ten-acre spread, speaks for the farmers. "Unless a program is implemented to slow down and control urbanization," he said in the August 19, 2002, edition of the *Miami Herald*, "within two or three decades South Dade's agriculture will disappear."

Potatoes, tomatoes, squash and pole beans make up the staple crops of the Redlands. But dozens of other money crops, such as guavas, mangos, avocados and starfruit, are also harvested on area farms.

There are few serious crimes committed in the Redlands, although a serial killer named Marshall Lee Gore had once kidnapped and murdered a woman there. And while dozens of small towns exist within the area, some boasting a deputy or two, the Metro-Dade Police Department is responsible for maintaining law and order.

While South Dade presents a façade of tranquility, a dark strain runs beneath the surface. Thousands of undocumented workers, simply called "rafters" by residents, work the fields. When it comes to migrants, farmers turn their eyes away from legal niceties, claiming that they could not survive without the cheap labor.

Many who perform the backbreaking work in the fields once braved the Gulf Stream in leaky boats or clung to sinking rafts to come to America. They perform dawn-to-dusk manual labor so their sons and daughters can take advantage of the education and freedom found in the new land. In their own way, they're as noble and as rejected as earlier immigrants.

But sometimes a bad seed is found among the good.

At 3:07 P.M., September 11, 1995, Barbara Harrick stopped her school bus at a corner in Redland. She knew she had a "cush" job—she didn't have to drive incorrigible street kids into the ghettoes of Miami like some of her co-workers. She'd heard the horror stories and seen the war-shocked eyes of drivers who had faced down gun- and knife-wielding students.

Harrick's route took her through the colorful countryside with a dozen well-behaved students. All had IQs above 130 and were enrolled in gifted programs. Many were the sons and daughters of lawyers, doctors, engineers and so-called "gentleman farmers."

Harrick watched as nine-year-old Jimmy Ryce got off the bus. He wore a blue backpack that was heavy with books. She waved and he smiled back. *He is a handsome young man,* she probably thought. *Give him a few years and his smile will melt the heart of any girl.* She waited until Jimmy moved away from the road and began walking home. His house was only a couple of hundred yards from the bus stop.

When Barbara Harrick pulled away that afternoon, she had no way of knowing that she would never see Jimmy again.

At six o'clock that afternoon, the Metro-Dade Police Department received a call from Jimmy's eighteen-year-old stepbrother, who said that Jimmy hadn't come home from school. He was always very prompt, arriving sometime between 3:15 and 3:20. His stepbrother had checked the bus stop several times and spoken with neighbors, but Jimmy seemed to have vanished into thin air. When asked where their parents were, he stated that they were out of town. Don and Claudine Ryce were both lawyers, he said, and they were attending a conference in central Florida.

The first officers arrived at 6:25 P.M. With less than two hours of light left, they immediately began searching the surrounding area.

At around 7:00, Metro-Dade Police Aviation Officer Michael Mann began an aerial search for the missing boy. He leveled his helicopter a few hundred feet above the earth's surface, circling out from the bus stop to surrounding fields and farms. "I start at the location of dispatch," he later testified, "and generally orbit that particular direction in a larger, ever-increasing diameter of circle, paying particular attention to areas I think are of special interest, that being playgrounds, rock pits, areas that a child might go to play."

Just before nightfall, his flight pattern took him over an avocado grove less than five miles from Jimmy's house. Circling the grove several times, he saw nothing suspicious. There was a house, a few outbuildings, a small trailer and some horses running free.

After two hours, investigators felt a growing concern. Not a single trace of Jimmy had been found. Cops who initially thought the child might have run away or become lost now realized this was more serious. Since the initial call, police units from all areas of Dade County had been swarming to the location. Even the FBI had sent an agent to begin a preliminary investigation.

Earlier that afternoon, Claudine Ryce had called home. When she was told that Jimmy wasn't there, she immediately sensed that something was wrong and, with her husband Don, packed up and headed home. During the two-hour drive, a bitter memory kept eating at her.

"I had tried," she later wrote, "[on] the first day of school, to get the bus to let Jimmy out in front of our house rather than on the corner where traffic is heavy. This did not involve a route change or an additional stop; the bus drove right in front of our home. When I telephoned officials, I was told that no changes could be made, for any reason, for the first two weeks of school. I was passed from one bureaucrat to the next, until the last one hung up the phone on me."

Reluctantly, Claudine had decided to wait for the two weeks, then she would try again. Now she sobbed in frustration.

At first, Don attempted to put on his lawyer's face and think logically. Deep down he was panicking. This was like some horror movie in which the on-screen monster suddenly transmogrified into a real-life nightmare.

Don and Claudine Ryce arrived home at about 7:30 P.M. Light was fading, but they found Jimmy's stepbrother and several neighbors still searching. Working with police, they scoured fields, groves and the many snake-infested canals that crisscrossed the area. Police cars with flashing lights prowled the neighborhood and a helicopter clattered above. Somehow, instead of reassuring Claudine, all the activity chilled her. It only reinforced the reality that her son was missing.

Don and Claudine, as well as nearly everyone across America, had heard or read of the abduction of Adam Walsh fifteen years earlier. They'd learned that the seven-year-old son of John and Reve Walsh had been snatched from a department store in nearby Hollywood. A few weeks later, his severed head was found in a canal sixty miles away. The mystery magnified the horror. How could a child just vanish? What happened to Adam after he was abducted? Where was his body? No one had ever learned the answers to those questions. Adam's murderer still had not been apprehended.

And now it was happening again.

Since the Adam Walsh case—in fact, *because* of it—new techniques of investigating child abductions had been instituted in most major law enforcement agencies. Investigators now forego the "twenty-four-hour rule" and begin an immediate search. Then cops focus on eliminating family members and close friends as suspects. They also interview neighbors and acquaintances while simultaneously interrogating known sex offenders in the area. Finally, if all "local" leads fail, cops consider every parents' worst nightmare: abduction by a stranger.

That night, police interviewed the Ryce family. Each family member was given a polygraph and quickly eliminated from suspicion.

During the night, someone told Don and Claudine about the National Center for Missing and Exploited Children. Claudine called and the organization offered to help distribute missing child posters nationally. Locally, friends, family and strangers volunteered to go door-to-door handing out the posters and taping them to storefront windows. Claudine found a picture of Jimmy holding a baseball bat and wearing a big smile. This was placed on the flyer and was designed to tug at the heart of someone who may have seen something suspicious.

Claudine later wrote in *The Magazine of Stetson University*, "I was able to tell the police exactly what [Jimmy] was wearing, because I knew what I had left out for him to wear. We also gave police a full set of Jimmy's fingerprints. Don represents companies and municipalities in employment and labor matters, and he had taken Jimmy on a business trip to Winter Haven, where the police chief had his prints made."

That morning, the media showed up. They parked their vans and trucks in front of the house, clogging the road for blocks. The family felt that perhaps publicity might generate some leads to their son, so they granted dozens of interviews in those first hours.

In the meantime, the search continued. "At noon Wednesday," Claudine wrote, "nearly forty-eight hours after Jimmy was kidnapped, more than 100 volunteers began an organized grid search...Through Saturday, hundreds of people, most of them strangers, took time off from work to search a five-mile area covered with thick tropical undergrowth and algae-coated canals."

In addition to the continued searches, the family tried other avenues. They offered a $100,000 reward, hoping to shake information out of someone who had knowledge of the crime. A week after the disappearance, on September 18, during a *Monday Night Football* game, Jimmy's picture was displayed on the electronic screen at Joe Robbie Stadium in Miami along with a request for information about the "little Dolphin fan."

In desperation, the family sent postcards with Jimmy's picture to every home in Florida. And Don and Claudine appeared on radio and television shows, including *America's Most Wanted*, hosted by Adam Walsh's father, John.

However, as the weeks went by, not a single clue was found. Claudine felt the weight of despair. How could a little boy get off a school bus and just vanish? Where could he be? Is he still alive, pleading with his captor to release him? Other dark possibilities, almost too horrible to imagine, ate into her mind. What she didn't know was that although the publicity they had generated would eventually lead to some of the answers, the darkness of one soul would be impenetrable.

The caretaker was a thief.

His employer, Susan Scheinhaus, was sure of it. A few months before, she'd noticed her .38-caliber revolver was missing. She'd bought it for protection when she'd moved to the Redlands and kept it in a drawer in her nightstand. Susan called police to report the crime and informed a responding officer of her suspicions about Juan Carlos Chavez. But when asked to provide proof, the employer said she had none. The officer stated that he couldn't arrest Chavez based only on suspicions.

Then the woman's heirloom jewelry disappeared. The rings, necklaces and bracelets were worth several thousand dollars, but the sentimental value was worth more than gold. Again, she called police and again ran into a stone wall.

As more and more items went missing, the situation became intolerable. Tools, her son's .22-caliber rifle, perfume, a calculator, a tape recorder, even some of her panties vanished. Her possessions, she told police, had only begun to "wander away" after she hired Chavez. It irritated her that investigators brushed off her complaints when she believed he was stealing from her.

The more she thought about it, the angrier she became.

She decided to gather the evidence needed to have Chavez arrested. "Cops need proof," she told her twenty-eight-year-old son. "We'll get them proof."

Susan knew very little about her caretaker. Farmers rarely got a resume with their hired help. For the last six months, she'd let him live in a small trailer on her property. After she gave him a duplicate key to the trailer, her own disappeared. Chavez had been employed to perform odd jobs and do electrical work and carpentry. He was also expected to feed and exercise her horses. He turned out to be an excellent worker and, at first, Susan was glad she'd hired him.

The caretaker was bilingual—in fact, he spoke English with little accent. Susan never said it out loud, but she considered him to be one step above the field hands she routinely employed.

On December 5, she arranged for her father to take Chavez out for the morning. Then she called a locksmith and she and her son headed for the trailer.

After the door was unlocked, the employer entered, followed by her son. Before she even got all the way inside, she spied her gun on a table in the living room. Her son hung back while his mother looked around. Susan quickly located her jewelry and Ed's rifle in a closet. There had been no effort to hide her possessions.

A police report explains what happened next. "As she continued to look inside the trailer, the woman discovered a book bag in the closet...The book bag was partially unzipped. Looking inside the bag, she discovered papers and books. She looked at some of the work which appeared to be in a child's handwriting and noticed the name 'Jimmy Ryce.' She also observed his name on a book."

The woman was puzzled.

"Why would a rafter have a book like this?" Susan asked her son.

"What do you mean?" he returned.

"It belongs to a child," she said. "The kid wrote his name on it."

"What's the name?" her son asked.

"Jimmy Ryce."

"Oh, my God!" her son replied. "I recognize that name."

Something in his voice made the woman turn and look at him. He was pale and shaking.

"What?"

"Jimmy Ryce is the name of that kid who got kidnapped a few months ago," her son said. "They've got posters out everywhere."

Susan stared at her son in disbelief.

"Are you sure?" she asked.

He nodded.

"Let's get back to the house," she said.

Thumbing through the telephone book, Susan found the telephone number of the local FBI office. With trembling hands, she dialed and asked to speak with an agent.

When Juan Carlos Chavez returned home that afternoon, Metro-Dade officers met him. He was asked to accompany them to headquarters for questioning on the theft charge.

Homicide Detectives Luis Estopian and Juan Murias were two of the investigators assigned to conduct interviews with Chavez. Each detective was fluent in both English and Spanish.

Estopian noticed that Chavez was about average in height and weighed around 180 pounds. He had thinning hair and dark eyes. During the initial questioning, he stated that he was thirty years old, had been born in Cuba and completed the twelfth grade "on the island."

Estopian began by asking if the gun found in his trailer belonged to his employer.

"Yes," Chavez replied. "It's my duty not only to work on her property, but to protect it. She gave me the gun as part of my job."

The suspect struck Estopian as intelligent and very familiar with English.

"How did the book bag get in your possession?"

"I found it at a horse ranch where I used to work," Chavez said. "I just picked it up and brought it home, but I never opened it."

Bingo! the detectives must have thought. In just a few minutes of questioning, Estopian had already caught the caretaker in two lies. According to Susan, he'd stolen her gun—she had not given him permission to take it. And Estopian knew Chavez had opened the bag, because investigators had found his fingerprints on one of the books.

The detectives were sure they had identified Jimmy's abductor, but they decided to build their case slowly. Moving from the theft of Susan's property to the disappearance of Jimmy Ryce, Estopian noticed the caretaker's ever-changing stories. At first he stated that he'd never seen Jimmy, then claimed that "the kid" had been at the farm several times to play with the horses.

Then Chavez dropped a bombshell. The last time Jimmy came over, he said, Chavez had accidentally killed the boy "as he [Jimmy] stepped out to close the gate and was pinned between the truck and the fence."

When asked what he did with the body, Chavez stated that he became frightened and placed the child in an empty feed barrel. After sealing it, he placed it in the bed of a pickup truck. The following day the truck and the barrel had vanished. Chavez said he never saw either again.

The story was so bizarre that detectives stared at the suspect in disbelief. They asked him to accompany them to the farm. He agreed. Once there, Chavez pointed out the gate where he said he'd accidentally killed

Jimmy. A team of forensics experts examined it, but found no marks on the gate or the adjacent fence. When Chavez was confronted with this, he stated that he was ready to tell the "real" story.

Estopian asked where Jimmy's body was located. "The family needs to be able to conduct a proper burial," the detective said.

Chavez began to sob. "Let's go back to the office," he said. "There's no need to stay here, because Jimmy's body no longer exists."

On the ride back to headquarters, Chavez was silent. The detectives hoped that his conscience was bothering him and that he would finally confess. However, as soon as they entered the interview room, their hopes were dashed.

Chavez now claimed that after accidentally killing Jimmy, he burned the body. He'd totally destroyed it, he said. There was nothing left, not even ashes. In fact, he stated that he'd dumped the ashes in a canal that ran through the property.

During the night, the suspect was given two polygraph tests. On both, he was shown to be deceitful.

In addition to the ongoing interrogation, forensics units were working around the clock. A technician discovered a spot of dried blood near the front door of the trailer. This was removed and sent to the lab for DNA testing. DNA tests later revealed that the blood belonged to Jimmy Ryce. A cartridge found in the trailer was determined to have been fired from the gun Chavez had stolen.

As investigators disproved each lie and gathered more evidence, the suspect came up with new tales. Now he claimed that he had a homosexual lover who had accidentally shot Jimmy. The killer then fled the country. According to Chavez, he had no choice but to get rid of the body. If he'd called police, he said, they would've accused him of killing Jimmy.

Estopian told Chavez point-blank that he didn't believe him. In fact, the detective stated that he didn't believe any of the stories he'd been told.

Again, he asked Chavez to do the right thing by the Ryce family.

"They need to give their son a Christian burial," Estopian said.

The suspect bowed his head on the table. For several minutes he remained motionless. Then he looked up and began to sob. He finally agreed to tell authorities what really happened.

According to the suspect, the murder of Jimmy Ryce was conceived in the mind of Juan Carlos Chavez when he saw a group of preteen boys swimming in a nearby canal. Using his employer's pickup truck, he'd been to a hardware store to pick up items for a deck he was building.

Several of the swimmers wore only undershorts. As he drove by, Chavez became aroused. After he arrived home, the caretaker unloaded the lumber, then drove back to the canal and watched the boys until they left.

On the way back to his trailer, Chavez saw a young boy walking home from school. The child wore a backpack and had bright, carefree eyes. The caretaker pulled the truck across the road and stopped in front of Jimmy. Chavez got out, holding his employer's gun.

"Do you want to die?" he asked.

Jimmy was startled. He shook his head and said, "No."

"Get in the truck."

Chavez grabbed Jimmy by the arm and forced him inside. Then he got in behind the child.

"Get down," he ordered.

Jimmy ducked and the truck sped off.

It was just that simple, Chavez said. His need was so great that he hadn't even looked to see if anyone was watching. He hadn't yelled at Jimmy, but Chavez had made it very clear that if the boy didn't obey, he would shoot him.

The abductor drove back to Susan's farm, about five miles away. He checked to make sure no one else was around, then pulled Jimmy out of the truck and ordered him to go into the trailer. Jimmy left his backpack on the floor of the truck.

"Sit down on the bed." Jimmy moved to the bed. Chavez pulled up an office chair and sat in it, facing the boy. The caretaker was breathing hard as images of the boys at the canal played in his mind. Jimmy had tears in his eyes and was glancing around, as if he was trying to find a way out.

"What's your name?"

"Jimmy Ryce."

"Do your parents work?"

"They're lawyers."

"Stop crying."

Jimmy gulped, trying to swallow his tears. "Why did you take me?" he asked.

"Why do you think I took you?"

Jimmy hesitated. "Cause you want a little boy?" he said.

The innocence of the remark stopped Chavez in his tracks. He later told detectives that it reminded him of the first time he'd been molested in Cuba. He was about the same age as Jimmy and he didn't understand it either. Instead of being empathetic to his captive, Jimmy's comments filled him with rage.

"Take off your clothes," he ordered. Jimmy had no choice. He took off his shoes and socks, then slowly removed his shirt and pants.

"Take off your shorts."

Jimmy, sobbing, pulled down his underpants.

"Lay down on your stomach," Chavez said.

As Jimmy lay across the bed, the caretaker walked into the bathroom and found a bottle of lubricant.

Chavez raped the boy, then ordered Jimmy to put his clothes back on. It was over in less than five minutes.

The caretaker then drove Jimmy back to the scene of the abduction. During the drive, he forced the child to keep his head down. He told detectives that he was planning to release Jimmy, but by the time they drove back to the bus stop, police were searching for the missing boy.

All the cars and activity frightened Chavez, so he drove his captive back to the trailer. They got out and went back inside.

When asked why he didn't release Jimmy somewhere else, Chavez was silent.

According to the statement Chavez gave police, Jimmy was upset. "He said [that] once inside the trailer, Jimmy is trembling and crying. And Jimmy asked, 'What's going to happen to me? Are you going to kill me?' So [Chavez] begins to speak to Jimmy in order to calm him down."

The kidnapper asked the boy about his family. Jimmy told him that his parents were at work. He also mentioned that his brother had a red car and a box full of cassette tapes. (Investigators knew that this was information that Chavez could only have learned from his victim.)

Detective Estopian later testified, "The next thing Chavez mentions [that] happened is he heard a helicopter fly over the horse ranch…He believed the helicopter belonged to the police, that the police were searching for Jimmy. When he heard the helicopter flying over him, he held Jimmy close to him so the boy wouldn't go anywhere. Eventually, as the chopper circled above the trailer, Chavez got up and looked out the window to see if he could see it."

Estopian also spoke about the final moments of Jimmy's life. "While he was looking for the helicopter," Estopian said, "Jimmy is still close to the front entrance of the trailer. He said that Jimmy made a dash for the door. Jimmy ran to the door trying to escape. [Chavez] said that he tried to reach up to [grab] Jimmy, but he got tangled on the floor [mat] of the bathroom and at that point he said he took the revolver belonging to Ms. Scheinhaus. He pointed the handgun in the direction of Jimmy [and] fired one time, hitting him."

As the shot rang out, Jimmy screamed, then collapsed. He'd barely managed to get his hands on the doorknob.

The detectives were amazed at the courage of Jimmy Ryce. Captured by a grown man with a gun, then taunted and raped, Jimmy managed to keep his wits about him until he saw an opportunity to try to escape. With a little luck, the brave boy with the genius IQ might have made it.

After shooting Jimmy, Chavez scrambled to his feet and ran to the boy. He stated that he held Jimmy in his arms as he heard the child's last gasps.

Hardened investigators wept as they heard about the last minutes of Jimmy's life. But when they heard how the kidnapper disposed of the body, they were outraged.

"I want to die," Chavez said. "I want to be executed."

Detectives couldn't guarantee anything, but most thought that if anyone deserved the death penalty, it was Juan Carlos Chavez. He refused to look the detectives in the eye and in the middle of a sentence, often broke down and sobbed uncontrollably.

Finally, investigators were able to get the whole story.

After murdering Jimmy, Chavez found a fifty-gallon metal barrel and brought it to the trailer. He placed the body in the container and sealed it with a metal lid. Then he placed the barrel in an unused van that was on the property.

He took Jimmy's book bag out of the truck and brought it into the trailer. That night, Chavez opened the bag and sorted through the boy's books and papers.

The next day, he noticed blood on his clothes and threw them into the canal. Chavez spent the day trying to work, but he agonized about what to do with Jimmy's body. Susan owned a backhoe, so Chavez decided to dig a deep hole and bury the body. He knew that the deeper the hole, the less chance anyone had of ever finding the remains.

But when he tried to crank up the backhoe, it wouldn't start.

Two days later, Chavez still hadn't figured out what to do with the body. According to a police report, "He eventually began to smell a foul odor coming from the back of the van and he felt that eventually someone else would smell the foul odor and discover Jimmy's body inside the drum. So he decided that he wanted to find a way of disposing of Jimmy's body."

Chavez went to check on the body and discovered that gases had blown the lid off the barrel. The smell was disgusting, but he knew he had to do something. He waited until the owners of the property left, then pulled Jimmy's body out of the barrel and dropped it onto a piece of plywood. Taking a pruning tool, the killer began to dismember his victim.

He worked most of the day, vomiting time and again. His body became so wracked with nausea that he could barely move. But he knew that if he didn't continue, he would be caught.

Once Chavez had cut off the arms and legs, he attacked the torso. He eventually cut it into three sections.

Inside the stable, Chavez had seen three plastic planters, each about three feet high and as big around as a large tub. He also found several bags of concrete. The killer stuffed the body parts into the planters, then sealed the tops with wet cement.

After it dried, Chavez dragged the planters in front of a row of hedges where they stayed for three months. He informed his employer that he'd placed them there to keep the horses from eating the hedges.

Detectives and forensics investigators once again made the trip to the residence, this time to recover Jimmy's body.

Chief Medical Examiner Dr. Roger Mittleman decided to take the planters back to the laboratory where he gingerly tapped the cement until it crumbled. Eventually, he was able to recover most of the decayed body.

Jimmy still had some of his clothes on, as well as one of his shoes. Part of a bullet was found lodged in the area of the heart. According to court documents, the bullet "entered right where the sixth rib is located, went upward in the body, through the lung, through the heart and exited from the upper left chest."

It would have taken Jimmy just seconds to die.

On September 18, 1998, Juan Carlos Chavez was convicted of first-degree murder, sexual assault of a victim under the age of twelve and kidnapping with a weapon. The jury quickly voted twelve to zero to sentence Chavez to death.

He currently awaits his execution at Union Correctional Institution in Raiford. He has changed his mind about wanting to be executed and now claims to be innocent.

Still reeling from the trauma of burying their son, Don and Claudine Ryce turned their energies toward helping other children escape the clutches of pedophiles.

They established The Jimmy Ryce Center for Victims of Predatory Abduction. One of the missions of the center is to donate bloodhounds to police departments. Claudine felt that if the investigators had a trained dog to search for Jimmy's scent, they may have been able to track him to his abductor's trailer in time to prevent his murder. The center has donated more than 400 dogs to police departments around the country. Several lives have been saved because of this program.

Don and Claudine also wrote one of the most controversial laws ever passed by the state of Florida. The Jimmy Ryce Act allows the court to mandate hospitalization of violent child predators once their prison sentences are completed. According to an *Associated Press* article, the act provides for "two psychiatrists or psychologists [to] review the files of every child molester who is about to be released from prison. If they determine the [inmate] is a 'sexually violent predator' who would likely attack other children if released, prosecutors can ask a judge to involuntarily commit the prisoner to a treatment facility until it is determined he no longer poses a threat."

Some groups claim that the Jimmy Ryce Act is unconstitutional, because it continues to punish criminals who have already served their sentences. Once a convicted felon serves his time, they argue, he should be released.

Don Ryce disagrees. "They say the molesters' rights are being violated," he said. "But what about the victims' rights?"

Claudine wrote, "When Jimmy was five years old, he asked me why God let a little boy burn up in a fire. The somewhat glib answer I gave was that maybe God wanted him to come home to Him. Jimmy thought about it a moment and said, 'What if the little boy wanted to live with his family first?' Jimmy, too, had many things he wanted to do before he died."

On January 23, 2009, Claudine Ryce passed away. According to local news sources, several bloodhounds and their handlers attended the funeral service in Palmetto Bay. They were there to memorialize Claudine's work on behalf of missing children. "She did not ask for any of this," Don said. "She did not ask to be a crusader. But she took it with grace, courage and determination."

Speaking about the killer of Jimmy, Don Ryce said, "It's not that we are dominated by thoughts of him, but justice requires he give his life for what he took."

Claudine Ryce was buried next to her son.

Unfortunately, too many child abductions occur with regularity in the Sunshine State. Many of these go unsolved. Jimmy Ryce was an unlucky victim, in the wrong place at the wrong time. Although his courageous escape attempt may have cost him his life, it is probable that his abductor would not have released him. Juan Carlos Chavez had never been tried for a crime, so it would have been difficult to stop him from committing his first one. The kidnapping was also a spur-of-the-moment decision, acted out in a burst of sexual passion. This random act could have been committed in any jurisdiction in the country. While most child predators have long rap sheets, occasionally, there's just no way to predict murder.

Chapter 5
An American Monster

"The situation that we have endured is beyond a parent's worst nightmare."

John and Reve Walsh, commenting on the murder of their son.

O ttis Elwood Toole was a smelly, murderous pervert who had few redeeming qualities.

Toole's mother had nine children, three of which died during childbirth or shortly thereafter. Several of her surviving offspring ended up doing hard time. From 1954, when her husband left forever, to her death in 1981, she scrounged a threadbare living in a slum section of Jacksonville called Springfield.

In later interviews with police and psychiatric professionals, Toole claimed that during his early childhood, his father arranged for neighbors to sexually abuse him. His penchant for truth-telling was never high. In fact, he claimed to have had sex with just about everyone he met. The gangly, gap-toothed teen learned to lie early on and used this lone skill later in life to enhance his living conditions in prison.

According to his own biography, when he was a child, Toole's sisters found it amusing to dress him up like a girl and play "house" with him. By the time he was ten, he claimed to have had sex with one of his sisters as well as several male neighbors. As he grew into adulthood, he developed a fetish for wigs and cross-dressing.

He asserted that his grandmother was a Satanist and that he'd taken part in ritualistic "celebrations" of the Evil One. In fact, according to him, she renamed him "Devil's Child." On the other hand, his mother was a strict Christian who took her children to church every Sunday.

Toole had numerous learning disabilities including dyslexia and attention deficit hyperactivity disorder (ADHD). He was also afflicted with grand mal seizures due to epilepsy. Psychiatrists eventually concluded that Toole suffered from a schizoid personality.

The young man had no interest in intellectual pursuits and quit school in the seventh grade. Obsessed with sex, he began turning tricks. On many nights he walked to nearby Confederate Park, sometimes dressed in drag, and tried to pick up men. Beneath the "Women of the Southland" monument, Toole consummated brief encounters with transients or businessmen. Sometimes he was paid a few dollars. On several occasions, cops arrested him for soliciting or loitering, but he served little time and was quickly back on the streets.

Local police thought of him as a quirky nuisance, someone to keep an eye on, but not a danger to others. Although Toole could barely write his name and couldn't read, he was streetwise. He worked occasionally in low-skill jobs, but rarely lasted for more than a few weeks. His passion for alcohol, drugs and gay sex was more important to him than money.

Toole claimed to have committed his first murder when he was fourteen. He told cops that when a traveling salesman made advances toward him, the teen ran the man over with his own car, killing him. As usual, however, investigators could find no proof of the murder.

Although he married twice, neither union lasted. His passion for male-on-male sex did little to keep his wives interested in continuing matrimonial relations.

Still in his teens, Toole developed yet another obsession—starting fires.

The Springfield area had once been one of Jacksonville's most stylish and prosperous communities. But after World War II, some of the two- and three-story Victorian homes gradually became havens for crackheads and prostitutes. Houses that had once hosted the cream of Jacksonville society were now rat-infested cinderblocks.

Toole was aroused by fire.

The flame-engulfed buildings excited him. Each fire he started was like a self-made carnival. The arsonist was entranced by the wailing sirens and sweaty firefighters who leapt from their trucks with hoses spewing streams of water toward the blaze. He usually targeted abandoned buildings, but occasionally burned down occupied boardinghouses. A prototypical sexual arsonist, he blazed his way through hundreds of orgasms.

By the time he was a teenager, Toole had developed a wanderlust that couldn't be sated. He hitchhiked all over the country, trading his own body for food and money. When that failed, he learned that he could steal or panhandle or even sell his blood for cash. He found that homeless shelters always provided a meal and a bed for a night or two. Many nights he slept under the stars, but all in all, he was satisfied.

His mother's home was in Jacksonville and Toole always returned. After a few weeks or months on the road, he often showed up unannounced. He stayed for a week or two, then disappeared again.

In 1979, Toole noticed a drifter named Henry Lee Lucas at a soup kitchen in Jacksonville. They'd met before, either in Pennsylvania or Michigan, depending on who told the story. Toole was taken by the one-eyed vagabond and invited him home. They quickly became sex partners.

Lucas had had a horrific upbringing. He grew up in a dirtfloor cabin in the backwoods of Virginia. His mother and his stepfather administered severe beatings for little or no reason. He was sometimes sent to school dressed up as a girl. Once, during a fight, his older brother stabbed him in his left eye and the wound went untreated for days. From that time on, Lucas wore a leaky glass eye that gave him a sinister look. He rarely bathed or changed clothes and, like Toole, lived on the far-out fringes of society.

When he was fifteen, Lucas was arrested for burglarizing an auto parts store. He was sent to a training school for boys. Because of several escape attempts, he spent two years there. After he got out, he began wandering the country. Lucas was soon picked up for burglary once again, but escaped. In Michigan, he was sentenced to eighteen months in a federal prison for violating the Dyer Act, which criminalized the transportation of stolen vehicles over state lines.

On January 11, 1960, after a long, bitter argument with his mother, Lucas murdered her. The Tecumseh, Michigan, medical examiner reported that he'd stabbed her in the neck after strangling her. For that crime, he was sentenced to forty years in prison—but only did ten.

After getting out, Lucas attempted to kidnap two teenaged girls and served another five years in prison.

Once he was released, he headed south.

His childhood, his long stays in prison and his aimless wanderings had hardened his soul.

Lucas and Toole teamed up—two rudderless drifters on an aimless journey. They made a loathsome couple. If their confessions were to be believed, they committed hundreds of gruesome murders in their travels.

On January 4, 1982, Toole burned down a row house on Second Street in Jacksonville.

Several tenants who rented rooms by the week were inside when the fire started. As smoke filled the hallway and filtered into the rooms, panicked residents jumped from second-story windows to save themselves. Sixty-four-year-old George Sonnenberg, however, was trapped in his room.

Outside, Toole reveled in the chaotic scene as firemen broke down the front door. Crackling flames licked high into the sky and black smoke boiled upward. Toole saw a man being wheeled away on a stretcher toward a waiting ambulance. The screams of the half-burned victim didn't bother the arsonist, however; they just added to the excitement.

Two years later, after being arrested for the murder of a kindly woman who'd tried to help him, Lucas ratted out his only friend. Documented in the book *Confessions of Henry Lee Lucas*, he told a Texas Ranger that "[Toole] set fire to an apartment house and we were hiding over there in the back alley there when he set the fire. We went around back...and the Fire Department was there fighting it. They brought the old man out on the front porch and tried to save his life, but they couldn't."

Although he was pulled from the burning building, Sonnenberg suffered severe burns and smoke inhalation. He died a week later.

Soon after, Toole and Lucas picked up Toole's ten-year-old niece, Becky Powell, and high-tailed it out of Jacksonville. They didn't hang around long enough to learn that officials had ruled the blaze had been accidentally started by a smoldering cigarette.

Lucas, a serial child molester, fancied that he and Becky were in love. Driving an old rattletrap Lucas had picked up somewhere, they wandered aimlessly about the country.

Lucas preferred sex with preteen girls while Toole liked men, especially Lucas. The strange "love" triangle couldn't last. Toole finally got angry because Lucas wanted almost constant sex with Becky, ignoring him. He ditched the couple and hitchhiked back to Jacksonville.

In Texas, Becky grew homesick. She asked Lucas to take her home, but he refused. By now, she was twelve and knew she had sexual power over him. When she insisted on going back to Jacksonville, Lucas became enraged and stabbed her to death.

In October 1982, Lucas was arrested for the murder of Mary Rich. He soon confessed to that murder, as well that of Becky Powell. In the Powell murder, he claimed self-defense, but no one bought that story. When Lucas led investigators to the body, detectives found that Becky had been dismembered and scattered across a field in Denton, Texas. Within weeks, the ex-con would be confessing to hundreds of murders. And he would be implicating his cohort, Ottis Toole.

The following year, Toole, along with two teenage boys, was arrested in Jacksonville for arson. A few months later, he was sentenced to fifteen years in prison for that crime.

After Lucas informed Texas investigators about the fire that killed George Sonnenberg, they relayed the information to the Jacksonville Police Department. When he was questioned, Toole readily admitted to the crime. He was tried and sentenced to death.

Since Toole was said to have been involved in some of the murders Lucas claimed to have committed, cops arranged for Lucas to call Toole. They recorded the conversation in order to obtain evidence against both men. The two prisoners spoke for the first time in two years.

Lucas told Toole that he planned to lead cops to all the bodies of victims they'd murdered, as long as the investigators treated him right. He planned to implicate his cohort, he said.

"I just don't want you to feel that I'm doing it for revenge or anything else," Lucas said. "I'm doing it because I know that what I'm doing is right."

In one of the strangest responses in the annals of crime, Toole said, "And I don't want you holding nothing back now, Henry. If you know I was involved, I don't want you just to say it—I want you to spit it out."

By now, Lucas had confessed to hundreds of murders. With each confession, his life got better. Unlike other inmates who had to live with the tedium and fear of being locked away from society with other violent felons, the self-proclaimed serial killer got special treatment. He had a television set with cable channels in his cell and was fed pizza and steak on a daily basis. He was constantly shuttled to faraway places like Illinois or Kansas or Nebraska to point out locations where bodies could be found. Lucas was the center of attention. He was living better now than he ever had in his entire life.

In fact, he'd become a celebrity. He was regularly on the six o'clock news. Shunned for most of his life, Henry Lee Lucas had become "somebody." On his trips away from prison, he got to eat at fast food restaurants and was plied with candy, cigarettes and even beer.

For the cops, the payoff was a closed case, even if the confession was vague and the suspect was unable to remember exactly where the crime had been committed.

Toole saw the treatment Lucas was getting. He soon figured out that he could raise his standard of living even if he was in prison.

Ottis Toole was to gain nearly as much notoriety as his cohort with his own confessions of murder.

One day in 1984, a former Hollywood, Florida, marketing executive named John Walsh received a letter that had a return address from Union Correctional Institute in Raiford, Florida. He knew that the prison was the home of all of the state's death row inmates. Curious, he opened the envelope and spread the letter in front of him. It read:

"Dear Walsh,

I'm the person who snatched, raped & murdered and cut up that little prick teaser, Adam Walsh, and dumped his smelly ass into the canal. You know the story but you don't know where his bones are. I do. Now you are a rich fucker, money you made from the dead body of that little kid. Oh, he was a sweet little piece of ass! I want to make a deal with you.

Here's my deal. You pay me money and I'll tell you where the bones are so you can get them buried all decent and Christian. I know you'll find a way to make sure I get the electric chair but at least I'll have money to spend before I burn. If you want the bones of your little cockteaser you send a private lawyer with money for me.

No cops. No State Attorneys. No FDLE. Just a private lawyer with
a written contract. I get $5,000 as 'good faith' money.

Then when I show you some bones I get $45,000.You get a lawyer
to make up a paper like that.If you send the police after me before
we make a deal then you don't get no bones..."

The letter concluded with an obscenity-filled paragraph detailing how
the writer had raped and murdered the six-year-old boy.

It was signed by Ottis Toole.

The words, meant to cause pain and extort money, referred to the most
notorious crime ever committed in Florida.

For John Walsh, now a well-known advocate for crime victims, the
letter brought back a flood of bitter memories.

On the steaming hot morning of July 27, 1981, Reve Walsh drove to
the Hollywood Mall. Her son, Adam, went along. Reve planned to purchase
two lamps for their home. Her husband, John, was at work.

Reve and Adam walked hand in hand across the north parking lot and
entered the department store. To get to the section that sold appliances, they
had to pass through the toy department. Several kids were playing a brand-
new video game and Adam asked his mother if he could watch.

Since she would be only a short distance away and Adam was an
obedient child, Reve agreed. She pointed out where she would be and left
him there—just like thousands of shoppers do every day.

After learning that the lamps were unavailable and would have to be
ordered, Reve walked back to the toy department. Where there had been
four or five children, now there were none.

Reve felt like she'd been sucker punched.

As she began to frantically search the store for Adam, staff didn't seem
helpful. They ignored her or tried to soothe her by saying that her son

would soon return. Reve told anyone who would listen that Adam was wearing green running shorts, a short-sleeved shirt and yellow flip-flops. He also had on a white captain's hat. The captain's hat should make him easy to find, she probably felt.

No one seemed to have noticed Adam. As the search stretched on, Adam's grandmother showed up. Gram, as they called her, lived nearby and just happened to have come to the store that day. Together, they searched the store, the mall and even the parking lot. They walked to Reve's car several times, hoping Adam would show up there.

As the minutes dragged by, their panic increased.

About thirty minutes later, someone in the store called the Hollywood Police Department. John Walsh was also notified and rushed to help.

The situation was so far beyond the pale of reality that the close-knit family had trouble believing that it had really happened. How can a child just disappear? No one else, even the police officers who showed up, believed it was serious. Just a missing kid, they said, he'll show up. He's probably hiding somewhere or wandering around unseen.

But that pit in Reve's stomach wouldn't go away. She instinctively knew that something wasn't right.

A seventeen-year-old security guard was located. She told cops that four boys playing the video game had gotten into a scuffle. The guard had ordered them to leave the store. She sent two of the boys out of the mall on the north side and the other two boys out on the west side. She thought Adam was one of them. If so, he would have been unfamiliar with that area since he and his mother always used the north entrance.

The investigation into Adam's disappearance was difficult almost from the start. The local cops had no experience in a high-profile kidnapping. Despite all evidence to the contrary, detectives spent several crucial days treating Adam as a runaway—even though six-year-olds rarely run away and certainly not from the toy department of a store.

As cops chased phantoms, John and Reve Walsh cooperated with their every request. The parents took lie detector tests, endured hours of grueling interrogations and opened up their lives and homes to the strangers whose jobs it was to find their child. But when no real suspects emerged, the Walshes contacted the media. Instinctively, they believed that publicity was the key to finding their son.

It was while they were in New York for a television interview that they learned that the severed head of a child had been found in a canal in south Florida. When it was determined that the head was Adam's, John and Reve were devastated.

They returned home and learned that the boy's head had probably been severed with a machete or bayonet, probably while he lay on his stomach. Fishermen had found the head in Indian River County, on a dirt road off the Florida Turnpike. It was approximately 100 miles from where he'd been abducted.

Other than the head, there was no evidence at the scene and the killer remained unknown.

By the time John Walsh received the extortion letter from Ottis Toole, he had become a well-known advocate for missing children.

Somehow, John and Reve Walsh kept their marriage together. Their grief, frustration and anger were documented in two made-for-television movies and a book entitled *Tears of Rage*.

Did Ottis Toole kidnap and murder Adam Walsh?

Unfortunately, he was a drifter who never kept any solid records of his wanderings. Over the years, Hollywood police worked to learn as much as they could about his activities in the weeks before and after Adam's abduction. Many of the records were obtained from arrest reports, soup kitchen records and documents from homeless shelters.

However, police were never able to reliably document Toole's whereabouts during the week that Adam Walsh went missing.

When he was in Jacksonville, which was his home base, Toole stayed at his mother's house. After she died in 1981, he bunked with relatives, slept in abandoned buildings or rented a room when he had money.

Toole's first arrest took place when he was thirteen. He stole a neighbor's bicycle and was charged with theft. Over the years, he was arrested in various states, including Georgia, Kentucky, Alabama and, of course, Florida.

Many of the crimes he was charged with were "nuisance" crimes—others were more serious. A list of charges included auto theft, larceny, lewd behavior, propositioning a police officer, indecent exposure, cross-dressing, window-peeping, breaking and entering and theft. He was also known to make obscene phone calls. Until his arrest for murder in 1983, Toole served most of his short sentences in local jails. Up to that point, the only hard time he served was when he spent two years in a federal prison for interstate transportation of a stolen vehicle.

After having spent two years on death row for the murder of George Sonnenberg, Toole's sentence was reversed. The Florida Supreme Court ruled that during the sentencing phase of the trial, the presiding judge did not inform jurors that "emotional disturbance" could be used as a mitigating factor. Toole was then re-sentenced to life in prison.

He was also convicted of murdering nineteen-year-old Ada Mildred Johnson in Tallahassee. While serving a life sentence for that murder, he was suspected of several others. In fact, he was indicted in four murders: Jerilyn Peoples of Bonifay; John Perry McDaniel, Jr., of Campbellton; Brenda Jo Burton of Bonifay and Ruby McCrary of Washington County. Although police had confessions and some evidence linking both Toole and Lucas to those homicides, they were never tried, because both recanted their earlier statements of guilt.

In 1983, Jack Hoffman and Ron Hickman, two detectives from the Hollywood Police Department, drove to Union Correctional Institution in Raiford and interviewed Toole about Adam Walsh's murder. He'd implicated himself in earlier statements to detectives from other jurisdictions when they were interrogating him about previous murders. Those investigators contacted Hollywood police and Hoffman and Hickman took a series of recorded statements from the alleged serial murderer.

Toole readily admitted his guilt.

In the first interview, he claimed that he and Lucas were together when they kidnapped Adam. He stated that they drove Toole's white car that had a black top. After leaving Jacksonville, they traveled straight to Fort Lauderdale. That night they slept in the car, then drove around until they found a mall that had a department store in it. Toole stated he went to the wig department to browse, but claimed he never went inside the store.

While looking at wigs and no doubt dreaming of more cross-dressing exploits, Toole told the investigators that he spotted a young boy in the parking lot. The child seemed to be between seven and ten years old and was alone, he said. When describing the clothes the boy wore, he got it wrong, recalling that the boy had on blue jeans, a blue shirt and sneakers.

Toole said he had a handheld video game and lured the boy to the car in order to show him how to use it.

Detective Hoffman asked, "Was the child in the front seat with you and Henry or was he in the back?"

"If you snatch up somebody," Toole replied, "you damn sure ain't going to let them in no backseat." The comment was typical of Toole and Lucas— it illustrated the fact that they thought the cops were stupid. The two killers who had a combined IQ of slightly above 100 thought themselves superior to everyone else.

Toole said that he was drinking beer and popping pills when the abduction occurred, so he couldn't remember much about it.

He stated that the kidnappers placed Adam between them and drove north on the Florida Turnpike. The turnpike had toll booths spaced at intervals, but cars with no money could go through without paying.

(Video cameras recorded the license plates of non-payees and they were billed later.)

In Toole's confession, he claimed that after driving for about an hour and half, Adam became unmanageable. He was crying for his mother and begging his abductors to take him home.

Toole, who was driving, said he pulled onto a dirt road, away from traffic. The kidnappers forced the boy to lay face down on the ground, then Lucas used a "bayonet" or "machete" to chop off Adam's head. It took three or four blows to complete the grisly job.

Then he was shown an aerial photograph of the canal, but he didn't recognize it. When he was shown Adam's photograph, he also claimed that it wasn't the same boy.

So far, the interview wasn't going well for the detectives. It got worse. Buddy Terry, the Jacksonville cop who was coordinating the interviews with Toole, told the detectives that Lucas couldn't have been involved. Terry had learned that in July of 1981, he was in a Pikesville, Maryland, jail. Lucas remained in custody until October, when he was released. Therefore, it would have been impossible for him to have been involved in the abduction of Adam.

The detectives decided to try again.

In the second interview, Toole admitted he'd lied. He wanted to "get [Lucas's] sorry ass," he said, so he'd tried to implicate his former partner. Toole now claimed that he'd kidnapped Adam by himself. As they were driving north on the turnpike, the child began crying and screaming so Toole punched him in the face several times, knocking him out. He said he decided to kill the boy, because he thought Adam could identify him.

In *Tears of Rage*, John Walsh described what the medical examiner had found. "Hoffman and Hickman," he wrote, "were of course familiar with Adam's autopsy report. Ronald Wright, the medical examiner, had made a number of findings two years before: that before death, there had been a broken nose and injury between the eyes. That Adam was already dead, and lying facedown, when he was decapitated. That there were five blows to the base of the skull. That the killer was right-handed and would have had to use both hands."

That fit exactly with what Toole was now telling the investigators. The twice-convicted killer was indeed right-handed, but said he'd used both hands and had made "four or five" chops near the base of the skull. He then drove for about ten minutes more with the head on the floor behind the front seat. He pulled onto a dirt road, he said, and drove a short way to a "little bridge" that went out into a canal. There he threw the head into the water. Toole was unclear about what he'd done with the rest of the body.

On October 21, Hoffman and Hickman drove Toole from Raiford prison to Hollywood in an attempt to retrace the kidnapper's route. They took him first to the Broward County mall. Toole correctly stated that it wasn't the right one. Then they transported him to the Hollywood Mall and he identified the west entrance as the place where he picked up the boy. Now he claimed that he had used toys and candy for bait.

Toole was asked to show the investigators the route he'd followed when he had abducted the boy. He directed them through town and to the turnpike. After driving for about an hour and a half, Toole told them to stop at an access road. This, they must have thought, was the place where Toole had decapitated Adam. It did indeed have a "triangle," or a branch in the road, as Toole had previously described. It was also the only place on the turnpike where a driver could get off the highway toll-free. Toole had also mentioned that fact in his earlier interviews.

Then he led the investigators up the turnpike to another cutoff road. It was about four miles farther north. He pointed to a dock and stated that this was where he'd thrown the head.

Hoffman and Hickman were elated.

Toole had indeed picked the exact spot where fishermen had located Adam's head two years before!

It seemed to be the proof needed to convict Toole of kidnapping and murdering Adam Walsh. How could he have known the location if he hadn't been there? At long last, the detectives may have thought, the case that had haunted south Florida and a nation had been solved.

Cops delivered Toole back to Raiford. The Hollywood Police Department held a press conference and announced to the world that they had solved the most infamous kidnapping case since Charles Lindbergh's son was abducted out of his own home. It seemed reasonable to believe that charges would soon be leveled against the drifter who had confessed to the crime.

Police quickly impounded Toole's car. It was filthy and cluttered with trash. A forensics team discovered that there was blood on the passenger seat and on the passenger door handle. There was also blood on a floor mat behind the driver's seat. Both coincided with the killer's statement that he'd knocked Adam out in the front seat, then placed his head on the backseat floor.

The blood was tested and determined to be human, but before the advent of DNA testing, a positive identification of the source of the blood was impossible.

Carpeting from the floor in the back was sent to the lab at the Florida Department of Law Enforcement in Tallahassee for further testing.

Meanwhile, police conducted a background search, attempting to develop a timeline of Toole's movements for the weeks before and after Adam went missing. Investigators knew that Lucas and Toole had been on the road for most of the summer of 1981. Records indicated that they'd been in Louisiana, Texas, Florida and Maryland. On July 22, Lucas had been busted in Pikesville, Maryland, and spent three months in the city jail. Toole had moved on to Delaware, where a Salvation Army paid for a bus ticket to Jacksonville.

It was known that the killer was in Jacksonville on July 25. However, his whereabouts were unknown from then until July 31. Cops obtained receipts showing that he rented a room in Jacksonville on July 31. So it was indeed possible that the drifter could have been in Hollywood on the day of Adam's disappearance. He was known to have traveled to Miami occasionally to hustle, because tricks there paid better than those in Jacksonville. It's possible that he may have traveled to south Florida looking to make some quick cash and spied Adam outside the department store in the Hollywood Mall. Despite the circumstantial evidence, months passed, then years. No charges were filed. John Walsh received the extortion letter from Toole (actually written by another inmate, serial killer Gerard Schaeffer, since Toole was illiterate) and again contacted police about the case. His questions went unanswered.

As Walsh's advocacy for crime victims grew, he and Reve worked to establish the National Center for Missing and Exploited Children. They had three more children, but Adam was never far from their minds. They continued to lobby for laws that were designed to prevent children from being victimized by predators.

In 1994, the Hollywood Police Department began yet another investigation into the case. By this time, DNA was being used routinely to convict murderers and rapists as well as to exonerate innocent inmates. Since the case was but then thirteen years old, new investigators felt that there should be no problem testing the car and the floor mat recovered after Toole's confession. DNA tests should have quickly determined whether the convict was telling the truth.

But there was an unexpected problem.

Both the car and the carpet had disappeared.

How did investigators lose such critical evidence? Especially something as big as a car? The new detectives working the case determined that the vehicle had been sold to a man in St. Augustine. He had eventually junked it in an automobile salvage yard.

Likewise, FDLE was unable to find the floor mat. While it had been sent to the Florida State Crime Lab for testing, it was never returned to the Hollywood Police Department. It was assumed that at some point the mat was destroyed. But no one could account for why it had been lost.

With the possibility of collecting DNA lost forever, the Walshes once again began asking why the case was never prosecuted. Even without the DNA, there seemed to be enough evidence to go forward. Cops said that one of the reasons they had shelved the case was the timeline. When Toole arrived in Jacksonville in July after an eleven-hour ride, it was thought he would have been so tired that he would never have hopped into a car to travel to Miami when he could have hustled a few bucks close to home.

On the other hand, the new investigators thought that the air-conditioned bus ride could have, in their words, "invigorated him"—for months, he'd been living in Lucas's car or on the streets in strange places. Refreshed from the bus ride and needing money, he may indeed have driven to a place where he'd been successful raising needed cash before.

Another reason for not indicting Toole was that he had recanted his confessions. He'd stopped cooperating with investigators and, without his own words, prosecutors felt he could not be convicted.

On September 15, 1995, Toole died at Union Correctional Institute in Raiford, Florida. Unlike the heady days when he was confessing to every murder brought his way and reaping the benefits, his last years weren't pleasant.

Since Toole had confessed to murdering a child, he was reviled by other prisoners. They urinated on him in his cell and dumped food on him. After a documentary about Adam's case was televised, Toole was attacked by a group of inmates.

While incarcerated, Toole developed Hepatitis B and C, cirrhosis of the liver and AIDS. His stomach had become distended and he was always exhausted. Prison personnel, medical workers and detectives who visited him wore protective gowns and surgical masks. Few people, even medical personnel, wanted to be around the notorious monster who had caused so much pain.

A pariah even among the worst human beings Florida had to offer, in later years Toole clammed up when approached by investigators attempting to resolve old cases.

In the waning days of his life, did his memory rewind back to his soul mate, Henry Lee Lucas? Did he recall the words of his fellow murderer? "We killed them most every way there is except poison," Lucas once bragged. "There's no possible way that anybody in the country could do what me and Ottis have done. [We killed them] by shooting them, hanging them, running them down with cars. We've beat them to death. There's crucifixions, filleting people like fish, people that have been burnt, shot in their cars."

Most investigators eventually concluded that Lucas was good for only a handful of murders. It could be proven that he killed three people. Though there was some circumstantial evidence implicating him in a few of the murders to which he confessed, most of his confessions could not be proven or were obviously untrue.

There's little doubt that Toole murdered George Sonnenberg and Ada Johnson. Cops in the Florida panhandle still insist that there is evidence connecting Toole and Lucas to four murders there. But they were never tried.

And then there was Adam Walsh. It's hard to imagine a frightened six-year-old boy inside that filthy car with a monster like Toole.

When asked why he abducted Adam, he said, "I wanted a little boy to keep."

That's a horrifying thought.

Ottis Toole's body was never claimed.

He was buried in the cemetery inside Union Correctional Institute at Raiford.

Toole's niece contacted John Walsh after the prisoner died. She stated that she visited him as he lay dying and that Toole confessed that he had indeed murdered Adam.

On December 16, 2008, twenty-seven years after the abduction and murder of their son, John and Reve Walsh received a telephone call. It was newly-appointed Hollywood Chief of Police, Chadwick E. Wagner.

"Through a lengthy process of exclusion over the entire investigative period of twenty-seven years," Wagmer said, "the direction of this investigation has always continued to focus upon Ottis Toole as the perpetrator of this horrific crime...Prior to this year, I never actually had the opportunity to review the entire Adam Walsh investigation. I did observe the investigation handled by others in the department and admittedly realized, even years ago, that this investigation had flaws. This fact was confirmed when I recently had the opportunity to digest the entire investigative file. Nevertheless, in the first few months into my appointment as Police Chief, I committed as a priority to resolve and conclude this investigation."

In a statement issued to the press by John and Reve Walsh, they wrote:

"It has been more than twenty-seven years since our son Adam was abducted from a Hollywood, Florida mall, then murdered.

"Despite an ongoing, twenty-seven year investigation, our son's murder case has remained open—until now.

"Although Adam's killer never served one day in prison for destroying our son's life and almost ruining ours, nor will he ever because he died in prison serving time for an unrelated murder, we are satisfied that the main suspect in Adam's murder—Ottis Toole—has now been positively identified and this chapter in our lives is now closed..." John Walsh had become the anchor for *America's Most Wanted*, perhaps the most popular true crime show ever created. By the end of 2008, the show had helped local, state and Federal authorities capture more than 1,000 dangerous felons.

This crime happened before law enforcement learned how to more effectively investigate such cases. Because of the abduction and murder of Adam Walsh, new procedures were developed to track down child-killers not only in Florida, but also nationwide. Even so, the Hollywood Police Department was remiss in their investigation. The loss of two key pieces of evidence (Ottis Toole's car and the floor mat) was, from our view, inexcusable. Their insistence on going it alone, even refusing to accept the help of the FBI, hindered the search for Adam.

Part Two
A Pall on the Sun

Introduction

Now we turn to two heavily publicized cases and several lesser known cases, which exhibit Florida's growing list of murdered children.

Caylee Anthony, "The Lost Child", received day-to-day "special alerts" and "breaking news" advisories on all the true crime talk shows for as long as she was reported missing. Once she was found murdered, "bombshell" became the lead-in. Night after night, the case exploded over the cable news channels. The Anthony case was so compelling that the public, though horrified, was drawn to it. The unusual characters and weird twists and turns made us decide to include the case in our accounts of shocking murders in the Sunshine State. In the middle of it all, two parents were caught in a maelstrom of hate and accusation.

What happens when a gang member invades Spring Break? "Intruder in Paradise" describes the encounter of a beloved Panama City Beach police officer and a dangerous parolee. The disparity between two lives was never more evident.

"Bloody Murder in A-Dorm" describes the brutal night a Charlotte County Correctional Officer was supervising inmates on a late-night work crew. Little did she know that they were planning to murder her. The case deserved more media attention than it received.

Long hours and low wages are just part of the difficulties faced by workers in the service and food industries. Robbery, assault and even murder are common occurrences to convenience store clerks, delivery drivers and restaurant workers. The so-called "Waffle House Murders" illustrate those dangers.

Each year, many Floridians use guns to ward off violent criminals. "The Wrong Victim" was short, had high blood pressure and looked vulnerable. But when he and his daughter were attacked in their Fort Myers motel room by two gun-wielding career criminals, he fought back. The confrontation between good and evil should have received national publicity.

"Stone Cold" recounts the sad story of a beautiful child named Tiffany Eunick and a violent twelve-year-old thug named Lionel Tate. Lawyers conceived a bizarre defense that gained much media exposure. The jury, however, wasn't convinced and Tate was sentence to life in prison.

Norman Mearle Grim was known as the "Tattoo Man" in his Milton, Florida, neighborhood. Almost every time he committed a crime or attempted to cover one up, his tattoos gave him away. For that reason, he'd spent most of his life in prison. While out on parole, he was involved in one of the most senseless crimes imaginable.

In "Death Row Granny," we delve into the tragic life of Josie Davenport. The life of the middle-aged divorcee and grandmother from England was floundering when, on impulse, she wrote a letter to an inmate on Florida's death row. Ronald Clark responded with roses and gifts. Josie fell hard for the self-styled "Death Row Poet," but she had no idea the trouble that she'd soon land in.

Women who are put on trial have an advantage over men. There seems to be a natural sympathy toward femininity. "The Diary" illustrates that disparity. Did Valessa Robinson really help her boyfriend murder her mother or was she forced against her will?

For at least two decades, fugitives made their home in the Ocala National Forest. In "The Dark Forest", the authors describe what happened when college students John and Pam Edwards met two hardened criminals on an alligator trail in the Forest. The heart-wrenching brutality of the crimes that occurred there should have produced changes in the Park Service's operations. But they didn't.

According to the Florida Law Enforcement Agency Uniform Crime Reports, in 2007 there were 1,201 known murders in the Sunshine State.

However, the very best statistical analysis of crime can never be totally accurate. How many missing persons were murdered and their remains never found? How many murder victims were never known by law enforcement to be missing at all? How many abducted teens were written off as runaways?

The case of two-year-old Trenton Duckett is an example of statistics gone awry. Where do you place someone who was at his home one minute and gone the next, never to be seen again?

On August 27, 2006, Trenton's mother, Melinda, reported him missing from his bedroom. A cut window screen seemed to indicate that he was taken from his home. However, as police delved into the background of Melinda and Trenton's father, Josh, they found the divorced couple engaged in a hate-filled custody battle. Josh and Melinda fought for the custody of Trenton with every trick they could muster.

Melinda became the chief suspect when investigators could not nail down a timeline for her whereabouts on the last two days Trenton was known to be alive. She refused to take a polygraph test and her cooperation with police ended when she obtained a lawyer. Finally, after an intense verbal confrontation with CNN's talk show host Nancy Grace, Melinda went to her grandparents' home, placed a shotgun to her head and pulled the trigger. Any information about Trenton's fate seemed to end with his mother's suicide.

Where is Trenton? Cops seem to have focused on two major theories: The first is that Melinda murdered her son and hid his body, so that it couldn't be located; the second is that she found a go-between and shipped him to her native South Korean homeland. But what if someone really did take the child from his room?

Trenton Duckett's case was not listed in the Florida murder statistics even though he may very well be dead.

The same can be said for Zachary Bernhardt, Sabrina Paige Aisenberg, Amy Billig, Marjorie Christina Luna, Jennifer Marteliz and Rilya Shenise Wilson. These are just a few Florida children who went missing under suspicious circumstances and have never been found. Some may well have been murdered. But they will never be listed in the statistical data released each year by the state unless their remains are found.

Chapter 6
The Lost Child

"It should be noted that at no time during any of these interviews did the defendant show any obvious emotion as to the loss of her child. She did not cry or give any indication that she was legitimately worried about her child's safety."

Detective Yuri Melich, observing in his report the behavior of
a woman who reported her daughter missing.

The first 911 call, placed on the afternoon of July 15, 2008, was simply a plea for police to be sent to the Anthony residence in Orlando. Cynthia "Cindy" Anthony told the dispatcher that she wanted to have her daughter, Casey, arrested for stealing her car and her money.

The second call, a few minutes later, would rock the nation.

"What is your emergency?" the dispatcher asked.

"I called a little bit ago...My granddaughter has been taken. She has been missing for a month. Her mother finally admitted that she's been missing. I want someone here now."

"Okay, what is the address you're calling from?"

"We're talking about a three-year-old little girl. My daughter finally admitted that the babysitter stole her. I need to find her."

Raw emotion garbled Cindy's voice.

A confused dispatcher asked, "Your daughter admitted that the baby is where?"

"That the babysitter took her a month ago—that my daughter's been looking for her," Cindy said. "I told you my daughter was missing [for] a month. I just found her today, but I can't find my granddaughter. She just admitted to me that she's been trying to find her herself. There's something wrong. I found my daughter's car today and it smells like there's been a dead body in the damn car."

As the conversation continued, Cindy put her daughter on the phone. Twenty-two-year-old Casey claimed that her daughter, Caylee Marie Anthony, had been missing for thirty-one days and that her nanny, Zenaida Fernandez-Gonzalez had taken her. She had been Caylee's babysitter for one-and-a-half to two years, Casey said.

When asked why she didn't report it when the child first went missing, Casey said, "I've been looking for her and have gone through other resources to try to find her, which is stupid."

When deputies from the Orange County Sheriff's Office arrived, they found a modern three-bedroom ranch-style house. Casey Anthony, a striking brunette with deep green eyes, stood beside her mother. Cindy explained to the deputy that she hadn't seen her granddaughter since June 9. (That date would later prove to be incorrect; it was actually June 16.)

Casey explained to the deputies that she'd dropped Caylee off on that date at an apartment. Since then, Casey said, she hadn't been able to locate the nanny or Caylee.

Cindy told deputies that Casey had taken her car and left home days before. Cindy hadn't heard from her until she'd tracked Casey down. During the time she'd been gone, Casey abandoned Cindy's car on the side of the road and it had been impounded. Cindy said that Casey had also stolen one of her credit cards and run up thousands of dollars in bills on it.

As deputies attempted to get a handle on the confusing story, they contacted the Orange County Sheriff's Office Child Abuse Division. Detective Yuri Melich was assigned to the case.

Shortly after interviewing Cindy and Casey Anthony, deputies drove to the apartment complex where Casey said she dropped off her daughter. There they interviewed the manager and learned that the apartment had been vacant for 142 days, since February.

This was just the first of dozens of alleged lies Casey would tell investigators as they attempted to determine the whereabouts of Caylee.

The next day, Detective Melich met with her. He told Casey that he was suspicious of her original story, because it didn't make sense. When asked if she wanted to change it, Casey claimed that what she'd told the original deputy was true. "That's the story I'm gonna stick with," she said.

In a taped interview, Casey claimed that on the morning of the ninth, she went to work and left Caylee at the apartment complex with Zenaida. Melich's report read: "She says she's known Zenaida for four years and Zenaida has babysat Caylee for the past one and a half years. When the defendant left work around 1700 hours and came to pick up Caylee, she says she got no answer at the door. She tried calling Zenaida's cell phone (number unknown) and got no answer. She started going around to places that Zenaida was known to frequent but didn't locate her child." Casey told investigators that the reason she didn't report Caylee missing was that she'd seen movies where children who'd been abducted were murdered after the parents reported it to police.

Meanwhile, Detective Sergeant John Allen, Melich's supervisor, had located an Orlando woman with the name Zenaida Gonzalez. (Allen made use of the DAVID System, a law enforcement database that brings up photographs and information on any person who has a Florida driver's license.) Melich called Zenaida and arranged for two female detectives to meet with the woman. "She was open and responsive," their investigative report read, "and when asked, denied knowing Casey, Caylee or babysitting for anyone at all." After viewing photographs of the missing girl and her mother, she said she'd never seen either of them.

As Melich continued his interview with Casey, she was shown photographs of every woman with the nanny's name found in the DAVID database. She said that none was the woman she knew.

As the inquiry proceeded, detectives were alarmed at Casey's lack of concern for her daughter. He wrote in his report, "She remained stoic and monotone during a majority of our contacts."

Because of Casey's unusual behavior, Detective Melich decided to cross-check everything she told him. He drove her around Orlando and interviewed people at the locations where she said Zenaida had lived. They found no one who had ever heard of her.

In one particularly bizarre incident, Casey claimed that she'd regularly dropped Caylee off with Zenaida at a ritzy housing complex. When the detectives took Casey to the subdivision, Melich wrote that "[Casey] said she didn't remember the exact house, claiming she stopped paying attention to which one it was since she came here so many times."

Detectives questioned her about Caylee's father, but Casey would only tell them that he was a man who had died in an automobile accident in Georgia. She had no further knowledge about him, she said.

Since Casey claimed to be an "events coordinator" at Universal, Melich called her personnel office and was informed that Casey was not employed there. She'd worked there in 2004, but had been fired. When confronted with this inaccuracy, however, she insisted that she still worked there.

Her boyfriend with whom she'd been living the last month, Tony Lazzaro, told investigators that she rarely went to work. Casey claimed her boss let her work out of her home.

Casey told cops that the only people she'd told about Caylee's disappearance were two co-workers. When Melich again checked with personnel, he discovered that neither worked there. Casey also claimed to have been issued a cell phone by the company, but couldn't produce it.

Melich asked Casey if she would take him to her office. She agreed, although she said she'd also lost her ID card. After meeting with security guards, Casey, Melich and two other detectives were allowed to go to the office complex where she said she worked. Melich wrote, "We followed her into a building nearby and down the building's inner hall. She walked with purpose and acted like she knew where she was going. Halfway down the hall, she stopped, turned and told us she hadn't told us the truth and she was not a current employee."

The boldness of the lie chilled investigators. What else could she be hiding?

By now, Cindy and George, Casey's father, had provided the sheriff's department with dozens of up-to-date photographs of the missing child. When the images were released to the media, one was so powerful that it struck those who saw it as a picture of pure innocence. Caylee, a beautiful child with brown hair and hazel eyes, posed with her arm propped on a pillow. Holding her chin in her little hand, she seemed to be looking in wide-eyed wonderment at the world around her. That photo was selected to be placed on her missing person poster.

Casey's older brother, Lee, was interviewed by detectives, but added little to what they already knew.

The media descended on the case. Here they had a perfect storm of mystery, intrigue and an oddball character whose devious schemes seemed straight out of the twilight zone. A beautiful child was missing and an attractive mother, whose outlandish stories never matched, hadn't reported her daughter gone for a month. As the case unfolded, stories of sex, booze and wild parties surfaced. The press couldn't seem to get enough of the story.

As the case burst onto the national scene, detectives began receiving calls from various individuals who knew Casey. Almost every person who phoned in claimed that she was a "habitual liar." According to some friends, former friends and former lovers, she also was a thief. Amy Huizenga, a onetime friend, stated that Casey stole checks and $700 in cash from her. None of the callers claimed to have ever heard of Zenaida.

Investigators subpoenaed Casey's cell phone records and couldn't find one single call or text message to the nanny.

On the second day of the investigation, deputies impounded a vehicle from the Anthony home. This was the car that Casey had driven and abandoned when it ran out of gas.

"Once the car arrived at our forensics bay," Melich wrote, "Sergeant John Allen and I met with Crime Scene Investigator Gerardo Bloise to inspect the car and investigate a 'smell' [that] George and Cindy Anthony noticed when they picked up the car. Upon opening the driver's side door we all immediately noticed a strong smell of decomposition coming from inside the car."

Investigators gathered the contents of the vehicle into a trash bag. Among the items found were food, maggots and an empty pizza box. Melich claimed that the odor from the discarded food was different from the smell of decomposition that all the detectives noticed.

Items taken from the car were sent to the FBI and the National Laboratory in Oak Ridge, Tennessee. Air samples from the trunk were sent to the world-famous "Body Farm" at the University of Tennessee in Knoxville. In what was referred to as "cutting-edge technology," scientists would allege that the air contained decompositional matter.

Orange County Sheriff's Office officials also claimed that testing on the root of a hair found in the trunk showed it was in a state of decomposition. Dr. Michael Baden, a forensic expert, explained how the test worked. "Just putting the hair under the microscope," Baden said, "one can tell the difference between a normal hair root and one that's been infected with bacteria after death."

Even worse for the defense, DNA extracted from the root was said to have matched Caylee's DNA. Chloroform residue was also found in the trunk.

A computer in the Anthony home that Casey used was searched and detectives learned that someone had looked up "chloroform." They knew that even a small amount of chloroform could be fatal to a child.

Investigators learned that two weeks after Caylee went missing, Casey got a new tattoo. It read: "Bella Vita," which is Italian for "Beautiful Life."

George Anthony met with detectives. It was obvious that he cared for Caylee and his daughter, but he seemed to suspect that Casey might be responsible for harming his granddaughter. "I don't want to believe," he said, "that I have...raised someone and brought someone into this world that could do something to another person."

On the second day of the investigation, detectives brought in cadaver dogs to search the Anthony backyard. The yard backed up to a tree line and had an above-ground pool, a sandbox, a tiled patio with chairs and a purple and green playhouse stuffed with children's toys. The dogs "alerted" to an area near the pool.

On July 16, Casey Anthony was arrested by the Orange County Sheriff's Office for child neglect, making a false official statement and obstructing an investigation.

Jose Baez, a local attorney hired by Casey Anthony, entered a not guilty plea on behalf of his client.

Photographs began to appear on Internet Web sites showing Casey and her friends cavorting at local nightclubs. When it was learned that some of the suggestive photos were taken after Caylee went missing, the public rage grew to a frenzy.

Night after night on the national talk shows, viewers watched the slick exterior of the Magic Kingdom being gutted and a sordid nightmare belching from its belly.

As ground searches for Caylee stepped up, Casey appeared in court. She was remanded to the Orange County Jail with a bond of $500,000. Neither Casey—who had no job—nor her parents, from whom she had stolen an estimated $45,000, could afford the 10 percent necessary to spring her. Baez asked that the court lower the bail, but his petition was denied.

In a jailhouse meeting, Casey confidently informed her parents that Caylee would be home in August, her third birthday. No one except George and Cindy seemed to believe her.

While Casey's attorney complained about the sheriff's department leaking information about the case, the media kept digging. Every aspect of the Anthony family came under public scrutiny. (How many other families could withstand such a dogged investigation?)

Casey Marie Anthony made her arrival on this planet on March 19, 1986. She attended Colonial High School, but never graduated. After quitting school, she worked odd jobs. Her longest stint was for a year-and-a-half at an entertainment company.

As detectives and reporters continued investigating the strange case, the image of Casey as a narcissistic party girl grew stronger and stronger. Drinking and carousing seemed to have made up a large part of her life. The public wondered if Casey murdered her daughter so she would have more time to party.

As videotapes of her jailhouse conversations with her parents and brother were released, many people found it hard to believe that Casey seemed to have little interest in finding Caylee. Cindy, who had an Internet page, wrote a piece entitled, "My Caylee is missing." It had been published July 3, two weeks before she tracked her daughter down. Cindy's anguish was palpable.

"[Caylee] came into my life unexpectedly," she wrote, "just as she has left me. This precious little angel from above gave me strength and unconditional love. Now she is gone and I don't know why. Where did she go? Who is watching out for the little angel?"

These were questions that all of the world wanted answered.

On August 18, Tropical Storm Fay blew into Florida near Naples and made its way up the coast. It stalled for a day around Daytona Beach, then moved out into the Atlantic and re-entered the state near Melbourne. After five days of intense rain, severe flooding made many areas uninhabitable. After the storm passed, the weather reverted to its usual pattern of near-daily summer rains, compounding the flooding problems.

Less than one half of a mile from the Anthony home, a patch of dirt drowned in four feet of floodwater. For more than a decade, this heavily wooded area had been a hangout for children in the neighborhood. Teenagers partied there, while younger children sometimes buried their dead pets on the high ground.

Tim Miller, Director of Equusearch, a search and recovery team, had been trying to find Caylee for weeks. He attempted to search the patch of woods near the Anthony home, but found it covered with water. He eventually called off the search, stating that he felt Caylee's body might never be found.

Watching the case from afar, a California bounty hunter decided to post Casey's bail. At a press conference, he said he believed Caylee would never be found as long as Casey was in jail—the bounty hunter seemed to think he could get her to confess to him. Three days later, Casey was released from jail when he put up a $50,000 bond. He and Baez accompanied Casey to the Anthony home.

Casey was met by a throng of protestors. Even though Florida and United States law allows people who are not indicted of a capital offense to post bail, the mob ranted for the hated mother to be placed back in confinement. Their screams and taunts were replayed night after night on many national talk shows.

While Casey spent a tense time at home, investigators were busy drafting new indictments. Amy, the former friend from whom Casey had allegedly stolen checks and cash, decided to press charges. Casey was rearrested days later. This time the charges included "uttering a forged instrument, fraudulent use of personal information and petty theft."

Even after Casey was placed back in jail, the protestors continued to disrupt the community and the Anthony home. By now, George and Cindy couldn't go outside without being verbally attacked. The scene got even uglier when agitators began violating the Anthonys' property rights. Day after day, hundreds of people who were incensed by the case harassed the family. Rushing up the driveway, they cursed and banged their fists against the garage door. Then they threw rocks at the house.

Cindy and George repeatedly called 911 in their attempts to get the trespassers thrown off their property.

On September 4, an anonymous benefactor from Tennessee posted Casey's bail and, again, she was released. She was rearrested for the third time during that month on additional charges relating to the Amy Huizenga case.

In October, Jose Baez entered a not guilty plea for Casey on the most recent charges.

Exactly two weeks later, Casey Anthony was indicted on a charge of first-degree murder.

On December 11, meter reader Roy Kronk walked into a wooded area near the corner of Suburban Drive and Hopespring Drive. He worked for the Orange County Public Works Department and had been reassigned to the area after having worked there in early August. At that time, he'd used the patch of woods to relieve himself. Now, as he again walked into the woods to "take a leak," Kronk was curious about a plastic bag that he'd seen in August. On three separate occasions, Kronk had called 911 to report seeing the suspicious bag, only to encounter widespread disinterest from dispatchers and cops alike.

The rattlesnake-infested woods would be a good place to dump a body, he thought. And since the Caylee Anthony case was still on his mind in December, he decided to see if the bag had been moved. It hadn't. Detective Melich's report related what happened next. "While there," it read, "he noticed a black plastic bag with a dome shape underneath. Using his meter reading tool, he hit the dome shape and heard a hollow sound. He then used his tool to lift up the plastic bag and that's when he noticed the dome was actually a human skull. Roy backed out of the area and used his radio to notify his office and report what he found. They in turn notified the Orange County Sheriff's Office."

Kronk later described the cursory search undertaken by a deputy after his third call in August. "[The deputy] went to the water's edge," he said. "I pointed to where [the bag was] at. He just swept his head back and forth and said, 'I don't see anything.' And pretty much, that was it. I guess the deputy didn't want to go into the water to look at the bag. The cop was— I would say—he was kind of rude to me."

Proving the old adage that no good deed goes unpunished, Kronk soon became a target for conspiracists and hatemongers.

Investigators descended on the patch of woods where the child's body had been located. While the media set up their portable vans, campers and trucks along the road about a hundred yards away, Detective Melich went to the scene. He walked down a path alongside a fence. "Within a short distance down this path," he wrote, "was a black plastic bag and lying next to it what appeared to be a human skull. The skull was void of flesh but quite a bit of hair could be seen on or around it. The skull appeared to be that of a child or small adult. I immediately noticed that there appeared to be a piece of silver duct tape across the mouth area of the skull. The tape appeared to have been purposely placed there."

Two bags lay next to the skull. One was a black plastic trash bag. The other was a canvas laundry bag—it had a name brand written on it and was reinforced with a wire rim across the top. Beside the skull there was also a pair of children's shorts with pink and white stripes.

Inside the canvas bag, forensics personnel found a second black trash bag (both had yellow ties).

In addition to the bones of a child found inside the first trash bag, other items were located including a stained blanket, a pair of "one size" shorts with pink and white vertical stripes, a pink size 3T shirt that had the saying "BIG TROUBLE comes small" written across it and other bits and pieces of rotted clothing.

As investigators continued to collect evidence, Detective Melich drafted a search warrant for the Anthony home. Orange County Sheriff's Office detectives and agents from the FBI found several incriminating items. Possibly the most significant was a canvas laundry bag matching the one found near Caylee's remains.

Investigators also located a metal gas can with a piece of tape on the top—it was similar to the tape found in the woods. Both had the same word—"Henkel"—written on them. George Anthony had told detectives that Casey was the last to use the can.

In Casey's bedroom, Melich found a photograph of Caylee dressed in "pink and white vertical striped shorts." It looked identical to the shorts discovered at the scene. Other items located in the home were pull-up diapers identical to a pair found at the crime scene and a shirt with the brand and the number "RN 74299," the same as that written on the shirt found at the scene.

The remains were sent to District 9 Medical Examiner Dr. Jan Garavaglia (the "Dr. G" of television fame).

A few days later, the FBI made a crucial discovery. "FBI Analyst Karen Cowan gave me an update on the duct tape from the body that was sent to the FBI lab in Quantico," Detective Melich wrote. "While processing the duct tape the latent print unit noticed residue in the perfect shape of a heart. The heart was not hand drawn and residue appeared to be consistent with the adhesive side of a heart-shaped sticker. It appears that the sticker was put on the duct tape intentionally. In the search area, investigators located a small heart-shaped sticker similar in size to the residue found on the duct tape. The sheet from which this sticker came from was not discovered on the scene."

A later search inside the Anthony home yielded a sheet of heart-shaped stickers with several missing.

"Dr. G" concluded the cause of death was a homicide of undetermined means. DNA testing conclusively established that the skeletal remains were those of Caylee Marie Anthony. Although it was obvious from the moment the little skull was found, a stunned nation grieved for the lost child.

Documents released by the Orange County Sheriff's Office revealed that investigators concluded that Caylee was murdered somewhere between June 16 and June 27. She was last seen by her grandfather on the sixteenth when Casey left without saying where she was headed. Detectives believe that after Caylee was killed, she was kept in the trunk of the car "for a period of time but removed prior to June 27."

Investigators concluded that the evidence found at the crime scene and at the home pointed directly to Casey Anthony.

If Casey had killed her child, why did she do it? Investigators theorized part of the reason was so that she could enjoy her freedom without the burden of a child. It was also believed that she had a deep-seated hatred of her mother. The venomous anger she felt toward Cindy was obvious from the recorded jailhouse conversations between the two. Had Casey murdered her child to hurt Cindy?

The defense, however, had hired a "dream team" of attorneys and forensics specialists. (Many people wondered how an indigent client could afford such high-priced hired guns, but the funding for the team was never divulged.)

In addition to Jose Baez, the team consisted of Linda Kenney Baden, a high-profile New York attorney; Terence Lenamon, a Miami defense attorney; Dr. Henry Lee, Chief Emeritus for Scientific Services for the State of Connecticut and well-known television personality; Dr. Lawrence Kobilinsky, an expert in forensic biology, serology and DNA analysis; Dr. Kathy Reichs, a bone specialist who once taught at the FBI Academy; Dr. Timothy Huntington, an entomologist and Dr. Werner Spitz, a professor of entomology and frequent guest pundit on television true crime talk shows.

According to members of the team, most of the evidence collected was suspect. The duct tape, for instance, found on the remains and on the gas can was "the most widely sold duct tape in the nation." There were no fingerprints on the tape or on any of the other items located.

As for the air samples found in the trunk and said to have proved a decomposing body was there, the defense team called it "junk science."

The pain became too much for George Anthony. Family attorney Brad Conway called 911 to report that the grieving grandfather was missing. The family was afraid.

Using his cell phone pings to guide them, the Orange County Sheriff's Office was able to track the distraught grandfather to a hotel in Daytona Beach. He sent text messages saying he was depressed about Caylee's death and his daughter's incarceration and pending trial.

A five-page letter that he had written was found but not released.

The "real" Zenaida Gonzalez filed a defamation lawsuit against Casey Anthony. Through her attorney, she claimed that because of her association with the case, she was fired from her job and couldn't find anyone who would rent her an apartment.

After Caylee's remains were released, George and Cindy held a memorial service at First Baptist Church in Orlando. According to estimates, more than 1,200 people came to pay their last respects. Casey wasn't there—she was in jail. For months, Casey had refused to allow her parents to visit her. Now she criticized them for holding a public memorial. "I still don't want the public with cameras and everyone around for Caylee's funeral service," she said. "[But] I can't stop my parents from doing what they want."

Inside the church, George, Cindy and Casey's brother, Lee, wept.

"It's God's day," George said. "It's Caylee Marie Anthony's day."

"[Caylee] wouldn't wake up crying," Cindy said. "She would wake up laughing."

Perhaps the pastor said it best. "If you want to know where Caylee is," he said, "[it's] wherever Jesus is."

At the memorial, a videotape of little Caylee singing "You Are My Sunshine" touched all who were there.

Shown on television, it touched the hearts of millions.

    You are my sunshine, my only sunshine,

    You make me happy when skies are gray.

    You'll never know, dear, how much I love you,

    Please don't take my sunshine away.

The sunshine from the Anthony family was gone and someone needed to pay for killing her.

Circuit Court Judge Stan Strickland set Casey Anthony's trial date for October 12, 2009.

When the remains of a pretty little girl named Caylee Anthony were found, many had already decided who killed her. Her mother, Casey, appeared to be strange, seemingly a pathological liar and a party girl. Did she murder her child to spite her mother or to get rid of a burden so she could continue the year-round party, as many have speculated? Or is Casey innocent? Prosecutors have said they will seek the death penalty, but Casey Anthony has a formidable team of attorneys who could make it difficult for prosecutors.

Chapter 7
Intruder in Paradise

"I'm not going back to prison. Ain't happening, dude."

Robert Bailey, speaking to a friend as result of a traffic stop.

Robert Bailey was a time bomb ticking away toward an explosion.

While most citizens of Milwaukee, Wisconsin, lived peaceful, productive lives, Bailey inhabited a parallel universe of gangbangers, ex-cons and dopers. His past was littered with arrest warrants and his future had a poison needle waiting.

At age twenty-two, Bailey had already done hard time—three years in a Wisconsin prison. A member of the Brew City Royals street gang, he was on probation and under house arrest when he decided he needed to take a vacation. On March 26, 2005, he climbed into an SUV his grandfather had rented and fled the freezing climes of the Midwest for sunny Florida.

Numerous gang tattoos emblazoned Bailey's pale-white body. On his back, a huge emblem read, "Saint, Royal Family." (Among the Royals, his street name was "Saint.") Other tattoos, almost all gang-related, decorated his neck, arms, legs and fingers.

On Easter Sunday, Bailey, his friend John Braz and D'Tori Crawford, a friend of Braz's, pulled into Panama City Beach. They'd driven for twelve hours straight. Beneath the seat of the SUV, Bailey kept a loaded Taurus nine millimeter semiautomatic pistol.

The city was packed. During mid-March through mid-April of each year, several hundred thousand college students descend on the sandy beaches of the Gulf Coast to party. On Spring Break, the partiers have wild dreams of getting drunk and getting laid. They hang out in bars and attend rock concerts on the beach and bikini parties. If they get lucky, they might meet someone and hook up.

Panama City Beach Police Department Sergeant Kevin Scott Kight could not have been more different than Robert Bailey. Kight was born in Washington and grew up in Springfield, Ohio. He earned his degree in psychology from Wright State University and then joined the Lawrenceville, Ohio, police department. In 1995, Kight transferred to the nearby Germantown PD. While there, he received a Medal of Valor for making a dramatic rescue of an infant who was drowning in a pool. He quickly worked his way up to the rank of sergeant.

In 1998, Kight and his wife moved south to be near his father, a retired Air Force pilot. Three days later, the couple had a son. Kight joined the Panama City Beach Police Department and quickly worked his way up to detective. During his time as an investigator, he received several letters of commendation. But he liked being on the street more than sitting in an office. Soon after making sergeant, Kight requested reassignment to the Patrol Division.

The religious significance of that Easter Sunday was lost on most of the revelers. At 10:20 P.M., the party was just beginning.

Traffic on Front Beach Road was stop-and-go. The two-lane street runs parallel to the beach but is separated from the ocean by condominiums, restaurants and other businesses. On that night, frolickers strolled from bar to bar and the sidewalk was almost as crowded as the road.

As Kight, now a shift supervisor, made his rounds, he noticed a white SUV stopped in the middle of the street. It had Wisconsin plates and a rental decal. Two men in the vehicle were so busy flirting with girls on the sidewalk that they didn't realize traffic was stacking up behind them. Kight, hoping to disperse the logjam, maneuvered his police cruiser through the traffic and pulled up behind the vehicle.

Bailey, Braz and Crawford had guzzled beer and smoked pot for most of the twelve-hour trip south. When they arrived in town, they registered at a motel. Then, wandering through the city, they came upon an inviting bar. The three spent an hour imbibing, but their dreams of hooking up still hadn't materialized.

Bailey and Crawford left the bar, determined to find some women who were willing to go back to the motel with them. They told Braz, who decided to stay, that they would come back for him later.

As the officer approached the vehicle, Crawford noticed that Bailey was getting nervous. He barely knew the man—Crawford and Braz were long-time friends, but he'd only met Bailey once before their trip. He wasn't impressed by the foul-mouthed braggart who seemed oblivious to anything outside his own gang world lifestyle.

The officer asked for a driver's license and registration. Bailey, who didn't have a license, handed him a Wisconsin ID card.

Sergeant Kight walked back to his car to run a check on Bailey. He was suspicious. The driver acted nervous and his lack of a license and registration activated Kight's crime-dog antenna.

Kight didn't have a computer in his car, so he called the dispatcher and asked her to run a background check on Bailey. When dispatch couldn't bring up any information on him, Officer Michael Rozier, who was just a few blocks away, offered to run the check on his computer. Because of the three-way conversation with the dispatcher, the radio frequency was tuned so that many of the police officers in the city could hear it.

In the white SUV, Bailey was panicky. It scared Crawford.

"I don't have a license," Bailey said.

"Chill out, man," Crawford said. "He'll just give you a ticket and we're on our way."

Bailey's eyes bulged. "You don't understand, man," he said. "I'm on parole. I'm not supposed to be out of my house."

Crawford's father had been a cop years before and he knew a busted parole wasn't good.

"Just chill out," he said, still trying to calm down the agitated gang-banger.

Crawford noticed that the tough ex-con had tears in his eyes.

"If he tries to arrest me," Bailey said, "I'm gonna pop this cop."

"Man, don't do it," Crawford entreated.

Bailey reached under the seat and pulled out the gun. He placed it beneath his right leg.

"You'll probably just get a ticket," Crawford said, still trying to placate him.

Bailey was shaking. He pulled his cell phone out of his pocket and tried to place a call. His hands were trembling so hard that he couldn't dial. He gave the phone to Crawford and ordered him to speed-dial his girlfriend. Crawford punched the button and handed the phone to Bailey.

"I'm gonna pop this cop," Bailey kept repeating as he spoke into the phone. Crawford figured his girlfriend was arguing with him, because he kept reiterating the same line over and over. Bailey begged her to come down to Panama City and pick him up after the shooting.

Crawford had seen enough. It was taking a long time for the officer to run the background check and he figured the result wasn't going to be good. Crawford glanced back and saw that the police officer, still in his cruiser, was looking down. He eased out of the passenger seat, quietly shut the door and walked away. Blending into the crowd, Crawford was soon out of sight. Later he told investigators he didn't warn the officer, because he thought Bailey would kill him.

Sergeant Kight began walking back to the SUV. He had one hand on his gun and handcuffs in the other. It was clear what he intended to do.

At exactly 10:30 P.M., Officer Tonya Miller, who was only a couple of blocks away, heard three loud thuds on her radio. She knew immediately that they were gunshots.

"I've been shot," Kight exclaimed.

Seconds later, the dispatcher informed deputies that an officer was down and relayed the location. Miller was the first officer to respond. She got to the scene in less than a minute.

Kight was lying on his back. He looked to be unconscious.

As Miller began to administer CPR, Officer Lorah Buchanan arrived. "Sergeant Kight was laying on the ground with Officer Miller on his chest calling his name," Buchanan later testified. "His eyes were open and he was staring at the sky. I dropped down beside him and tried to wake him up. I told him, 'This is not funny. Get up.'"

Paramedics arrived within minutes. They found no pulse.

Panama City Beach Police Sergeant Kevin Kight was dead.

Robert Bailey's identification card was found in Kight's citation holder, along with a ticket for driving with a revoked license. Two fired cartridge casings were discovered on the ground next to the fallen officer, along with a set of handcuffs.

Over the static of the radio, the dispatcher broadcast Bailey's description.

Officer Rozier was making a traffic stop when he heard the call. As he headed to the scene, he saw several officers assisting their fallen comrade. Rozier noticed tire tracks a few feet in front of Kight's cruiser. It appeared that a vehicle had driven onto the grass beside the road.

He followed the tracks into a dead-end road that led past a twelve-story condominium. Behind the building, he saw a vehicle identical to the automobile that dispatch had said may have been used by the shooter. Rozier approached it with his gun drawn, but the vehicle was empty. He called for backup and waited until detectives arrived.

Inside the van, forensic investigators found a fired shell casing. They also impounded a cell phone, a vehicle rental contract and a membership card from a fitness gym with Robert Bailey's name was on it.

While police fanned out in a frantic search for the suspect, detectives pieced together what had happened.

A seventeen-year-old witness, Jarrod Schalk, told investigators that he'd been sitting in a minivan next to the vehicle. Traffic was slow, he said, not quite bumper-to-bumper—but not fast. He was from Tennessee and was visiting Panama City with friends. When the shooting occurred, he was about five feet away.

"I was parallel to the SUV when I noticed how mad [the driver] looked," Schalk told detectives. "I saw the gun and I said, 'Oh, no!' I saw him fire the first shot and I ducked. It was almost like slow motion. I heard stuff breaking and I was hoping I wasn't getting hit."

The glass on the passenger side window where Schalk was sitting had been shattered by a bullet.

He described Bailey and later identified him as the shooter.

Police recovered a nine millimeter round from the door of the van. It was too mangled for ballistics experts to match to a single gun, but it confirmed the witness's story.

A second witness, Hillary Chaffer, was a resident of Panama City Beach. She'd been out shopping and turned onto Front Beach Road on her way home. Her sister was with her and they noticed a police officer had stopped an SUV. In the slow-moving traffic, they watched the horrific scene unfold.

Chaffer later testified that the driver looked pale. "He was clammy," she said. "He was like, almost looked like he was starting to sweat and he was very scared...[he] almost [had] a grayish color."

The driver of the white SUV looked in the rearview mirror, she said, then started to drive off, but stopped when the officer got out of his patrol car. The witness confirmed that the policeman had one hand on his gun and the other on his handcuffs. As he approached the vehicle, she began to drive away. Suddenly, Chaffer heard two gunshots. Looking back, she saw that the driver of the SUV was holding a gun out the window. She saw the flash from the barrel of the gun and heard breaking glass.

Chaffer stated that the shots were in quick succession, one after the other.

She quickly turned her car around and drove back to help. The officer was lying in the road and she got out and rushed to him. Several other people had already come to his assistance and, in just a few seconds, Officer Miller arrived. Chaffer immediately backed away.

As detectives were taking statements from witnesses, a strange scenario was playing itself out several blocks away.

A college student was sitting in the bed of a pickup truck along with several friends. They were on Front Beach Road, barely moving since the traffic was backed up. Suddenly, a man ran from the beach and jumped into the bed of the truck. It seemed kind of crazy to the student, but not totally unheard of, at least in a place like Panama City Beach.

The stranger was obviously nervous. His hands were trembling, and he seemed scared.

He picked up a towel from the back of the truck and placed it over his body. The college student asked the man what he was doing and he said he'd just "popped a cop."

The student told the man he didn't believe him. He changed his mind when the stranger pulled up his shirt and motioned to a gun in his belt.

"I gotta get off this road," he said. "I don't care where I go, but I need to leave."

Now it was the student's turn to be frightened. He figured it was better to play along with the stranger than confront him, so he let the man talk. He said his name was "Saint," and he seemed like a "loose cannon," willing to shoot anyone in order to get away.

The stranger used his cell phone to make a call. Then he started telling the student which direction he wanted to go. The student leaned up to the driver's window and told the driver that a stranger was in the back with a gun. He relayed the man's directions and told the driver to get there as soon as she could.

As they traveled in slow-motion along the crowded street, the stranger rambled on. "If I get caught," he said, "I'm going to jail for life. This cop tried to arrest me and I had to pop him." The student noticed that every other word seemed to be followed by an expletive.

They finally arrived at their destination, the bar where they'd left Braz. The stranger pulled a wad of cash from his pocket and handed the student a one hundred dollar bill. With that, he hopped out of the truck and vanished into the crowd.

The college student and his friends quickly found a Panama City Beach police officer and reported the incident.

Bailey, Braz and Crawford met up at the bar. Braz was also carrying a gun and informed Bailey he planned to get rid of it. He stated that the cops would eventually track them down and he didn't want to be arrested for carrying an unlicensed weapon. Braz suggested that Bailey get rid of his gun, too, because the police could match the bullets from the officer's body with the nine-millimeter. Bailey disagreed.

"I'm going out in a freakin' blaze of glory," he said.

They argued all the way back to the motel. Along the way, Braz saw a small pond and flung his pistol into the water.

Braz and Crawford decided to wait at the motel. They knew the cops would eventually be coming for them.

Within a few hours, both were taken into custody. Crawford would face no charges—he became a state's witness and testified against Bailey. Braz was also released. Since witnesses confirmed that he was at the bar when the shooting occurred, he could not be charged.

The manhunt for the killer of Sergeant Kight continued without letup through the night.

Early on the following morning, March 28, deputies from the Bay County Sheriff's Office were searching a row of motels and condominiums west of the motel where Bailey was staying. Deputies Jim Jenkins and Donna Land were paired up.

As Land began to climb up a set of stairs at one of the motels, Jenkins spotted a man peering at her from the corner of the building. He was hiding behind a thicket of bushes and closely resembled the suspect.

The man didn't see Jenkins. The deputy noticed him reach into his waistband and tug at something. It has to be a gun, the deputy probably thought.

Deputy Land was scanning the area in front of her, unaware of the danger. Jenkins raced forward and shouted for the suspect to raise his hands. Bailey glanced at the approaching cop, but continued to tug at something in his clothing. Jenkins, his gun drawn, yelled again. Suddenly, more deputies appeared.

Bailey, as if he were unsure of his next move, turned toward them. Finally, he raised his hands in the air.

He was quickly handcuffed and patted down. Jenkins found a fully loaded handgun in the suspect's waistband, as well as a pocket filled with bullets. He also found a key to the vehicle.

While he was being transported to the Panama City jail, Bailey asked if the officer he'd shot had died.

Early that morning, Dr. Charles Seibert performed an autopsy on Panama City Beach Sergeant Kevin Kight. The report stated that there were "two gunshot wounds to the upper chest just below the collar bone, and the wounds were about two inches apart. The bullets traveled through the weaker material of the upper left chest portion of the protective vest Kight wore. A stippling pattern was found on the chin and neck consistent with the barrel of the gun being within eighteen to twenty-four inches."

Seibert concluded that Kight was ambushed at point-blank range. He was probably leaning down when the bullets tore into his heart, liver and kidney. According to the report, he would have lost consciousness almost immediately.

The Simon City Royals gang was formed in the 1960s in Chicago. Over the years, they established brief alliances with other gangs, such as the Popes, the Gaylords and the Black Gangster Disciples. They also fought turf wars with rival groups. During the 1970s, several members moved to Milwaukee. In 1997, the Milwaukee chapter split from the Chicago chapter and renamed themselves the Brew City Royals.

According to Milwaukee police, the gang was involved in the distribution of cocaine and marijuana, armed robbery, burglary, extortion, racketeering, loan sharking and murder. In fact, just two days before Robert Bailey headed down to Florida, he was a participant in the armed robbery of a local Milwaukee watering hole. As was the gang's custom, part of the money went into the organization's coffers.

In addition to having served three years in prison for armed robbery, Bailey also had arrests for automobile theft, burglary and the use of illegal drugs. While he was on his way to Florida, a warrant had been issued for his arrest for violation of probation.

While much of the violence perpetrated by the Royals was inflicted on outsiders, the savagery could turn inward. In case of a violation of any of the gang's rules, the punishment was severe.

For instance, when a gang member, Smithson, decided to leave the organization, leaders issued an "SOS"—Smash on Sight—on him. A few days later, several gang members spied Smithson at his girlfriend's house. They pulled him from his car and began beating him, using baseball bats, tire irons and steel pipes. When the wayward gang member broke free and ran, he was chased down and pummeled into unconsciousness. Although he survived the attack, Smithson was permanently scarred.

An article in the October 2, 2008, edition of the *Milwaukee Journal Sentinel* identified Anthony Lubrano as the head of the Brew City Royals.

He ran the outfit from prison, where he was serving a long term for multiple offenses. "Angela Schleicher, twenty-seven, of Franklin, is portrayed as the gang's treasurer," the article stated. "Her job...was to keep the ledger, collect monthly dues and control 'the box,' from which members could borrow money for guns, drugs and personal use. Loans were expected to be repaid promptly with 10 percent interest. Those who failed to repay were beaten—twenty seconds for every hundred dollars owed."

After the negative publicity following the shooting of Kevin Kight, police in Milwaukee cracked down on the Royals and arrested most of its leadership. Members were convicted under the Wisconsin Organized Crime Control Act (similar to the Federal RICO Act) and sentenced to long prison terms.

While awaiting trial in the Bay County Jail, Robert Bailey maintained a cocky, self-assured attitude. Four months after he arrived, on August 8, 2005, he was charged with attempted escape when hacksaw blades were found in his cell. It was never determined how the blades entered the prison, but within a week, one supervisor was fired and another demoted. Bailey was sentenced to five years for the offense.

In March of the following year, Bailey threw an "unknown liquid" at nearby maintenance workers. The liquid was thought to have been urine. When corrections officers entered his cell, Bailey pulled out a "shiv" (a homemade knife made from a toothbrush and barbed wire) and attacked them. Before he was restrained, a corrections officer suffered severe cuts to his head. Before his murder trial even began, Bailey was convicted of aggravated battery on a law enforcement officer and sentenced to thirty years in prison.

Although most people avoided Bailey, his friend Braz continued to call him. Those conversations, unknown to the friends, were recorded.

At the trial, the evidence against Bailey in the murder of Sergeant Kight was overwhelming. Two witnesses identified Bailey as the shooter.

The third witness, Braz's friend Crawford, related the events that occurred in the SUV until the final moments when he left. He testified that Bailey kept repeating, "I'm gonna pop this cop." The motive, Crawford testified, was so that he would not go back to prison.

The college student identified Bailey as the stranger who hijacked the truck he was riding in. He testified to what Bailey said, including his confession that he had "popped a cop" and the fact that he'd seen a gun in the stranger's belt.

Bailey's identification card and a citation were found on the ground beside Officer Kight.

Two bullets removed from the fallen deputy matched groove marks inside the barrel of the murder weapon.

A shell casing located in the white vehicle was matched to the gun used to kill officer Kight.

It was obvious to all, even his defense attorneys, that Robert Bailey had murdered Sergeant Kevin Kight. On April 11, 2007, he was found guilty of first-degree murder.

Before sentencing, Bailey's attorneys attempted to mitigate the sentence. They portrayed him as retarded and mentally ill. "Bailey suffered from a number of mental problems," the defense contended, including: "(1) Low intelligence with no IQ score...above 77; (2) Brain dysfunction and likely damage; (3) Attention deficit hyperactive disorder diagnosed in childhood; (4) Bipolar disorder symptoms noted in prison psychological evaluations; (5) Substance abuse; (6) Anti-social personality disorder; (7) Borderline personality disorder. These problems impacted Bailey's ability to make decisions, learn from experiences and to control impulses."

Unfortunately for Bailey, the court played back the recordings of his telephone conversations with Braz.

Bailey told Braz he was playing his "crazy card." He told Braz that when faced with his own legal problems, he should "start talking to the walls."

After stating that he wouldn't even be tried if he could convince officials he was "insane," Bailey stated that he would only be sent to a mental health facility for five years. After that he would be released, he said.

Even the ever-gullible Braz didn't buy that argument. "The problem is you're going to be in the nuthouse for the rest of your life," he said. "No, brother," Bailey corrected him. "You ain't understanding. You go to the nuthouse for five years, brother. If they don't find you competent within five years, after five years they legally find you not guilty by reason of insanity and then you stay in the nuthouse and if you ever get better after that, they let you go home."

"For real?" Braz asked.

(Bailey's interpretation of the law was misinformed. In Florida, as soon as a mentally ill suspect is deemed competent, he can indeed be tried.)

Prosecutor Steve Meadows made the following remarks in his closing argument: "I ask that as you sit down in the jury room to deliberate [that] you do two things before you take a vote. I want you all just to put your finger eighteen to twenty-four inches away from each other's face and see how close you are when your eyes are meeting, as [Bailey's] met those eyes [of Officer Kight] on an Easter night in our community...firing once, twice and three times."

Several members of the jury later stated that Bailey's own words had been one of the deciding factors in their decision.

Circuit Judge Michael Overstreet sentenced the gangbanger to die. Two aggravating factors compelled the judge to impose the lethal sentence: first, Bailey was on parole when he shot Officer Kight and secondly, he murdered the officer to avoid being arrested.

Panama City Police Sergeant Kevin Kight has not been forgotten. One year after the murder, family and friends dedicated a memorial to him at the intersection of Front Beach Road and Beckrich Road, at the very spot where the murder took place. Kight's wife and their son were present to honor the fallen hero.

Beginning the same year, the Thunder Beach motorcycle rally named a parade in the fallen officer's honor. Hundreds of motorcyclists and thousands of spectators showed up. The Kevin Kight Memorial Parade has become an annual event, raising money to help needy children.

Spring Break at various locations (Daytona Beach, Fort Lauderdale, Panama City Beach, etc.) has always been big business in Florida. In some places, such as Daytona Beach, the arrival of thousands of horny college students has occasionally exploded into rape and even murder. In the same area, serial killers have been known to stalk and murder visiting girls. Panama City Beach was generally regarded as a more peaceful Spring Break haven. But when a visiting gang member with little regard for human life invaded the place, he wrought havoc on the small town. As long as we have college students, we'll have Spring Break in Florida. And while the visitors are generally peaceful, there seems to be no way to keep out the fraction of troublemakers who incite violence.

Chapter 8
Bloody Murder in A-Dorm

"It's on. We're leaving tonight."

> Tommy Eaglin, who had planned a jail break,
> commenting to another inmate.

It was another day just like any other. Darla Lathrem entered the Charlotte Correctional Institution on the evening of June 11, 2003, and reported to work. She was scheduled for the third shift—from four to midnight. She was still a "rookie," having been hired as a correctional officer only ten months before.

At six feet tall and attractive, thirty-eight-year-old Darla was a striking figure. Soft-spoken and personable, she'd made a positive impression on her supervisors. She was serious about her job, yet she liked to joke with her fellow officers. She never cursed and she faithfully attended the McGregor Baptist Church in Fort Myers, where her father was the minister. Certainly, Darla Lathrem seemed out of place working with rapists and murderers.

At 4:10 P.M., she entered A-Dorm, a building that was being renovated. Inmate work crews were assigned to help with the project and Darla's job was to supervise them. As usual, she would be alone with a crew of five until ten o'clock, when they were scheduled to return to their own dorms. Like all other officers inside the prison, Lathrem was armed only with pepper spray. A radio with a "panic button" was clipped onto her belt, but no other prison guards were assigned as backup.

The rookie correctional officer could never have guessed that a murderous escape attempt was planned for that night.

On that night, the lone officer went about overseeing the inmates on the work crew: Tommy "The Fighting Irishman" Eaglin, a former boxing champion who was serving a life sentence for first-degree murder; Stephen V. Smith, who had racked up dozens of convictions for violent crimes, including the rape of a ten-year-old girl during a home invasion; Michael Jones, a rapist and repeat offender also serving life; John Beaston, who had been convicted of trafficking in cocaine, burglary with a firearm and escape and Charles Fuston, who was serving a thirty year sentence for various crimes, including home invasion with a firearm and resisting arrest.

All seemed quiet, but the mix of violent characters and lax supervision was a cinder box waiting to explode. Eaglin and Smith hated Fuston, because he had "snitched them out" in a previous escape attempt. Beaston would be getting out soon and was trying to stay clean until his time was up. But he was deathly afraid of Eaglin, who had beaten several inmates into unconsciousness in the two years he'd been locked up. So, even though Beaston was aware that the escape was going down that night, he kept quiet.

Eaglin, Smith and Jones, who'd been planning the escape for months, knew that this was the last night for a possible breakout. The following day, the dorm was scheduled to be completed and the inmates would all get new assignments.

Charlotte County, in southwest Florida, has only one incorporated city: Punta Gorda. It is rural, with just a few small towns scattered among the swampy terrain. The state prison is its second largest employer, providing several hundred jobs. In the summer, sand gnats (tiny, biting insects that savor human flesh) and mosquitoes plague the county residents. Although the prison has modern architecture, with the heat and insects it can be a miserable place to live and work.

County residents and local politicians never really wanted the prison. But state politicos thought the remote swamps would be a good place to house incorrigible inmates. Thus, after several years of fighting it, the county caved in. The prison opened in 1989. By 2003, it housed about 1,200 inmates.

From the beginning, it was bedeviled with problems. In 1990, an inmate was stabbed to death. In the same year, two correctional officers were charged with assaulting prisoners. Then the warden was demoted for spending an "outlandish amount" of money on his living quarters.

Two years later, an angry prisoner somehow smuggled a gun into the lockup. Instead of attacking the hated guards with it, however, he shot three other inmates in a dispute over a soccer game. A year later, the new warden was demoted and the following year a prisoner stabbed two other offenders to death with a two-foot sharpened pipe.

Through the years, correctional officers were charged with abusing inmates and inmates routinely assaulted prison guards. The problems never seemed to end. Seven correctional officers were charged with conspiracy in the death of an inmate. Administrators were accused of sexual harassment. The warden and assistant warden seemed unwilling or unable to provide the structure needed to maintain the safety of staff and inmates.

Darla Lathrem was unaware of many of the problems, because they were routinely covered up. So, on that steamy summer night she went about her job as she'd been instructed, never knowing that dozens of procedural violations would leave her vulnerable to a violent attack.

At 8:55, Officer Kenneth George met Lathrem on the sidewalk outside A-Dorm and picked up the "count slip." It was the moment Eaglin, Smith and Jones had been waiting for.

The jobs being performed by the inmates that night were welding lockers underneath beds, pressure washing the walls and painting the cells.

They used a variety of tools, including a sledgehammer with a fourteen-inch handle.

While Lathrem was still outside, Eaglin sucker punched the hated Fuston, knocking him to the floor. In revenge for having been a snitch, the former boxer continued to beat Fuston until he was nearly unconscious. He then dragged the hapless inmate up a set of metal stairs, depositing him in an already completed cell. He knew that Lathrem wouldn't be able to see the prisoner there.

Eaglin walked back downstairs to get the sledgehammer. As he did so, he passed by Smith.

He informed Smith what was planned. The rapist wasn't very bright, but he'd already figured it out.

Eaglin ran back upstairs carrying the sledgehammer. He stood over Fuston, striking him in the head three times, crushing his skull.

When Lathrem walked back inside after giving Officer George the count slip, Smith asked her to open the tool closet.

"I need to get something out of there," he said.

As Lathrem turned to open the door, Eaglin walked up behind her. Raising the sledgehammer, he swung it with all his might, smashing the back of her head. Lathrem went down in a shower of blood.

Eaglin opened the closet door and, grabbing her arms, dragged her inside. Then he hit her again, once in the skull and once in the face.

"Why'd you have to hit her in the face?" Smith asked.

"Bitch gotta die," Eaglin said.

Smith cursed out loud. For weeks, he'd planned to rape Lathrem when she was incapacitated. But he couldn't go through with it now, because of all the blood and gore.

With Lathrem and Fuston out of the way, they had to move fast. The inmates had only an hour to carry out their plan.

While Jones and Smith went outside to get the ladders they planned to use for the breakout, Eaglin led Beaston into a nearby cell. The convicted cocaine dealer had asked Eaglin to strike him in the head so he could claim

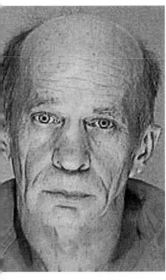

Jessica **Lunsford** (right) was kidnapped from her own home and then raped and murdered by **John Evander Couey** (above).

Here are the **charred remains** of the house where Couey committed his dastardly deeds on an innocent young girl after it was torched by an arsonist.

Photo courtesy of Sarasota County Sheriff's Office

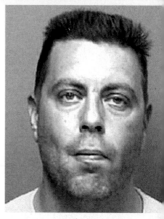

In a first for American crime, as **the security camera of a Sarasota car wash** was taping the entire scary event (above), **Joseph Smith** (middle right) walked off with eleven-year-old **Carlie Brucia** (middle left).

Photo courtesy of Sarasota County Sheriff's Office

The site where Carlie's body was found has now been reconfigured as a **beautiful garden** (above) constructed in her name created by members of the Central Church of Christ in Sarasota.

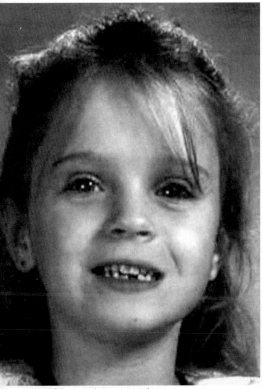
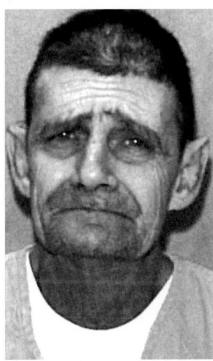

Seven-year-old **Amanda Brown** (left) was kidnapped by crab fisherman **Willie Crain** (right) after Crain invited Amanda and her mother, Kathryn Hartman, to his Tampa residence. Her body was never found.

Immigrant drifter **Juan Carlos Chavez** (right) kidnapped **Jimmy Ryce** (left) in broad daylight as he got off the school bus and then savagely raped and murdered him in cold blood.

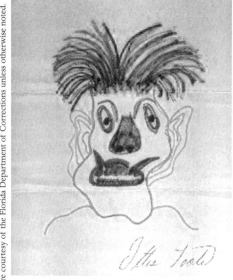

In one of the most infamou kidnapping cases in America history, **Adam Walsh** (left the son of *America's Mo Wanted* host John Walsh, wa snatched from a departmer store in Hollywood, Florida. was later confirmed that **Ott Elwood Toole** (above), seri killer, arsonist and accompli of fellow murderer Henry Le Lucas, was the culprit in th little boy's brutal slaying.

Two examples of some of th **twisted jailhouse art** (top) Tool created while he was in prison

lave You Seen Me?

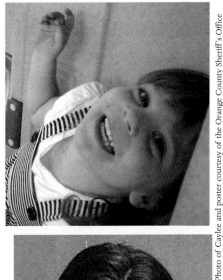

Caylee Marie Anthony

Year Old, White Female, Brown hair, Hazel eyes,
irthmark on left shoulder, Approximately 3 feet tall.

e Orange County Sheriff's Office is currently trying to determine the
whereabouts and well being of this child. If you have seen
Caylee Marie Anthony in the company of another
since June 9, 2008 call 407-254-7000.

ww.HelpFindCaylee.com

Please Contact The
ange County Sheriff's Office 407-254-7000
or Crimeline 1-800-423-TIPS (8477)

Flyer Design Courtesy of: Kid Finders Network   1-877-One-Lost

e mysterious disappearance of three-year-old
ylee **Anthony** (top) garnered national
idlines. After she was reported missing,
picions were raised about the girl's mother,
sey (right).

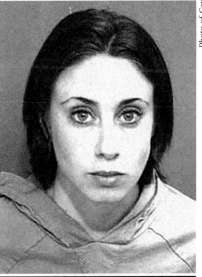

nest **Major** was a career
minal sentenced to life
prison for home invasion
obery and numerous
ier crimes.

Gerhard Hojan (left) was sentenced to death for the
Davie Waffle House murders. **Jimmy Mickel** (right)
was convicted of being the mastermind behind the
murders.

Robert Bailey (top left), member of a notorio Milwaukee, Wisconsin, gar shot and killed Panama C police sergeant **Kevin Ki** (top right) during the reve of Spring Break.

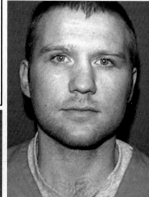

Darla Lathrem (center), the first female correctional officer in Florida to be killed in the line of duty, was viciously murdered in a botched prison break orchestrated by **Dwight Eaglin** (middle top right) and another inmate, **Stephen V. Smith** (below Eaglin).

The brutal murder of **Tiffany Eunick** (bottom rig was portrayed by the media as an accident involvi playmate **Lionel Tate** (bottom left), who in tru willfully murdered the young girl.

Norman Mearle Grim, called the Tattoo Man by his neighbors, murdered attorney Cynthia Campbell.

Adam "Rattlesnake" Davis (middle) received the death penalty for murdering Vicki Robinson, the mother of **Valessa Robinson** (top).

nald Clark (above), a y prisoner awaiting cution, was dubbed 'he Death Row Poet".

Loran Cole's (right) Internet essays protesting his innocence would be humorous if it weren't for the savage brutality of his crimes.

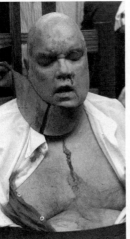

Allen Lee Davis's bloody murder of three innocent people earned him a ride on the notorious Son of Sparky. Allen Lee Davis's **execution photos.**

Above is the gurney used for **"Old Sharpie"**, the nickname given to the needle used for let injections in Florida. Below it is **"Son of Sparky"**, one of the most infamous electric chairs in United States.

that he wasn't involved in the plot. Once inside the cell, the former boxer bashed Feaston's skull with a hammer, knocking him out.

Using an assortment of aluminum ladders, brackets and nuts and bolts that they'd already stashed away, Eaglin, Jones and Smith began to construct a "super ladder." In order to complete their plan of getting over the two razor-wire fences that encircled the prison, the ladder had to be at least twenty-four feet long and thirteen feet high. It would be shaped like an inverted "U".

By now, A-Dorm was a bloody mess, but the three inmates dutifully began to attach brackets to the ladders. They found that they needed additional parts for the project, so Eaglin went outside to get them while Smith and Jones worked. During the entire process, none of the correctional officers inside the prison noticed anything suspicious.

The inmates labored for forty-five minutes constructing their contraption. Finally, as they had planned, they carried the components outside and finished bolting the ladders together. It was nearly ten o'clock.

Time was running out as the three inmates lugged the super-ladder to the fence.

Dwight Thomas Eaglin stood five feet seven inches tall and weighed about 150 pounds. Muscles rippled on his body and soon after he arrived in Charlotte Correctional Institution, a much larger inmate challenged him to a fight. Out in the yard, where the encounter took place, prison guards had to pull Eaglin off his beaten opponent. He was placed in solitary confinement, but it didn't stop him from fighting. During his two years at CCI, he was placed in solitary twice more for violent incidents.

In 1990, at the age of fifteen, boxing under the name of Tommy "The Fighting Irishman" Eaglin, he won the Illinois State Golden Gloves championship. Moving to St. Petersburg, he tallied a seventeen win and five loss professional record with ten knockouts. Eaglin fought as a welterweight during his entire boxing career. Before his arrest, he was being considered as an opponent for a championship bout in a division which boasted such superstars as "Sugar" Shane Mosley and Antonio Margarito. A match with either fighter could have netted Eaglin a million dollar payday.

"Before the prison world," he said in a later interview with reporter David Karsh, "I'm happy-go-lucky, class president, captain of the football team, state Golden Gloves Champion, professional boxer. Mr. Popular everywhere I go. Everybody knows me."

However, Eaglin had a dark side. After one particularly grueling match, he was introduced to cocaine. Soon he was spending all his money on the stuff and it still wasn't enough. Eaglin began committing petty thefts to finance his growing habit.

The murder that sent him to prison for life seemed senseless. Eaglin was stealing a CD player from a car outside a topless bar in Pinellas Park, when John Frederick Nichols drove up. Prosecutors theorized that Eaglin attacked the unarmed Nichols when he tried to call police to report the crime. The boxer stabbed Nichols thirteen times and slit his throat down to the spinal column. At trial, Eaglin claimed he killed Nichols in self-defense, but the jury didn't buy it.

Eaglin, never one to follow rules, had previously been convicted of battery, child abuse and DUI.

When reporter Karsh asked how he went from promising boxer to lifer, Eaglin said, "I started drinking a lot, doing drugs and it spiraled downhill from there. I don't have any excuses. I made the choices to shove that stuff up my nose and drink the drinks..."

Stephen Vincent Smith was serving seven life sentences for raping and beating an eighty-year-old Broward County woman to death when she caught him burglarizing her home. An equal opportunity rapist, he'd also been convicted of raping a ten-year-old girl during another armed burglary.

In fact, Smith had twenty-eight convictions in Florida alone. When he was arrested, investigators found that he was having an incestuous relationship with a relative.

In his home state of Rhode Island, he'd served time for raping his own sister and various other sex crimes.

Michael Jones was serving a life sentence for burglary and sexual battery with a weapon. He'd been listed on Florida's sex offender registry before going to prison.

Eaglin, Smith and Jones were dangerous characters. They were also desperate since none of them had any chance of ever being paroled.

About 10 P.M., Officer Mark Pate and other officers got a "red alert" on Zone 5 from the control room via radio. The perimeter fencing at the prison had been hit or touched. Officer Pate, who had just come out of B-Dorm, saw a ladder pushed up against the inner-perimeter fence.

In truth, five ladders had been bolted together in a giant inverted U-shape. Afterward, a guard commented, "It was almost...like a bridge."

The two perimeter fences were twelve feet high with coils of concertina wire (called razor wire by guards and inmates alike) rising from the ground and spiraling all the way to the top. The inner and outer fences were separated by a twenty foot walkway.

Officer Pate saw Stephen V. Smith a few feet up the ladder. Michael Jones stood on the ground. Eaglin had already climbed over the inner fence and was attempting to scale the outer fence. The maze of razor wire seemed to be blocking his progress.

A later investigation showed that the ladder had buckled under Eaglin's weight as he climbed over the inner fence. This had caused him to fall into the no man's land between the fences. The ladder touched one of the fences, causing the alarm to be activated.

Several officers, including Timothy Belfield, raced toward the escaping inmates. When Smith and Jones saw them coming, they abandoned the ladder and ran back to A-Dorm. Eaglin, still inside the two fences, was ordered to "lay down on the ground."

The only guns available to the guards were in a truck that patrolled the perimeter of the prison. The officers had only their physical strength and pepper spray to subdue the inmate.

Belfield and other correctional officers rushed through a gate in the inner fence and converged on Eaglin. Once the boxer realized he couldn't escape, he assumed his fighting stance.

"You're going to have to shoot me," he screamed. Eaglin knew that the only guns were in the truck circling the fence, but he may have assumed that the guards had gotten them.

"Get on the ground," Belfield yelled. "Get on the ground."

"I'll kill you," Eaglin said. "I'll make you kill me, too."

He backed away from the officers, tearing off his clothes. Two officers sprayed him with mace, but the "chemical agents" had no effect at all. The guards lunged at Eaglin, but he fought back. After several minutes, he was finally forced to the ground and handcuffed.

The official report describing the incident stated that "Mr. Eaglin was still angry and out of control. [He] tried to kick, bite and head-butt the offi- cers. After [he] was removed from the fenced area, another sergeant secured his legs with shackles."

Eaglin had a gash on his forearm and blood was streaming from the cut. He was treated and placed in a holding cell.

Officer Pate had rushed into A-Dorm with other officers. He attempted to radio Officer Lathrem, but heard only silence. Suddenly, he stopped in his tracks and stared at a ghostly sight. Seeping from a closet was a puddle of blood. Pate attempted to open the door, but it was stuck. He banged on it, yelling for Lathrem.

Calling for an ambulance and nurse, Pate backed off.

Someone arrived with a set of keys and unlocked the closet door. When it was opened, Pate saw Lathrem lying on the floor in a fetal position. A sledgehammer lay beside her head.

Paramedics placed the rookie officer on a gurney and transported her to the emergency room. They couldn't get a pulse and doctors pronounced her dead a few minutes after she arrived.

Guards began searching A-Dorm. Lathrem's keys and radio were found in the toilet bowl of a nearby cell. Ladders and tools were scattered everywhere. Officers moved through the blood and litter looking for the two inmates who had run back inside. They finally located them, hiding in a cell. Smith and Jones were handcuffed and taken to separate cells.

John Beaston was found holding a rag to his head. He was bleeding and stated that he had lost consciousness. "What's going on?" he kept asking. He was placed in a wheelchair and taken to the prison emergency room.

Officers found Charles Fuston in an upstairs cell. He was lying face-down, with a "massive amount of blood around him." Fuston, unresponsive, was also taken to the emergency room. He was later transferred to Lee Memorial Hospital. He was comatose and never regained consciousness. Fuston was taken off life support two days later.

A bloodbath had occurred in A-Dorm. A correctional officer and an inmate were dead. Three men, two having been convicted of murder, had nearly escaped.

How could it have happened?

The answers would leave the state's prison system reeling.

The plan to escape originated in D-Dorm where Eaglin, Jones and Smith were housed. It was an "open bay" dormitory—it didn't have cells; instead, it had rows of bunks. For that reason, several inmates heard the three discussing their proposed escape.

Two prisoners later testified that the three planned to put together a series of ladders sixteen feet high and twenty-three feet across. Once the first inmate got across, he would hook it to a light pole so it wouldn't fall into the fence and set off alarms.

Eaglin was chosen to go over first, because he was stronger and faster than the others. Once on the other side of the outer fence, he planned to wait in the ditch next to the road until the "gun truck" came by. As it passed, Eaglin was supposed to hit the driver of the truck and knock him out. "Once he had the gun and a truck," court documents revealed, "Mr. Eaglin would assist Mr. Jones and Mr. Smith over the fence. If that plan did not work, they were going to have knives and go to the officers' housing, which was less than a mile away and obtain a vehicle."

The plan all along was to kill Fuston and the correctional officer on duty. Other prisoners stated that the three had bragged about killing anyone else who happened to get in their way.

About a month before the escape attempt, Eaglin, Jones and Smith allegedly made another ladder large enough to go over the fence. They'd hidden it, but someone found it and cut it up. They blamed Fuston.

Special Agents Steve Uebelacher and Andrew Rose with the Florida Department of Law Enforcement interviewed Eaglin. "I'll make it easy on you," he said. "I tried to kill those three people." He stated that he wanted to "get the chair," meaning he wanted to be executed.

When asked by the detectives about the murder of Darla Lathrem, he refused to speak.

Later, however, in his interview with reporter Karsh, Eaglin gave an explanation:

Karsh: "Did you kill Darla?"

Eaglin: "Yes, I did."

Karsh: "Why?"

Eaglin: "I was trying to escape from prison...I wasn't trying to kill her. But how do you administer a sledgehammer to somebody's head—you know, just do it right so that they won't die?"

At trial, the evidence against Eaglin was so overwhelming that it took the jury just two hours before returning a verdict of first-degree murder against him in the deaths of corrections officer Darla Lathrem and inmate Charles Fuston. A week later, he was given two death sentences.

Stephen V. Smith was also sentenced to death and Michael Jones was given life in prison.

While the courtroom proceedings were complete, the investigation into what went wrong was just beginning.

Daryl McCasland of the Florida Department of Corrections headed the inquiry. He conducted over 100 interviews with corrections officers, administrators, inmates and others involved in prison operations. McCasland's final report was devastating in its accusations of malfeasance among officials.

Prison policy required that two corrections officers monitor five or more inmates inside a dormitory that was under construction. However, CCI rarely, if ever, followed this guideline. Officers had complained on numerous occasions about not feeling safe in such settings, yet no action was ever taken. (In some instances, the ratio was eight prisoners—many having been convicted of violent offenses—to one officer.) Many times, officers had to turn their backs on inmates, because "they would be working in different parts of the building, performing different tasks." It seemed to many that the murder of Lathrem should not have been a surprise.

While there were forty-one officers on duty that night (more than the required minimum), none ever checked on Lathrem. McCasland's report read: "No one from Charlotte's administration appeared to monitor the construction project beyond the normal duty hours..." In what was called a "common practice," supervisors never performed security checks on the officers working in the dorms at night.

Another breakdown in policy was the failure of officers to wear "body alarms," electronic devices that alert other officers to a "fallen comrade." The policy required that all officers wear the alarms, yet few did.

Like guns, dangerous tools such as sledgehammers, saws, grinders and pliers should have been stored outside the prison. There had been cases of missing equipment and tools that were never found.

In addition, prisoners were supposed to be wearing restraints when they were transferred back to their dorms at ten o'clock. This policy was routinely ignored.

Two weeks after Lathrem's death, Warden Warren Cornell retired. A media advisory from the Department of Corrections reported that "Assistant Warden A. W. Boyett requested a hardship demotion to Colonel at Brevard Correctional Institution immediately following the incident."

Later, he was demoted to sergeant. Two other officers were demoted and three additional officers received "counseling."

Although the entire Florida state prison system was said to have improved security on account of the Lathrem case, just five years later, an eerily similar murder occurred at Tomoka Correctional Institution in Daytona Beach. On June 25, 2008, Corrections Officer Donna Fitzgerald was stabbed to death by a convicted kidnapper and sex offender.

Late in the evening, thirty-seven-year-old Enoch Hall slipped away from a work detail and hid in a welding shed. At about 7:30 P.M., he was reported missing. As officers fanned out to search for him, Fitzgerald entered the shed alone. In the darkness, the veteran guard found Hall crouching behind a bench. She ordered him to come out, but he attacked, using a shiv (a homemade knife) to stab her eleven times.

Like Lathrem, Fitzgerald was armed only with mace and an alarm.

Hall, a career criminal, had been arrested for burglary, auto theft, battery on a law enforcement officer and rape. In 1992, he kidnapped a woman and raped her, earning himself a life sentence. He had been incarcerated in Tomoka since 1994.

The investigation into the murder faulted Tomoka for many of the same lapses at Charlotte. For instance, only one officer was responsible for as many as twenty-seven inmates on work details. That very night, Fitzgerald had worked with thirteen inmates—five were convicted rapists and seven were convicted murderers.

Dangerous tools and equipment weren't kept outside the prison and were within easy reach of inmates in the work detail.

It seemed that few lessons had been learned.

Dwight Thomas Eaglin is currently on Florida's death row. While he initially stated that he wanted to receive the death penalty, he now proclaims his innocence and claims that the state is "torturing" him.

Stephen V. Smith accumulated seven life sentences from previous convictions. In 2006, he received a death sentence for the murder of Officer

Darla Lathrem. At his trial, his defense counsel blamed the Department of Corrections for Lathrem's murder. The defense called the investigators, who lambasted CCI and got them to admit to the many breaches of security at the prison. Even so, Smith was convicted.

On June 25, 2008, Michael Jones died while in custody. He'd had health problems for several years.

Darla Lathrem's family still grieves her untimely death. Thousands of law enforcement officials attended her funeral. One of her co-workers offered this eulogy: "Officer Lathrem was such a blessing to work with. She could make you laugh over anything and everything. She always put her best into everything. Matthew 5, verse 8 says, 'Blessed are the pure in heart for they shall see God.'"

When Florida Corrections Officer Darla Lathrem was savagely attacked by three inmates with violent pasts, it seemed to be an inevitable consequence of the lax security procedures followed by Charlotte Correctional Institution. Then the breakdown turned out to be statewide. After the Department of Corrections claimed to have "fixed" the problems, a second prison guard was murdered at a Daytona Beach prison. Prisons are always dangerous places to work. Many inmates have committed violent crimes outside prison and, given the chance, will repeat their behaviors on the inside. Guards and other inmates are always at risk for violent encounters, and security lapses are numerous.

Chapter 9
The Waffle House Murders

"You know how easy it would be to rob this place?"

> Jimmy Mickel, discussing a robbery plan
> with his friend, Gerhard Hojan.

Waffle House restaurants are a southern icon. Based out of Georgia, the first twenty-four-hour-a-day cafeteria opened in 1955. It was an instant success. Now there are more than 1,500—they've even invaded a few northern states. Some cities may have a half-dozen or more of the restaurants in various locations, their colorful yellow and black signs beckoning many a hungry late-night rider. The restaurant's waffles and unique hash browns have been perennial southern favorites from day one.

"The Waffle House is everywhere in the South. It has inspired country songs, comedy routines, loving editorials,[and] a scene in the movie *Tin Cup*," wrote Jim Ridley in the *Nashville Scene*.

While on tour, famous country singers have been known to dine at the cafeteria. The South Carolina-based band Hootie and the Blowfish once did an album entitled *Scattered, Smothered and Covered*, referring to the restaurant's hash browns served with onions and cheese. Musician Kid Rock was involved in a brawl at a Waffle House outside of Atlanta when a customer made derogatory remarks about a female member of his entourage.

The Waffle House in Davie, Florida, was a clone of all the other restaurants in the chain. It had a group of regulars who bantered back and forth, argued politics or sports and enjoyed their food hot off the open grill.

Sometimes undesirables hung around: dopers, prostitutes, outlaw bikers. But as long as they didn't cause trouble, they were welcome.

In the early morning hours of March 11, 2002, three employees worked the night shift: seventeen-year-old waitress Christina De La Rosa, a pretty blonde high school dropout who was working to support her young son; cook Willie Absolu, an immigrant from Haiti who labored at two jobs and whose dream was to bring his wife and two children to the promised land of America and waitress Barbara Ann Nunn, who'd once done eight years in an Iowa prison for stabbing her boyfriend to death.

It had been slow most of the night. At 3:30 A.M., only two customers remained. They were regulars, known to the employees only as "Jimmy" and "Chip." Barbara Nunn had once worked with Jimmy when he was employed there as a cook, but she didn't know his last name. Now he worked with his friend Chip at a Ft. Lauderdale club —in fact, he'd gotten Nunn in free a couple of times.

Thirty-three-year-old Jimmy Mickel lived with his girlfriend in a mobile home not far from the restaurant. His buddy, Gerhard "Chip" Hojan, twenty-six years old, rented a room from Mickel. Hojan stood six feet tall and weighed more than 300 pounds. In public, he was quiet, preferring to remain in the background. Both were deep in debt and neither had a criminal history.

They sat in the smoking section, eating waffles and sipping coffee. As they'd done on many occasions, Mickel and his friend commiserated over their mounting debts. Mickel had two children from a previous marriage and owed back child support. Hojan was renting a pickup truck from a car rental company. His payments were $411 per month and he was two weeks behind. In the last couple of days, he'd started getting nasty phone calls— the company was demanding that he turn in the truck and pay up. In addition to being a defendant in several civil suits brought against him by creditors, Hojan also owed back rent to Mickel.

Mickel began discussing the possibility of robbing the restaurant. Although they'd talked about it many times before, the conversation always began that way. Mickel had told his friend many times that he understood how the restaurant operated. He knew where the receipts were kept and when the "slow times" occurred. Best of all, Mickel said, there was the fact that there was absolutely no security.

Hojan sensed that Mickel was serious this time and told his friend that he'd been studying up on killing. In fact, he said he'd borrowed a book about serial killers from Mickel's girlfriend, who was a law student.

Although neither said it out loud, they'd previously discussed the obvious fact that if they *did* rob the place, they couldn't leave any witnesses.

"Let's do it," Mickel said.

He stood up and walked outside to get bolt cutters out of Hojan's truck. For months, the knowledge of easy money had been burning a hole in his brain.

After Mickel went outside, Hojan moved to the counter and handed De La Rosa a ten dollar bill. As she reached for it, he stuck a gun in her face.

Barbara Nunn, who always referred to Hojan as the "Mexican," later described what happened. "[The] Mexican...pulls out his gun and tells us to go to the back..."

As soon as she saw the pistol, De La Rosa began shaking. Verging on hysteria, she handed Chip the cash from the register. "I have a six-month-old son," she blurted. "I want to see him again."

Mickel came back inside and used the bolt cutters to pop open the padlock to the drop-box beneath the counter. While he placed the cash in a transparent plastic bag, Hojan marched the employees single file to the back. Nunn, who had considered Mickel a friend, turned and asked, "Are we going to be okay?"

He ignored her.

Hojan continued to herd them to the back. "Get in the freezer," he said.

After the door slammed shut, De La Rosa began to sob. "God, I need to see my baby," she cried.

A minute later, Hojan re-opened the door. "Empty your pockets," he said. "Gimme your cell phones."

De La Rosa reached into the pouch that held her tips and pulled out $200 in small bills. She handed them to Hojan. Nunn gave him $80.

Absolu stated that he had no money.

"Hand me your wallet," Hojan said.

"I don't have a wallet."

A police report taken during a later interview with Nunn read: "Barbara Nunn stated that 'Chip' went into the cooler three times. The first was to put [the employees] in there. The second time was when Chip demanded they empty their pockets and the third time was to order them to turn around so he could shoot them."

When Hojan entered the freezer for the final time, he leveled the pistol, a .380-caliber semiautomatic, at them. "On your knees," he said. "Turn around and get on your knees."

They all knew what that meant.

De La Rosa's shrieks pierced the frigid air. "Please, please," she begged. "I need to see my child."

"Wait a minute," Nunn said, trying to remain calm. "Wait, can't we just talk?"

Absolu, who'd been silent during the entire ordeal, knew they were as good as dead. He suddenly reached out and snatched at the gun. He was much smaller than Hojan and stood little chance. The crack of the first gunshot unleashed a torrent of hell.

Absolu dropped to the floor. (Cops would later find a shell casing clutched in his hand, proving that he'd indeed grabbed the gun.) The cook was hit in the head. A second shot ripped through his left arm.

De La Rosa's non-stop wailing sounded like a dying animal. As the shots blasted into the tiny freezer, she frantically tried to scramble beneath a series of shelves that held boxes and cans of food. "The girl with blonde hair tried to crawl beneath the racks," Hojan later said.

At some point, she was hit. An autopsy later showed that one round shattered her spinal cord, paralyzing her. The second was a head shot.

"De La Rosa was lying on her right side," the police report read. "Her head was pointed westward lying against the back wall slightly on top of the boxes...It appeared as if she was in a curled-up fetal position. It appeared as if she attempted to cover her face and head with her hands."

Despite Hojan's demands, Barbara Nunn had refused to turn around. "I knew what that meant," she later said, referring to the fact that she knew he planned to execute them. He pointed the gun directly at her face and pulled the trigger. When the bullet hit her, Nunn's head snapped back and she slumped to the floor, fading into unconsciousness.

When she awoke, Nunn felt something heavy on her legs. It was part of Absolu's body. She pushed him off, opened the freezer door and peered out. Seeing no one, Nunn pulled herself up and staggered toward the back door.

Later she said that she didn't see any blood on her clothes, but she felt "wet." Her head throbbed and she could barely walk. Nunn knew she had to make it outside for help.

Most of the surrounding businesses were closed. However, she spied a gas station with its lights on about a hundred yards away in a strip mall.

Danish Khan, the night clerk at the station, looked up in utter horror as a blood-soaked woman burst into the store. He noticed that she was wearing a Waffle House uniform.

"We've just been robbed," she shouted. "Don't open the door for *anyone.*"

Khan picked up the phone and dialed 911. Nunn lurched toward him, then fell. As she lay on the floor, she asked him to lock the door. "Keep out any Mexicans," she kept repeating. "They're coming to kill me."

As Khan waited for the police to arrive, he tried to comfort her.

"Will you call my mother?" she asked.

Khan used his cell phone and dialed the number Nunn provided. He handed her the phone and she told her mother that she'd been shot in a holdup.

Within a minute or two, several police officers arrived, followed by paramedics. Nunn reiterated to the cops and the medics that a former co-worker named "Jimmy" and "a big, fat Mexican guy" had robbed the restaurant and shot her. She stated that she thought her fellow employees were dead.

The wounded woman was airlifted to a hospital in nearby Hollywood, where doctors removed a projectile from the left side of her head. (Because of the severity of the wound, Nunn lost much of her eyesight, hearing and balance.)

Investigators waited at the hospital for her to awaken so she could be questioned.

Davie Patrol Officer Lazaro Rodriguez arrived at the Waffle House at 4:50 A.M. He was the first cop on the scene. His report described what he saw. "I grabbed a napkin from the napkin holder," he wrote, "which was laying [sic] on the booth and began to conduct an interior search of the business using the napkin to open doors. I proceeded to walk behind the employee work area, which led me to the business supply room....As I was clearing the supply room of any suspect's [sic], I observed a trail of blood on the supply room floor which led from the west side door to a [black-colored] door which was closed. I then opened the door and observed a large silver door directly to my left..."

The silver door opened into the freezer. Rodriguez peered inside and saw two bodies, a male and a female, lying motionless on the blood-soaked floor. He backed out, closed the cooler door and called for a backup unit to set up a crime scene perimeter outside the restaurant.

The case was not a whodunit.

A witness had lived to identify the assailants.

The detective in charge, Davie Police Sergeant James Franquiz, called the Waffle House manager and informed him that the store had been robbed and at least two employees had been murdered. Since he'd hired Jimmy a few months before, the manager informed Franquiz of his former employee's last name and his address. The manager also knew that "Chip" lived with Mickel. A quick search of a police database confirmed that the second robber was Gerhard "Chip" Hojan.

In his report, Detective Franquiz wrote: "The front counter cash register drawer was missing. A small cash box under the front register counter was located. This cash box was also emptied. A small padlock which appeared to have been used to lock the cash box appeared to have been cut off and was found lying on the [floor] underneath the box."

As Franquiz entered the back room, he saw several menus scattered across the floor. A two-drawer filing cabinet was open and the contents, including loose change and unused receipt books, had spilled onto the floor. Two cash register drawers were nearby.

A further search of the freezer revealed a wallet hidden behind several boxes on a shelf. It contained identification cards and a driver's license in the name of Willy Absolu. It also contained several dollars in cash and business cards advertising a hair salon. It was later learned that Absolu's second job was as a barber at the salon.

A large pool of blood in the freezer contained more evidence. Shell casings and loose change were soaking in the blood and collected as evidence.

Later that morning, Palm Beach County Assistant Medical Examiner Linda Rush O'Neil arrived. In a preliminary examination, she determined that Willy Absolu had been shot in the head, neck and left arm. A later autopsy would confirm that one round had severed his jugular vein, causing him to bleed to death. A shell casing on the floor next to his body matched the shell found clutched in his hand.

Christina De La Rosa had also been shot in the head and neck. There was stippling underneath her chin which indicated she'd been shot at close range. She also had a gunshot wound to her upper left breast, which lodged in her spine.

Late that afternoon, Detective Franquiz learned that Barbara Nunn had regained consciousness and had identified Hojan and Mickel from a photo lineup. Franquiz drove to the hospital to interview his only witness. In his report, the victim describes the terrifying moments before she was shot. "So [Hojan] comes back and he says, um, on your knees," Nunn said. "All [of] you turn around and get on your knees." She tried again to reason with him. "Wait a minute!" she said. "You don't have to do this. Can't we talk?" Just before he fired, she screamed, "Wait!"

Nunn said she heard a "loud bang." She felt no pain, but began to drift away. She lost all feeling and collapsed. After she fell, she said she "felt people falling on top of her." Then she lost consciousness.

She stated that Willy Absolu "held them all together before 'Chip' came into the room for the third time."

Detective Franquiz obtained warrants for the arrest of each suspect. They had been under surveillance and were quickly taken into custody.

The next day, Franquiz interviewed Jimmy Mickel. While everyone who knew them said he led his friend Hojan around "like a puppy dog," Mickel claimed that he never knew the robbery was going down. He'd merely gone to Waffle House with Chip to get coffee and suddenly his friend pulled out a gun and robbed the place. He said he watched Hojan take the employees to the back and heard several loud thumps. They didn't sound like gunshots, Mickel said, and he didn't know the three had been shot until later.

Mickel said he followed Hojan's orders and went outside to get the bolt cutters. He cut the locks and dumped the money into a bag that Hojan was holding.

After collecting as much money as they could find—altogether about $1,500—they drove to the club in Ft. Lauderdale. Mickel said Chip got out of the truck and threw the murder weapon into some bushes behind the building.

After hiding the gun, they went to a convenience store where Hojan bought two money orders, each for $411. Then they drove to the rental car company so Chip could make his two car payments, but the place was closed.

Finally, they drove back to Mickel's trailer and went to bed. Mickel said he had no trouble sleeping and only woke up after his girlfriend returned home from law school late that afternoon.

"When I asked why they decided to rob the Waffle House," Franquiz wrote in his report, "Mickel stated that Chip was under a lot of pressure because of his ex-wife, bills and that Chip only works part-time. Mickel stated he went along with the robbery to be cool. He stated that he didn't want to do it but if he didn't go along, he was going to get his ass kicked [by Hojan]."

The pistol was located exactly where Mickel said it would be. It was later determined that the gun had been stolen and purchased "off the street" by Hojan.

Gerhard "Chip" Hojan was interviewed next. Detective Franquiz wrote a report describing his confession. "He and Jimmy went to eat breakfast," it read, "at the Waffle House around 3:00 A.M. during which time, Jimmy began bragging [about] how easy it would be to rob the Waffle House. Hojan stated that they were eating inside until sometime around 4:00 A.M. When they finished, Jimmy went outside and came back inside the Waffle House with a pair of bolt cutters..."

Hojan confirmed that he ordered the employees into the freezer and shot them. He also described Absolu's attempt to get the gun from him: "Hojan stated that the cook came at him as soon as he opened the cooler door [the third time]. The cook grabbed Hojan's hand which had the gun in it and that's when the first shot was fired. Hojan stated that as the cook was going down, he still had a hold of Hojan's gun and the gun fired again."

The evidence was overwhelming: an eyewitness who had survived against all odds and identified the robbers, shell casings and bullets that matched the gun recovered from behind the club and bolt cutters retrieved from Hojan's truck that were said by experts to match marks found on the padlocks at the scene. In addition, both suspects had confessed to the robbery. Hojan had also confessed to the murders.

The trials were held separately.

Gerhard Hojan refused to let his attorneys argue the case. He stated that he was guilty and wanted to receive the death penalty. On October 17, 2003, Hojan was convicted of two counts of first-degree murder, one count of first-degree attempted murder, one count of attempted felony murder, three counts of kidnapping and two counts of armed robbery. He was given two death sentences and is currently on death row.

Even though Barbara Nunn testified against him, Jimmy Mickel was acquitted of the murder charges and attempted murder charges. He was, however, convicted of three counts of armed kidnapping and two counts of armed robbery.

At his sentencing hearing, Broward Circuit Judge Paul Backman said: "There is no question having sat through both Mr. Hojan's trial and your trial that you were the mastermind behind this entire thing. You manipulated Mr. Hojan. He was there, he did your bidding and the three times that he left that freezer and went back to your location, there was no question what was going on. You were telling him no witnesses, no witnesses, no witnesses, and he went forth, and he went back and he went forth, and he went back and he pulled the trigger and that pull of the trigger was a cold, calculated, premeditated act that was precipitated by your direction."

Judge Backman also asserted that Mickel had never shown any remorse.

Mickel received five life sentences. He is serving his time at Hardee Correctional Institution.

Five lives intersected that night in an orgy of violence. The killers are behind bars, but the victims' families still grieve.

Christina De La Rosa was just beginning her life. She'd made some mistakes, but after her best friend overdosed and De La Rosa became pregnant, she'd reconsidered the direction in which her life was headed. She'd obtained a job, enrolled at a vocational school in order to get her GED and hoped to someday obtain a degree in nursing. De La Rosa's final moments, her final screams, her last thoughts before the darkness overtook her, were about the son she loved so desperately.

Willy Absolu had lived in Florida for two years. After having been raised in desperate poverty in his home country of Haiti, he emigrated to the Bahamas. But America called, and Absolu joined his brother in south Florida. He worked two jobs and saved money so he could send for his family to join him. The night before he was murdered, Absolu had called his mother in Haiti and promised to send her money. His brother, Dieumeme, who lived in Lauderdale Lakes and was best friends with Willy, said that he was determined to pull his own family out of the grinding poverty they knew so well.

After learning that Hojan had received the death penalty, Absolu's brother was satisfied. "I wanted [Hojan] to be dead," he said. "I lost my brother. If [Hojan] is in jail, he's still alive. There's no way I can get my brother back."

Speaking about the attempt by Willy Absolu to stop the robbery, Don Grimme, an expert on workplace violence, stated, "It's the first rule of what we train employees never to do."

Others disagreed. It was obvious that Hojan and Mickel planned to leave no witnesses and that the employees, who had no weapons with which to defend themselves, were like ducks in a shooting gallery. Many felt that it was an act of courage on the part of the cook to attempt to stop the slaughter before it began.

Barbara Nunn was permanently disabled because of the shooting. Barely able to walk or see, she is unable to work. She and her two children moved in with her mother.

Fast food restaurants and convenience stores have proliferated in our rootless state. Many businesses stay open all night. The majority of clerks in privately-owned stores are armed and, on many occasions, have stopped robberies by shooting back. But some chain restaurants have forbidden their employees to pack heat. Therefore, the workers are helpless when robbers such as Gerhard Hojan and Jimmy Mickel set upon them. The police reports and other documents related to this case highlight the distressing helplessness of the victims. But there has been no change and service workers in the state continue to be murdered in store robberies.

Chapter 10
The Wrong Victim

"[Major] grabbed my arm and pulled me...in the
bathroom and kind of gave me a shove into the bathroom...
I heard gunshots and seen 'em puncture the door...And then
I heard someone say, 'Get out. Let's go. Let's go. Get out.'"

Sarina Robey, describing her ordeal to
Detective Mike Rakestraw.

A t exactly 9:36 A.M. Steven Robey heard a knock on the door of his
North Fort Myers motel room. Robey had ordered room service
almost an hour before. It hadn't come and he'd grown tired of waiting.
He had walked down to the office for the hotel's advertised Continental
breakfast. After eating, he packed a danish and a cup of orange juice for his
sixteen-year-old daughter, Sarina, who was still sleeping on the second bed
and had just gone back to their room.

He didn't notice that it was a hard, rattling knock. Robey thought it
was a waitress bringing the room service breakfast he'd ordered to him and
Sarina. But when he opened the door, he saw a stranger.

Steven and his daughter were staying at the Howard Johnson motel
while they attempted to purchase a home in nearby Cape Coral. On the
previous day, they had driven down from New Smyrna Beach and met with
realtors.

On that sunny Florida Chamber-of-Commerce morning, as they
prepared for another day of house-hunting, Steven and Sarina Robey

hadn't heard that two serial robbers had been targeting visitors at hotels in the area.

"You got a couple bucks I can borrow?" the man at the door asked.

Steven shook his head and tried to shut the door. But the stranger jammed his foot between it and the frame, then put his shoulder to it. Steven, caught off guard, fell back. The intruder, later identified as Ernest Major, barged into the room while a second man, Phillip C. "New Wave" Nelson, swept in behind.

"Get down on the bed!" Major screamed.

He jerked a pistol from his pocket and put the barrel to Robey's temple. Robey knew about guns and guessed it was .22-caliber revolver.

"Get down! Get down!" the assailant repeated.

Robey, thin and only five feet five inches tall, was no match for the two-hundred pound Major. He sat down on the mattress.

Nelson, six feet tall and heavily muscled, slammed the front door shut. Now the room was a twilight nightmare—only the flickering television screen provided light.

Jacking tourists was a time-honored tradition amongst Florida criminals. Major and Nelson, both career criminals, were counting on the odds. Having been imprisoned numerous times, the two men were certain their luck had changed. After a couple of trial runs, which netted them enough cash for the drugs they craved, they felt that they had practiced their routine down to an art. And, following their successful streak of heisting unwitting visitors of the Sunshine State, they both had settled on hotel robbery as their golden ticket.

In fact, they'd successfully robbed a nun just two days earlier. They got a kick out of that. "Don't want *none*, ain't never had *none*," Nelson said, then paused dramatically for the punch line. "And ain't gonna get *none*." He always made sure to emphasize the word "none," which brought the house down. Well, at least it made Major laugh.

The day before they robbed the nun, they'd jacked a businessman. Now they were casing hotels again when they saw this little dude walking to his room. Nelson, forty-eight years old, winked at his younger cousin. The guy appeared to be preoccupied. Most of all, he looked weak. They had no doubt that this would be another quick score.

"Let's do it, bro," Nelson whispered.

They had no way of knowing it, but in this case, they'd picked the wrong victim. "[They] stuck a gun to my head and demanded money," Robey later said. "[They] told me to [get] down on the bed and I gave them my wallet. I assumed they were going to shoot me...and rape my daughter."

So far, the intruders hadn't realized there was a second person in the room. Sarina had burrowed beneath the covers when the men entered. She peeked out and stared wide-eyed at the scene unfolding in front of her. Her father sat on the other bed with a gun pointed at his head.

Can this really be happening? she probably thought.

In 1987, as the Florida legislature seemed poised to pass Florida's Right to Carry Law, the *Miami Herald* predicted disaster: "[A] pistol-packing citizenry will mean itchier trigger fingers...South Florida's climate of smoldering fear [will] flash like napalm when every stranger totes a piece and every mental snap in traffic could lead to the crack of gunfire." The "Gunshine State," according to the pundits, would become a statewide Dodge City.

The legislature ignored the predictions and passed the law. A coalition of Republicans and Democrats voted for the bill and Governor Bob Martinez signed it into law. A second bill, passed several years later as a companion piece, was commonly called "10-20-Life."

The 10-20-Life Law mandates that a felon will serve ten years without parole for any crime in which the offender has a firearm in his possession.

He will serve twenty years if the gun is discharged during the commission of a crime. If someone is shot, the felon will serve life in prison without the possibility of parole.

The rationale behind the two laws was simple: law-abiding citizens will obey gun laws while lawbreakers will ignore those same laws. Statistics collected over two decades show that almost everyone who obtains a concealed carry permit obey existing gun laws. In fact, the state has issued nearly one-and-a-half million permits—only 165 of those have been revoked, because a permit holder committed a gun crime.

Those same statistics show that recidivists commit more than 75 percent of all violent crimes. Taking them off the streets for long periods reduces crime. In fact, by 2004, violent gun crime rates in Florida had fallen by 30 percent.

The dire predictions for gun battles in the streets between permit holders never materialized. While thousands of Florida citizens carry concealed firearms every day, they generally obey existing laws.

Even many of the leading opponents of concealed carry laws admitted they were wrong. Hundreds of permit holders have used guns to stop violent crimes. When a deranged assailant stabbed two department store employees, a woman pulled a handgun from her purse and stopped the attack. She had a concealed carry permit. In January 2009, a permit holder shot and killed an armed assailant who tried to rob him at a car wash in Orlando. In Fort Myers, two masked ex-cons attempted to rob a pharmacy. When one jumped over the counter waving a firearm, the pharmacist, a permit holder, pulled his own gun and killed the assailant. The second man was held at gunpoint until police arrived.

Guns are a fact of life in Florida.

As in other places, they can be used for good or evil.

Each year, Florida hosts more than sixty million visitors. Whole segments of the state's economy are dependent on tourism. And while local

Chambers of Commerce and state officials would never admit it, many of the state's taxes seemed designed to fleece the travelers.

Tourism is vital to Florida's economy.

But in the 1980s and 1990s, a series of disasters rocked the state's tourist industry, causing visitors to question whether it was safe to visit the Sunshine State.

It began with the Mariel boatlift in which Cuba's premier Fidel Castro unloaded thousands of criminals onto the south Florida shores. It didn't take long for many of these desperados to end up in Florida's prisons. However, the brutality of some of their crimes shocked even the most hardened cops.

Then there were the so-called "Cocaine Cowboys," drug dealers from Jamaica who fought pitched battles on the streets of Miami.

Once the Cowboys were rounded up, Hurricane Andrew came calling. The devastation was shocking, but even a Category 5 hurricane couldn't dry up the tourist tree like the series of murders that began in 1993.

Uwe-Wilhelm Rakebrand, a German tourist, was the first to die, shot to death by robbers as he left Miami International Airport in a rental car. A few weeks later, Barbara Meller Jensen, another German, was murdered when she got lost and drove her rented car into the Liberty City ghetto. Soon foreign visitors were being slaughtered on a monthly basis.

A favorite technique of south Florida criminals was the "bump and rob" heist. (It was easy to spot tourists, because rental car license plates always had a unique "Y" or "Z" in the series of letters and numbers etched into the tags. If that wasn't enough, cars also sported stickers advertising the rental car company.) Once robbers zeroed in on a tourist, they drove behind the car and bumped it. When the driver pulled off the road to exchange insurance papers, she was relieved at gunpoint of all her cash, credit cards, jewelry and cameras. In a matter of seconds, the robbers were gone.

They had the bump and rob down to an art, but Florida criminals also targeted hotels, restaurants and stores near airports.

The 1990s crime wave intensified when two British tourists were shot at a roadside rest stop near Tallahassee. Gary Colley and Margaret Jagger had stopped to take a nap in their rental car before driving to south Florida when three teenagers with long rap sheets brandished handguns and ordered the travelers out. When the sleepy victims didn't respond quickly enough, the teens opened fire, killing Colley and wounding Jagger. The murderers later stated that they'd seen the rental car bumper sticker and figured the victims would quickly hand over their money.

This crime sparked an international backlash. "Slaughter in the Sunshine State!" screamed the headlines. In an article for *Investor's Business Daily*, Michael Fumento quoted the titles of several British tabloids: "Gunned Down Like Animals!"; "Shot Like a Dog"; "Come to Sunny Florida and be Murdered for Absolutely Nothing"; "Plan Your Trip Like a Commando Raid." Soon, American newspapers were also denouncing the violence.

The British government issued a warning to visitors advising them not to visit Florida. Germany followed suit and other countries across the globe joined in.

When tourism dropped by 20 percent, the boycott got the attention of Florida officials.

At first, tourism officials cranked up the spin machine. The Greater Miami Convention and Visitors Bureau hired a high-profile public relations firm and an advertising agency. They started by disseminating the view that "tourists are safer than Florida residents." It was almost slapstick. The spin machine did nothing to quell the concerns of tourists—in addition, Floridians began to wonder how safe *they* were.

The next tactic was for Miami to change its advertising slogan from "Miami—the city with a rhythm all its own" to the much more bland "Miami—spirit of the sun." Predictably, this blatant attempt to influence public opinion also failed.

In addition to the public relations campaign, an advertising blitz was launched. The public relations firm ran advertisements in major newspapers and in high-profile television markets throughout the country. The heart of their argument was that the tourist murders were overplayed by the media. In fact, they used sympathetic reporters and local editors to shill statistics that "proved" tourists were among the safest people on earth.

While tourism officials attempted to stick a band-aid on the bleeding, legislative efforts were more effective.

In a special session, the Florida legislature proposed that more than 20,000 new prison beds be built. Funding was allocated and within a few years, several new facilities were indeed constructed. In another move, lawmakers passed laws requiring that all violent offenders be required to serve a minimum of 85 percent of their sentences instead of 25 percent. The theory was that most criminals who are convicted of violent crimes are repeat offenders—if recidivists are locked up until they are too old to commit additional crimes, the crime rate will decrease.

The Department of Transportation was ordered to stop issuing the infamous "Y" and "Z" license plates. And rental companies were encouraged to stop placing bumper stickers and other advertising insignia on their cars.

Other attempts to remedy the problem included adding more police officers to local forces, instituting a rest area security system with armed guards and setting up a "Tourist Robbery Abatement Program," also known as TRAP.

All of these methods worked, at least to a degree.

Tourists continued to be robbed and murdered, but not at the rate of one death per month.

By 2002, ten years after the new systems were put in place, the laws and the spin machine had done their job. Florida once again was the beloved Sunshine State. "Its [sic] so cold everywhere else," read the new slogan, "and its [sic] warm and beautiful here."

Steven Robey sat on the edge of the bed with a pistol pointed at his head. He tried to keep his eyes from straying to the other bed where his daughter hid beneath the covers. So far, the intruders hadn't noticed her.

Ernest Major seemed unable to speak without screaming. And while his vocabulary was limited, he was proficient in the use of profanity. Steven knew this was meant to intimidate him and he was certainly frightened.

Major demanded Steven's wallet and car keys. But as he reached into his pocket, he wasn't fast enough. The intruder, still holding the gun to his victim's head, groped at Steven's back pockets and jerked out the wallet. Then he reached into the front pocket and located the car keys.

Steven, a family man, thought of his wife, son and his second daughter who had remained in New Smyrna Beach. They were all working, so only Sarina was available to help him in his search for a new home for the family.

Real estate magazines, business cards and newspaper classified ads lay on a table beside Steven's bed. A bank bag also lay on the bed. It contained more than nine thousand dollars in cash, enough to make a quick down-payment if he found a house he liked.

Because of the large amount of cash he was carrying, Steven was armed. He'd hidden a .45-caliber model 1911 semiautomatic handgun beneath his pillow. Six cartridges were in the magazine—none in the chamber.

Later he spoke to a detective about his decision to carry a gun. "The only reason I even got a concealed [weapons] permit," Steven said, "[was because] I went to a Tampa gun show and I tried to buy a rifle for target practice and they wouldn't even sell me a rifle cause I didn't have the permit. I [usually] choose not to carry a gun...but I just thank God that I had [it] with me this time."

In Florida, residents and tourists with a clean record can obtain a permit, or license, to carry concealed weapons. At any given time, tens of thousands of Floridians are secretly armed. They carry handguns in their pockets or their purses or even in holsters specifically designed to remain unobtrusive.

As Steven sat on the bed, Major noticed the bank bag. He picked it up, unzipped it and rummaged through the envelopes and papers in the bag. Somehow he missed seeing the cash. Cursing, he flung the bag back down beside Steven.

"Lay down!" he yelled.

Steven complied, dropping facedown on the bed.

Suddenly Sarina coughed. The sound startled Nelson, who was standing near her bed.

"Jesus," he swore. "Come out of there."

Fear paralyzed Sarina. She couldn't move.

Major turned away from Steven and raced across the room. Snatching the covers, he grabbed Sarina's arm and jerked her off the bed. She thought about trying to make a dash toward the door, but he pointed the gun at her.

While Major took charge of Sarina, Nelson moved over to cover Steven. The assailant kept his right hand in his pocket and Steven assumed he had a handgun hidden there.

"Don't you dare move!" Nelson said, glaring at his victim. But occasionally he glanced back at Major who was tugging at Sarina, forcing her toward the bathroom.

Steven took advantage of the confusion to reach underneath his pillow and grab his gun. Using the pillow for cover, he chambered a round and clicked the safety off. With all the shouting and scurrying around, the assailants never heard the rack of the gun as the cartridge slid into the barrel. As Major manhandled his daughter, Steven saw Nelson reach into his waistband. Convinced that his assailant planned to kill them both, Steven jumped up off the bed. Gun in hand, he charged toward the intruders.

Even in the twilight, he saw the panic in Nelson's eyes. The assailant, who had been standing over Steven, tried to back away, but the intended victim was able to squeeze off a round at almost point-blank range.

It sounded like a bomb exploding in the tight room.

"I fired at [the one closest to me] then this guy come running out [of the bathroom] shooting at me so I just kept firing at him..."

Major's little .22 sounded like a popgun compared to the massive reverberations of the .45.

Bang. Bang.

BOOM BOOM BOOM.

Sarina slammed the bathroom door and ducked behind the toilet. Steven heard her shrieking and prayed to God that she wouldn't be hit. He fired again and again as Major emptied his own gun in wild bursts.

Nelson backpedaled toward the other bed. In the half-darkness, the smell of cordite and the rocking explosions of the gunshots added to a surreal disbelief in Steven's mind. It seemed like just a minute ago that he was trying to get Sarina up so they could start their day.

As suddenly as they began, the guns went silent.

Somewhere far away, as if in a wind tunnel, Steven heard Sarina's screams. He tried to squeeze off another round, but nothing happened. He knew he'd run out of ammunition and assumed that his attacker had, too.

His next thought was to run outside and get help. "I assumed that I didn't hit either one of them cause they both [started] coming at me," he later said. "I kept trying to get out the door and they kept trying to [keep] the door shut. I didn't realize they had locked the bolt."

As Steven attempted to open the door, Nelson and Major attacked him. One of them punched him in the back of the head, knocking his face against the door. Knowing this was a life or death struggle, Steven wheeled around toward his assailants.

Using his gun as a club, Steven slammed it into Major's head. The intruder let out a howl, then began punching Steven in the face.

"I was hitting them as hard as I could, anywhere I could," he said. "[I hit them] with both my fist and the .45 cause...I knew they were gonna kill me if I didn't. So when one went down, I just kept pounding and the other one went [down] and I just hit him in the head too just as hard as possible...I know I hit him in the head, because I could see the skull under his flesh."

After knocking Nelson down, Steven again tried to open the door. But Major grabbed him and pulled him back. Steven hit his assailant again, then attempted once more to get to the door.

Blood gushed from Major's head. The intruder was grimacing, but he still came forward.

"I just kept trying to get away from them," he later told the detective. "And they were bound and determined I was not going to open that door. And I had just taken my blood pressure pills [because] I have extremely high blood pressure. I'm surprised that I'm sitting here now."

His second attacker went down again and Steven finally figured out that they had dead-bolted the door when they'd first entered. He unlocked it and stumbled out into the parking lot.

The sunlight nearly blinded him. But once he made it outside, Steven began yelling for someone to call the police. A woman on an upstairs balcony implored him to put the gun down. "My son's out walking," she said. "Please don't shoot him when he comes back."

Steven didn't even realize he was still holding the gun. He placed it on the hood of his car.

Suddenly, Steven saw one of the robbers lurch out of the room and stagger towards a gold car. It was Ernest Major. He was bleeding from the head and blood stained his shirt as he climbed into the car and drove off.

Sarina stood in the bathroom listening to the silence. She didn't know what was happening. Maybe her father had been shot. She cracked open the bathroom door. "I didn't hear anything else," she later told detectives. "So I [cracked] open the bathroom door to see if I could see anything, because the mirrors reflect the room. And I was looking into the mirrors and there was a man laying on the floor so I ran outta the room...My dad was standing in the parking lot yelling for someone to call the cops. And my dad told me to get the license number cause the other guy, the guy that came in first, was driving away."

In her panic, Sarina was unable to memorize the number. Instead, she ran into the hotel office.

Theresa Blue, a guest at the motel, was in the office when Sarina burst in. Later she told Detective Kevin Ferry: "[Sarina] came running in behind me screaming, 'Call the police. Call the police.' And she was, you know, nervous and she had her pajamas on...And she sat down on the sofa and [said her Dad had been robbed] and of course we were all just kind of in shock. And I thought I gotta get up and help this kid."

As the clerk called police, Blue walked over to the sofa and sat down beside Sarina. "I went over and I sat down next to her and I put my arms around [her]. I said, 'It's gonna be okay,' cause she was hysterical. And that's the way I remained for, like I think, forty-five minutes till the police came..."

Sarina told the guest that the robbery was a nightmare, that it was seared in her mind and would never go away. To add to the horror, she stated that when she came out of the bathroom, she'd had to step over a dead man to get out of the room. While she had been in the bathroom, she said, she heard bullets thudding into the walls and was sure she would be killed.

Blue later told Detective Ferry that Sarina was "a smart little cookie" and that she was impressed with how the teenager had held herself together in a life-or-death situation.

Lee County Sheriff's Office Major Crimes Robbery Unit responded to the barrage of 911 calls from hotel staff and patrons. At approximately 9:45 A.M., Detective Michael Rakestraw and Crime Scene Technician Phil Puglisi arrived at the scene. Sarina was in the office, but she was still verging on hysteria. Steven stumbled around the parking lot in a trance.

Spectators lined the second-floor walkway watching the scene unfold—more people were gathering in the parking lot. In the office, staff and patrons were still attempting to calm Sarina.

Rakestraw helped seal off the area around Room 104, where the crime had occurred. Then he and Puglisi opened the door. The first thing they noticed was a body lying motionless between the two beds. The room was a bloody wreck. Stained bedcovers lay on the floor. Bullet holes had penetrated the walls and doors and blood seemed to be everywhere.

After the detectives checked the room, a forensics team entered. They collected dozens of items including three .22-caliber projectiles embedded in the hotel room door; a .22-caliber revolver located on the floor between the double beds; blood located in the bathroom area and two .45-caliber bullets that had been fired into the bathroom door.

Phillip "New Wave" Nelson was so well-known to the Lee County Sheriff's Office that the first responding deputy identified him. Rakestraw suspected that Nelson's cousin and longtime partner-in-crime, Ernest Major, was the robber seen fleeing.

Rakestraw interviewed Steven and Sarina, then presented each victim with two photo lineups. Steven immediately recognized Major and Nelson. Sarina identified Major, but was uncertain about Nelson.

A few minutes after receiving the call about the hotel shooting, dispatch received a second call. Deputy Vallie Arvin arrived at a nearby residence to find a wounded man inside a tan car. He spoke so softly that she could barely understand him. Arvin observed bullet wounds to his stomach, arm and leg. When she got close enough so that she could hear him, Ernest Major stated that he'd been robbed and shot and that "New Wave" was dead.

Arvin had heard about the attempted robbery at the motel and knew the suspect was lying. Paramedics arrived and transported Major to the hospital, while Arvin sealed off the car until a warrant could be obtained to impound it.

Major's girlfriend came out of the house. She stated that the car was a rental that she used for business. She had given Major and Nelson strict orders not to drive it, because she suspected that they would use it to commit a crime. When she awoke that morning, she discovered that they had gone into her room and stolen the car keys. She told Arvin that she knew immediately that "something bad was going to happen."

After obtaining a search warrant, officers impounded the car. Two black ski masks were found along with a holster for a small-caliber handgun. Blood was smeared on the driver's door handle and the center console. Deputies also found a driver's license belonging to Ernest Major.

Detective Rakestraw drove to the hospital and attempted to interview Major. However, the suspect wouldn't speak—he'd been arrested so many times that he knew to request an attorney. Later that afternoon, the ex-con was charged with one count of armed robbery with a firearm, one count of felony murder and one count of attempted murder. He spent a week in the hospital in critical condition before recovering from his wounds.

In December 2003, Major was tried for a series of hotel robberies committed in the summer. In addition to the attempted robbery and murder of Steven and Sarina Robey, he was tried for the armed robbery of Episcopalian nun Sister Carol Andrew. He was convicted of all charges and sentenced to life in prison without the possibility of parole.

Ernest Major is currently serving a life sentence at Okeechobee Correctional Institution.

Phillip Nelson died on the floor of Room 104 at the motel in North Fort Myers. As one of the detectives observed, "You live by the gun, you die by the gun."

Steven Robey was not charged with any crime.

Florida criminals know that many Floridians carry concealed weapons. Therefore, the favorite target for many crooks are tourists and visitors to the

Sunshine State. As in this case, the two serial robbers targeted hotels. It just so happened that Stephen Robey was a Floridian with a concealed carry permit. His actions no doubt saved the lives of himself and his daughter. But as long as Florida's tourism industry is alive and well, there will be predators trolling the crowds looking for more victims.

Chapter 11
Stone Cold

"She was a beautiful little girl with a smile that would shine and innocent like a little angel. She was my daughter, my only child. And together, we traveled through the story that was life."

Deweese Eunick-Paul, mother of Tiffany Eunick.

At 10:30 P.M., one summer evening, the phone rang at the Fort Lauderdale Police Department's 911 Center.

"I have a child," the caller calmly stated. "She looks like she's not breathing. I tried to do CPR."

The dispatcher was surprised at the lack of emotion. He asked the caller her name. Kathleen Grossett-Tate identified herself and said that the child, Tiffany Eunick, was a friend. She explained that she was babysitting the girl.

"Is [Tiffany] breathing?" the dispatcher asked.

"No, she's not."

"Are you next to her right now?"

"Yeah. Uh, she has some food and that's all that was coming out of her mouth."

Since the call came from a Pembroke Park address, the dispatcher scrambled paramedics and deputies from the Broward County Sheriff's Office.

"She's not breathing," Grossett-Tate repeated.

"Does she have a pulse?"

"She's cold."

"She's cold? When did you see her awake?"

After a pause, the caller said, "I was sleeping. [Tiffany] was down here about three hours ago. She was down here watching television with my son."

The dispatcher noticed again that Grossett–Tate was calm. Too calm. He'd received dozens of calls about dead or dying children. Almost without exception, the caller was hysterical and incoherent.

"Do you want to try CPR?"

"Uh, yeah."

"Okay."

The dispatcher heard the caller start CPR again. Approximately three minutes later, the first paramedics arrived at the townhouse.

What they found would become fodder for one of the most sensational stories of the decade. And a child would become a "cause célèbre" for those who felt the criminal justice system was too harsh on juvenile offenders.

Pembroke Park had been pastureland until it was incorporated in 1957. The land area for the whole town was just one square mile and, by 1999, there were about 4,000 residents. Residents shopped in nearby Hollywood or Hallandale. Pembroke Park had no police force and was served by the Broward County Sheriff's Office.

Kathleen Grossett–Tate lived with her twelve-year-old son, Lionel, in a fashionable townhouse on the edge of town. A Jamaican immigrant, she was ambitious and anxious to achieve the American dream. She was a member of the Florida National Guard and had served a tour of duty during the 1991 Gulf war. At times, because of her military obligations, her son had stayed away from her with friends or relatives for a year or more.

Just three weeks before Tiffany's death, Kathleen met an old acquaintance, Deweese Eunick-Paul. They shared a lot in common. Deweese was a flight attendant and was also determined to enjoy the good life in southern Florida. She was a responsible employee, very religious and regularly took her daughter to church.

One thing they both required was help in caring for their children, because of the odd shifts they worked. The friends discussed the possibility of babysitting each other's kids and felt it would be to their mutual benefit.

Six-year-old Tiffany Eunick had warm eyes and a smile that lit up a room. She liked to wear pigtails—news photographs would later show a slim pretty girl smiling into the camera. She loved school and earned high grades. Her mom was pleased with her daughter. Tiffany was going to go somewhere in life.

On July 28, Deweese asked Kathleen to babysit her daughter while she worked. In return, Eunick-Hall promised to return the favor for Grossett-Tate's twelve-year-old son, Lionel. Deweese felt perfectly safe leaving Tiffany in the care of Kathleen—after all, her friend was a Florida state trooper.

The week before, Tiffany had learned several new songs at a church camp. Deweese heard her daughter singing as she walked out of her house and down the driveway to meet her friend.

As they drove, Tiffany, still upbeat after her camping experience, told her mom's friend that she was looking forward to a trip to Disney World that weekend.

When Kathleen and Tiffany arrived at the townhouse, they were met by Kathleen's son. At six feet tall and nearly 170 pounds, Lionel had the physique of a grown man. In fact, he still had not shed all his baby fat. He was watching cartoons, so Tiffany sat on the sofa next to him while Kathleen fixed supper. After eating, she told her son to watch Tiffany. Then she went upstairs to take a nap. After she left, Lionel turned on *The Flintsones* and later watched a cartoon entitled *Cow and Chicken*.

Sometime during her sleep, Kathleen heard a thumping from somewhere downstairs. It sounded like children running. Groggy, she didn't get up, but yelled for the two young people to stop making noise.

A few minutes later, a thud awoke her. This time she got out of bed, cracked the door and asked Lionel what was going on. While standing in the doorway, Kathleen heard Tiffany moaning. She didn't see the child, but her son stated that the girl was rolling around on the floor. Kathleen later testified that she thought Tiffany was sleeping on the floor and having a nightmare. She yelled for her friend's daughter to shut up. "If you don't," she said. "I'll come down and beat your butt."

Kathleen then closed the door and went back to bed. She soon drifted off to sleep.

She awoke to find her son standing over her, looking frightened. "Tiffany's not breathing," he said.

Kathleen rushed downstairs and found the lifeless body of her friend's daughter sprawled out on the living room floor. Later, she told police that she checked for a pulse, then attempted to resuscitate Tiffany. The child had vomited and was cold to the touch. Kathleen told investigators that she immediately called 911.

Police, however, weren't satisfied with her recall of the events.

As the case developed, detectives theorized that Kathleen had quickly concluded that Lionel had done something to harm Tiffany. She also called a co-worker at the Florida Highway Patrol before calling 911. A man rumored to be a former lover of Grossett-Tate's was later questioned by investigators. His answers were vague and shed little light on the investigation. At first he informed detectives that he never went inside the residence. In actuality, it was only when confronted by investigators that the man admitted that he did indeed enter the house. What he did there was never fully established.

Paramedics arrived within five minutes of Kathleen's call. According to one of the medics, he noticed a blood-soaked pillow lying on the sofa. Kathleen insisted that Tiffany had choked to death when vomiting the food she had eaten that night.

There were few outward signs of violence on Tiffany's body. Paramedics noticed a small bruise on her face and two more on her torso. Still performing CPR, they loaded her in the van and rushed her to the hospital.

A few minutes after 11:00 P.M., Deweese Eunick-Paul received a call at work. It was Kathleen. According to Deweese, her friend asked if Tiffany had asthma. When Deweese responded that Tiffany was perfectly healthy, Kathleen stated that her daughter was not breathing.

The statement rocked Deweese. Her knees went weak and she sank to the floor. She wailed and screamed and sobbed into the phone. Finally, Deweese calmed down and raced to the hospital.

There she learned that her daughter was dead.

Tiffany had never regained consciousness.

At first, investigators worked on the theory that Tiffany's death was due to natural causes. During an interview on the night she died, Lionel said that Tiffany had vomited, then lay down on the floor and went to sleep. Sometime later, he noticed she wasn't breathing and went up and got his mother.

Ken Kaminsky, a detective for the Broward County Sheriff's Office, stated, "We honestly believed [that] the child died of some kind of natural causes or some sort of accidental death. There was nothing to indicate whatsoever at the time of Tiffany's death that she died of foul play." However, during the initial interviews, cops were troubled by their perception that Grossett-Tate and her friend would not provide concise, detailed answers to their questions.

The autopsy report came back the following day.

It stunned the investigators.

Tiffany hadn't choked on her vomit or died of asthma. Instead, according to the medical examiner's office, she'd been murdered—brutally and systematically murdered.

Lisa M. Hannagan, M.D., Associate Medical Examiner, reported finding more than thirty-five internal injuries to the child. These included a cracked skull, brain hemorrhages, including multiple contusions of the left temporal lobe of the brain and cortical contusions of the left superior frontal lobe, lacerated liver and acute hemorrhaging of the inside chest area. Hannagan listed "homicide" as the cause of death.

Two days later, investigators questioned Lionel again. This time, he informed them that he and Tiffany had been playing tag together. "We were running in the house," Lionel said, "and I grabbed her like [we were] playing tag." Then he said he ran up behind Tiffany and clutched her to him, pinning her arms down to her side. He squeezed her, he said, but didn't think it was hard enough to harm her.

According to Lionel's second story, Tiffany ran into the bathroom and vomited. She came back out and lay down on the floor. After a few minutes, she went to sleep with her head on a pillow. Lionel asserted that at some point Tiffany's head flopped off the pillow. He said he "went to put it back on" and she hit her head on the edge of a coffee table. Shortly after moving her, he heard her yell, "Ow!"

Lionel told detectives that he hadn't told his mother about the injuries Tiffany suffered when she hit her head, because he thought he would get in trouble.

His story didn't make sense. Kaminsky now believed that Lionel had assaulted Tiffany and was lying to cover up the crime.

The following day, twelve-year-old Lionel Tate was arrested for the murder of Tiffany Eunick.

The more investigators learned about Lionel, the more troubling the case became. Here was a sixth grader who seemed unmanageable and yet whose mother never seemed to notice. As his body grew, his mind and moral compass lagged far behind.

Even in elementary school, Lionel was known as a bully and a disruptive force. He was known to pick on younger children. But he ran from older, more powerful kids. When teachers attempted to discipline him, his mother always took his side. According to educators, Grossett–Tate sometimes came to school for conferences wearing her state trooper uniform complete with her badge and gun—teachers thought she was trying to intimidate them.

When he was nine, Lionel moved to Mississippi to live with his father and his stepmother. While there, he attended elementary school. He lived there for a year until his father sent him back to Florida to live with his mother.

During that year, Tate terrorized classmates. Charlotte Stockstill, his fourth grade teacher, told reporters that he was uncontrollable. "He was kind of a loner," she said. "He was very loud and boisterous...like a bull in a china shop. He was almost out of control."

While doing group activities in class, Stockstill said that "nobody wanted to work with him." When she assigned him to a group, she stated that it "wouldn't be fifteen minutes and he'd be dragging his desk away, slamming his books." When he got into trouble, "he would usually hit the walls, stomp his feet and then totally withdraw into himself." Tate was suspended or written up fifteen times.

Eventually, Lionel's stepmother insisted that her husband send the disrespectful, troublesome youngster back to his mother.

Once he returned to Florida, the boy's behavior didn't improve. Lionel attended Watkins Elementary School in Hollywood. His fifth grade teacher said he was constantly doing things to antagonize other students. "One week he couldn't stand Boy X, and the next week it was Girl X, and it was a constant. Nobody liked him, that's what the children told me. Nobody wanted to sit next to him, because he stole their things—pencils, books, anything he could get his hands on. And under his breath, he would say things to the students, and they would become incensed and enraged and yell and scream."

All in all, Tate was a teacher's nightmare. In fact, one educator described him as the "worst student" she'd had in thirty years of teaching.

What investigators initially thought was an accidental death had turned into something much more sinister. Detectives were now convinced that Tiffany had been murdered in cold blood.

From the detectives' viewpoint, the case was complicated by the fact that Lionel's mother refused to even consider that her son might be guilty of any crime. She continued to insist that Tiffany's death was either accidental or from natural causes. Almost immediately, she hired one of south Florida's most flamboyant attorneys to defend her son. Jim Lewis, known for coming to court wearing leather-fringed jackets and bolo ties with Indian pendants, would be instrumental in catapulting the case into a national obsession.

Ken Padowitz, assistant state attorney, was chosen to be the lead prosecutor. He dreaded taking a twelve-year-old to court. No one, not even a prosecutor, could conceive of someone the age of Lionel going to prison for the rest of his life. On the other hand, the brutality of the crime cried out for justice.

Padowitz approached Lewis with the offer of a plea bargain. Much later, in a letter to the *Fort Lauderdale Sun Sentinel*, which was published in their September 17, 2002, edition, Padowitz explained his dilemma. "The evidence clearly supported the charge of first degree murder," he wrote. "I recognized the mandatory sentence for the crime was not appropriate in this case. The State Attorney's Office offered a plea to second degree murder with three years in juvenile detention, one year of house arrest and ten years of probation. Special conditions included one thousand hours of community service and psychological testing and counseling. It was rejected."

Padowitz claims that the defense was offered the plea deal many times. Again and again, he wrote, they turned it down. While many cops and others in the prosecutor's office thought the deal was top-heavy in favor of the suspect, Lewis, along with Grossett-Tate, seemed to think Tate would be found not guilty if the case went before a jury.

In fact, prosecutors felt Kathleen's conduct throughout the whole case was puzzling. She refused to consider what most insiders construed as a "sweetheart" deal, even though her son could be sentenced to life in prison

if he were convicted. Her continued insistence that he was innocent mystified cops and infuriated Tiffany's mother.

"I trusted a woman I thought was a caring mother," Eunick-Paul later
said. "I trusted a woman I thought would properly supervise my baby.
Kathleen says she went upstairs to sleep. She left my little first grader
with Lionel, at the time 179 pounds, alone, unsupervised... Kathleen knew
[that] Lionel had approximately twelve school suspensions or corporal
punishments for discipline problems over the last four years. Kathleen knew
he had trouble [with] fighting, destruction of property, [that he was] a
constant problem, always initiating [a] disturbance...Kathleen still left my
baby downstairs with him."

As the case moved inexorably toward a courtroom showdown, the
media whipped itself into a frenzy. Lionel Tate had become the hero of the
meta-narrative.

Deweese Eunick-Paul was rarely quoted. The preferred headline
seemed to be: "Child May Get Life in Prison." Anything that would make
Lionel Tate look guilty was not mentioned. Most Americans felt that he was
an innocent child who had accidentally killed his "playmate."

Then, when the defense team announced their unique trial strategy, the
case exploded onto the world stage.

The "wrestling defense" was the ace up their sleeve. According to the
defense team, wrestlers such as "Stone Cold" Steve Austin, Hulk Hogan, the
Rock and the Sting were Tate's heroes. While his mother was upstairs sleeping, Lionel and Tiffany were playing. Lionel decided to try out some
wrestling moves on Tiffany and, not knowing his own strength, accidentally
killed her. According to the defense, Tiffany was lying on the floor beneath
the stairs when Lionel jumped on her, like a wrestler leaping off a ring-post
onto his opponent. Lionel had seen the stunt a thousand times on
television. Even though he weighed nearly 170 pounds and she weighed
only forty-six, the defense contended that Lionel didn't realize that the leap

onto her body would harm her. Wrestlers, they said, did it all the time. So her death was, after all, nothing more than a tragic accident. This unprecedented defense, along with the age of the defendant, was just the type of case the media loves. For months, the story was front page headlines in every newspaper in the country. The cable news shows made it a daily staple and talk radio hosts and audiences couldn't get enough of it.

Just the thought of a twelve-year-old being locked up with hardened felons chilled most people. In the court of public opinion, Lionel would have quickly been acquitted.

On January 18, 2001, the spectacle began. Court TV carried the trial live as national and international news crews clogged the streets surrounding the Broward County courthouse. Media representatives fought for seats. The defense had threatened to call stars from WWE (World Wrestling Entertainment) as witnesses and many citizens showed up to see their idols.

Television stations in France, Japan, Germany and other countries also broadcast the trial live. The question everyone wanted answered was whether a child would receive a life sentence if convicted.

Judge Joel T. Lazarus presided over the proceedings. In the dock sat Lionel Tate, wide-eyed and nervous. Jim Lewis, his lawyer, seemed comfortable while District Attorney Padowitz looked tense and edgy.

Although the wrestling stars never showed up, the trial was a heavyweight slugfest from the outset. By the time it went to the cards, both fighters were bloodied.

Eleven days later, the jury returned a verdict. They weren't convinced by the defense's argument. Tears streamed from Lionel Tate's eyes as the foreman read: "Guilty." Reporters rushed in madhouse pandemonium for the doors. Outside, in front of banks of cameras and microphones, each of the reports had the same theme: Florida had done the unthinkable—it had convicted a child of first-degree murder.

The media and the public rose up in righteous indignation.

A few weeks later, though, as he sentenced Tate, Judge Lazarus had brought a sense of perspective to the grotesque scene: "Within...hours of the verdict," he said, addressing the court, "opening statements were being made in a new forum: the court of public opinion. Starting with the *Today Show* on that date and continuing unabated, there has been a barrage of appearances on talk shows, radio programs, pulpits in houses of worship and in any and every other forum imaginable. The media seemed to be trying this case for a second time in a court not governed by [the] laws of the state of Florida but by the feelings of sympathy and compassion for the young boy convicted of the highest offense known to mankind.

"And the effect was virtually immediate. Letters [arrived] from the north and south, east and west of this country. And these letters were almost universal in their tenor: have mercy on Lionel Tate, have compassion on this fourteen-year-old. The letters contained phrases such as 'horsing around,' 'boys will be boys,' 'playing,' and 'accident'...It is a truism that not one single letter writer or call-maker was privy to the horrific facts brought out during the trial, not one person sat through the pathetic testimony of the results of Lionel Tate's deeds upon the body of Tiffany Eunick..."

Judge Lazarus made it clear that he thought Tate had brutally murdered Tiffany Eunick.

Tate, now fourteen years old, was sentenced to life in prison.

The next day, one scribe articulated the sensibilities of many. Gary Kamiya published an article in the online publication *Salon Magazine* entitled "Childhood's End." It opened with two stark sentences: "Friday was a day of shame in America. A child was sentenced to life in prison."

That was the prevailing opinion on the case, both among Americans and internationally.

Tate was soon transferred to a maximum-security juvenile facility in order to await the outcome of his appeals.

He didn't adjust well. Within a few months, he was disciplined for fighting, using obscene language and disorderly conduct. In one violent outburst, he broke out a cell window. His mother Kathleen rushed to his defense. "Some [staff] at the jail are playing God," she said. She claimed that correctional officers were provoking Lionel, causing his outbursts.

Finally, after years of publicity, a "trial of the century" and the conviction and imprisonment of a child of first-degree murder, the story began to fade away.

But beneath the surface, a groundswell of lingering public sympathy and a barrage of legal appeals would soon free Lionel Tate.

Even with his freedom, however, the sad story would not end. In a stunning turn of events that had again garnered national headlines, Tate was released from prison.

Convicted of the murder of Tiffany Eunick, he'd spent three years in juvenile detention and was about to turn seventeen. During his incarceration, groups such as Amnesty International and the World Council of Churches organized massive letter-writing campaigns in an effort to have his conviction reversed. Thousands of interested citizens with no affiliation to any organization also got involved. Even the prosecutor agreed that life in prison without the possibility of parole was too harsh a sentence for the now teenaged killer. After several unsuccessful appeals, Lionel's murder conviction was overturned. An appellate court ruled that he may not have understood the charges against him. The District Attorney's office wasn't eager to retry the case, so the prosecutor offered him the same deal they'd initially proposed.

This time, he accepted.

It seemed as though Lionel Tate had dodged a bullet.

After agreeing to the deal, Tate was set free. For the next year, he would be under house arrest—after that, he would be on probation for ten years.

On September 4, 2004, a storm was brewing. Hurricane Frances had slammed into the Bahamas and was headed straight toward West

Palm Beach. With a huge eighty-mile-wide eye and wind speeds of more than one hundred miles per hour, it threatened to rip south Florida apart.

It wasn't a good time to be walking any street in south Florida. Especially at two-thirty in the morning.

On that night, coincidentally, a Broward County sheriff's deputy was cruising through Pembroke Park when he spotted two figures slouching along a deserted street. He stopped and asked their names.

The deputy later said they looked "sweaty" and were "panting," as if they'd been running. When asked what they were doing out on one of the most dangerous nights in recent memory, the teens told him they were "chasing girls."

According to the deputies, no girls were anywhere to be seen.

One of the teenagers was Lionel Tate. Since he was not supposed to be out of his house at that time of night, he gave the deputy a false name. When searched, it was found Tate was carrying a four-inch pocket knife. Another violation.

He was promptly arrested.

Judge Lazarus had explained during the plea deal that one violation could send Tate back to prison for life.

With that kind of time facing him, most people felt that Tate should have been grateful that the judge merely tacked on another five years to his probation for the knife incident.

In yet another case, later that year, three guns went missing from Kathleen Grossett-Tate's house. One of the guns, a 9mm Taurus Millenium, was her service revolver, owned by the state. The other two, a .40-caliber Beretta semiautomatic and a .357-caliber revolver, were her own.

The guns were never found, but cops suspected that Lionel took them.

Other incidents, including destruction of state property while awaiting trial on the probation violation charge, soured the public's perception of the once-sympathetic young man. Since his release, he'd broken his probation on at least two other occasions. In the criminal justice system, Tate was also down to his last chance.

One case in particular made headlines.

At 4:18 P.M., on May 23, 2005, a pizza delivery driver pulled up in front of an apartment complex nearby in Pembroke Park. A resident had called a pizza restaurant and ordered four pies.

Dressed in his striped uniform and carrying the pizzas, he walked up the stairs and knocked on the door. As always, he was cautious. There was no answer.

He stood there for a moment, then turned to leave. He later said he had a bad feeling about the call.

As he began walking down the steps, someone from the apartment yelled, "Hey!"

The driver reluctantly turned and started back. He saw the door crack open and suddenly he was staring down the barrel of a gun. He'd heard all the horror stories of pizza drivers who'd been assaulted or murdered for a few dollars in change. The networks had recently reported a story about a driver in Laurel, Maryland, who'd been kidnapped, robbed, tortured and mutilated. His killers still had not been caught. In the last few months, drivers across the country had been stabbed, beaten with baseball bats and crowbars and assaulted with fists.

A police report stated that when he saw the gun, the driver "immediately dropped the pizzas and ran down the corridor toward a stairwell where he tumbled down several steps, suffering minor injuries. He eventually made it to his car and back to the shop where he dialed 911."

A deputy picked him up and drove him back to the scene.

When they arrived, three people were sitting on the steps eating pizza.

The driver identified Lionel Tate as his assailant. Tate's own apartment was directly across the street from where the robbery took place.

After the driver identified Tate as the gunman, investigators questioned him. He admitted ordering the pizzas, but denied the robbery. (Police never located the gun, which the driver thought was a .38-caliber revolver.)

A twelve-year-old lived at the apartment where the robbery took place. In a videotaped statement, he told police that Tate had asked to use his phone to order the pizzas. Then Tate left for a few minutes. He told investigators that his neighbor returned and asked to enter the apartment to wait for the pizzas.

The boy said he knew Tate was going to rob the pizza driver, so he attempted to block his neighbor from entering the apartment. Tate pushed his way into the room and punched him several times. The boy broke away and ran into his mother's bedroom. Later, he claimed to have seen Tate rob the driver.

Soon after, he recanted his story.

Against his parole stipulations, Tate was also "hanging out" with two convicted felons. Willie "Little Will" Corouthers and Zawalski Edwards were both at the scene, either as participants or spectators. Both were Tate's friends. Corouthers' record dated back to 1982, with convictions for selling drugs, cocaine possession, burglary, grand theft and possession of a firearm by a convicted felon. Edwards had also spent time in state prison for drug and burglary charges.

Although neither was charged in the robbery of the delivery driver, Tate had sent Corouthers a text message earlier that day. "U still want to bust that lick after school?" he wrote. ("Bust that lick" is street language for committing a robbery.) Tate denied that the message had anything to do with the driver. He claimed it referred to a boy who was walking home from school. Still, to the investigators, the message showed intent to commit an armed robbery.

Tate was arrested and placed in the Broward County Jail.

As soon as the media heard about the child-killer's latest arrest, they rushed to back to Florida. That night, television newscasts once again echoed the name of Lionel Tate. The case would never end, it seemed. But this time, public opinion had changed. Previously publicized brushes with the law didn't help. While his mother and his paid attorneys continued to stand by him, many people now considered him a thug who would someday commit another violent crime if not sent back to prison.

A year later, Tate appeared in court to face the robbery charge. In a surprise move he pleaded no contest. Judge Lazarus sentenced him to ten years for the robbery and thirty years for violation of probation.

The judge who had originally sentenced Tate to life in prison had a few choice words for the prisoner: "In plain English, Lionel Tate," Lazarus said, "you've run out of chances. You don't get anymore."

By this time, Tiffany Eunick, the real victim in this case, had been dead and buried for nine years. Her mother handled the nightmare with dignity. Deweese had approved the original plea bargain and later plea agreements, even though a psychiatrist who examined him claimed Tate had a "high potential for violence, uncontrolled feelings of anger, resentment and poor impulse control."

As Tate accepted the plea deal, Tiffany's teary-eyed mother spoke to him. "I firmly believe in God and I believe in forgiveness," she said. "I so much believe in God and for that I have forgiven you, Lionel."

Lionel Tate is currently serving his time in Martin Correctional Institution in Indiantown, Florida.

When fourteen-year-old Lionel Tate was tried as an adult for first-degree murder, Florida was vilified. No one wants to see a child in prison with adults. Enabled by the media, the public viewed Tate as a sympathetic figure—the real victim, Tiffany Eunick, was largely forgotten. The killer's "future dangerousness" was also largely ignored. And so, when he was released from juvenile prison after three years, the young thug almost immediately began getting in trouble again. Many states struggle with the problem of what to do with violent youthful offenders. If the crime is vicious enough, as in this case, some think the murderer should be punished. But most agree that after a few years, the killer should be placed back in society. It's a tough call, and real answers seem hard to come by. One of the reasons these crimes by children seem to be occurring in Florida at such a high level may be the rootless lifestyle of many people who leave family and friends to move south for the fun and sun. High rates of divorce, drug abuse and child abuse in all segments of the population contribute to this growing problem.

Chapter 12
The Tattoo Man

"Something isn't right here. I want you to follow that guy."

Detective Blevin Davis, speaking to Detective Donnie
Wiggen, concerning his suspicions about an ex-con.

Despite being a career criminal, Norman Mearle Grim never gave much thought to avoiding capture after committing his crimes. Because of that, he'd spent more than half of his twenty-eight years in prison. He was known to local police as an "impulse" predator—when he decided to rob or rape or murder, it didn't matter how many witnesses were around.

Grim stood five feet six inches tall and weighed 130 pounds. He had short brown hair and blue eyes shaded by prison issued goggle-type glasses. Grim lived in Milton, Florida, a bedroom community about thirty miles east of Pensacola.

Deputy Timothy Lynch responded to a call from Cynthia Campbell at just after five o'clock on the morning of July 27, 1998. She stated that her residence, which was next door to Grim's house, had been vandalized. The well-groomed bungalow was set back among old oaks.

Campbell, a well-known Pensacola attorney, was dressed in a sweatshirt and blue jeans. She was barefoot. The homeowner, Grim and Lynch walked to the back of her house. Lynch got the impression that she didn't know her neighbor well. Behind the house, they found a cracked window. Using his flashlight, Deputy Lynch searched the ground and located a chrome lug nut in the bushes.

"Probably a bunch of damn kids," Grim said. Even this early in the morning, it was muggy. He was wearing blue jean shorts and no shirt. Beneath a film of sweat, tattoos flowered his body. An intricate pattern of fire-breathing dragons covered his entire back and a weave of smaller dragons decorated his right arm and chest. In fact, around his neighborhood he was called the "Tattoo Man."

Lynch asked Campbell how she'd found out about the broken window. She said Grim had awakened her. After showing her the window, Grim asked her to come over to his house for coffee. Instead, she called the police.

"My dog woke me up," Grim said. "I shined my light outside and seen the broken window." He had a high-pitched voice, almost like a girl's.

Lynch wondered how Grim could spot the small crack in the darkness all the way across the yard. The cop asked Campbell to step inside her house.

Grim, who was not invited, waited outside. He seemed agitated. He kept rolling his eyes and sighing loudly as he paced back and forth in the yard.

Deputy Lynch checked the other windows in the house and found that the back kitchen window was also broken.

It all seemed improbable to Lynch. If rowdy teenagers were going to throw lug nuts or rocks at windows, it would be at the front of the house. He'd heard no report of vandalism in the neighborhood and doubted that it had occurred.

The deputy sat at the kitchen table and wrote his report. Then he and Campbell walked back outside.

Lynch was suspicious of Grim, but had no reason to arrest him. He told Campbell that he would request that the sheriff's department step up its patrol of the area at night.

As he left, he heard Grim ask Campbell to come over for coffee.

A blood-red sun was beginning to rise over Pensacola Bay when Deputy Lynch left the residence at 5:51 A.M.

At about 7:15 A.M., Connie Kelley parked her car in the driveway of Campbell's house. Kelley, a freelance paralegal who did work for the attorney, noticed that the front door to the house was wide open. She pulled out a file folder stuffed with legal briefs and proceeded up the walkway. The signing of the documents by Campbell was a weekly ritual, but today she was nowhere to be found.

Kelley called out her employer's name, but Campbell didn't answer. The employee was concerned. She knew her friend as a responsible person who never missed a deadline or an appointment. For several minutes, she knocked on the door and called Campbell's name. Finally, Kelley stepped inside, placed the files on a table and left.

As she drove away, she noticed that Campbell's car sat in the driveway.

At 8:20 A.M., another employee, Cindy McGee, arrived at Campbell's law office in Pensacola. She didn't have a key to get into the building. After waiting outside for nearly thirty minutes, McGee decided to drive to Campbell's house to see if anything was wrong. Like Connie Kelley had, she stood at the open door calling Campbell's name. A small dog was barking somewhere in a back room, but McGee couldn't see it. Finally, she stepped inside. The place just felt weird, like it had been abandoned.

McGee later said, "I knew something was wrong, so I went to her house. She always goes to work. That's all she does." After checking every room in the house and finding no one at home, she was worried. She telephoned Campbell's landlady, who called the police.

Less than ten minutes after receiving the call, Santa Rosa County Deputies Calvin Rutherford and Steven McCauley arrived. They retraced the employee's steps and, finding no sign of Campbell, walked over to Grim's house and knocked on the door.

It took several minutes before he opened the door. Grim wore shorts but no shirt and was sweating profusely. The deputies noticed a rust-colored stain on his shoulder. He kept glancing back into his house.

"Have you seen Cynthia Campbell?" McCauley asked.

Grim adjusted his prison glasses. "She came over earlier this morning," he said. "We had three or four cups of coffee, then she left."

"Did she say anything about where she was going?"

"Said she had to go to work. That's probably where she's at."

"Does she have another car?" McCauley asked, pointing to the late-model sedan sitting in Campbell's driveway.

"I dunno," Grim said. "Some kids broke out a couple of her windows. She was upset."

Rutherford, standing on the porch, attempted to peer inside the house. Grim noticed and blocked his view.

"Can we come in and look around?" Rutherford asked.

"No way, man," Grim answered with eyes blazing at the cops. "Maybe if you weren't so rude, I might let you in."

He stepped back inside and slammed the door.

McCauley and Rutherford walked to their cruiser. Rutherford pulled Grim's name up on the computer.

McCauley looked over his shoulder as Rutherford read the police file out loud.

"Robbery. Kidnapping. Burglary. Grand theft. Aggravated battery." The cops shook their heads.

"Anything else?" McCauley asked.

"Yeah, that's just for Florida," Rutherford said. "Guy served time in Texas, too. But it doesn't say what for."

McCauley pointed to the back of the house. Grim was inside a shed, working. Finally, he walked back into his house. After a few minutes, he came out the front door and motioned the deputies inside.

Checking Grim's house, McCauley and Rutherford found no sign of a struggle, but they did notice some dark spots on the kitchen floor. They continued through the house. On the back porch, they saw a car in the backyard. Rutherford walked over to the car and peered inside.

"May we have permission to search the trunk?" he asked.

Grim stuttered for a moment, then said, "My ex has the keys."

"You divorced?"

"I'd let you look," he nodded, "but I can't get in myself."

"Why not?"

"Bitch took the keys just to screw me over," Grim winked, as if he was divulging some deep dark secret.

Rutherford asked Grim for the name, address and telephone number of his former wife. The cop wrote the information on a pad.

Something smelled. Nothing seemed right. The attorney who, according to co-workers, was never late for an appointment had missed two within an hour. Her front door was wide open, her car still in the driveway and she was nowhere to be found. While it was always possible that she'd left voluntarily, a more sinister scenario seemed more likely.

Then there was Norman Grim. By his own admission, the little ex-con had been the last known person to see Cynthia Campbell. His evasiveness, the rust-colored spots on his shoulder, the brown drops on the kitchen floor, the refusal to open the trunk of his car and his very attitude pointed to foul play.

Based on his suspicions that Grim might be involved in the strange disappearance of Cynthia Campbell, Rutherford radioed for a detective to come to the scene.

Santa Rosa County Sheriff's Detective Blevin Davis soon arrived, followed by several uniformed officers and plainclothes investigators. One of the detectives, Donnie Wiggen, assisted Davis.

Davis made a quick survey of Campbell's residence. Nothing looked out of the ordinary, so he walked outside.

Norman Grim was standing near the street chain-smoking cigarettes. The detective's impression of the nervous ex-con was the same as Rutherford and McCauley's. Davis began walking toward him.

Suddenly, Grim collapsed onto the ground.

"What's wrong?" Davis asked.

"Gonna puke."

The detective led Grim to Rutherford's cruiser and told him to sit in the backseat. Davis observed the stain on the ex-con's shoulder and several reddish-brown stains on his shorts. He also noticed that Grim wasn't wearing a watch even though there was a "tan line" from a watchband on his left arm.

After a couple of minutes, Grim got out of the car and approached Davis. "I gotta go pick up my dogs," he said. "They're running loose on the street and I'm afraid they'll get hit by a car."

Davis informed Grim that he was free to leave. The ex-con walked into his house and came out smoking another cigarette. He walked to his car, (the one he claimed he didn't have the key for) started it and drove slowly through his yard and out onto the street. It almost seemed as if he was laughing at the cops.

Davis asked Wiggen to follow him and Wiggen began to tail Grim. The ex-con drove to a nearby park and loaded his two dogs into the backseat of his car, then he took a winding route to a convenience store. He went inside and came out holding a paper sack. Wiggen saw a carton of cigarettes sticking out of the bag.

Grim, holding a can of soda, walked over to Wiggen's car. "I ain't going nowhere," Grim said.

Wiggen followed as Grim left the store and headed south, away from his home. He got on Interstate 10, then pulled off onto Scenic Highway. Grim scrupulously obeyed all traffic laws, including using his turn signals. It wasn't exactly a slow-speed chase—more like a game of cat and mouse. Grim made a right-hand turn, then a left-hand turn, then proceeded for a mile or two and suddenly veered off onto a side street.

Wiggen flashed his lights several times, trying to get Grim to stop. However, the ex-convict continued on until the detective got caught up in traffic and lost sight of him.

At mid-afternoon, seven hours after Cynthia Campbell was reported missing, Chris Farrell was fishing from the Pensacola Pier. The pier is actually part of the old bridge that once connected Pensacola with the town of Gulf Breeze. Today, it runs adjacent to the modern four-lane bridge and is used by locals for fishing. The pier on the Pensacola side is about a mile-and-a-half long. One of the bridge's attractions is that it offers "drive-on" fishing.

A convenience store and bait shop sits at the foot of the bridge. It opens early and closes late, offering lures, live bait and refreshments. It even rents tackle to novice fishermen.

Farrell, hoping to catch a redfish, flipped his line into deep water. He immediately hooked something. It literally felt like a whale, he later said. As he struggled to reel it in, a huge object boiled to the surface. Although it was wrapped in sheets, shower curtains and trash bags, the fisherman saw the unmistakable outline of a corpse.

"It kind of gave me a flashback of a body bag in Vietnam," he later said.

Farrell told his son, who was fishing with him, to call 911.

It wasn't long before a boat from the Florida Marine Patrol arrived. Detective Blevin Davis, on hearing of the discovery of the body, sped to the scene. Investigators from other jurisdictions followed and the corpse was taken to the morgue.

The remains were quickly identified as those of Cynthia Campbell. As the medical examiner began the autopsy, Norman Mearle Grim was the only suspect.

Detective Wiggen drove to the bait store located on the pier and spoke with the manager. He remembered Grim, because of his small size and many tattoos. The suspect had come into the store sometime in the middle of the afternoon, he said. As proof, the manager produced a surveil-lance videotape and gave it to the investigator. A quick scan of the tape confirmed that the multi-emblazoned ex-con had entered the store a few minutes after two o'clock.

Investigators were still trying to track Grim down, but he'd disappeared. It was discovered that he was currently on probation from a prior burglary conviction, which gave cops a reason to arrest him once he was located.

As the search spread out to other states, detectives began interviewing people who knew him.

Grim had worked at a manufacturing company for four years. The business manufactured toolboxes, roof racks and other equipment for pickup trucks. His employer stated that Grim was a good worker. In fact, he was the "lead person" in the fabrication department, supervising nearly a dozen other workers.

While being interviewed, one co-worker stated that earlier that afternoon, she'd seen Grim on the bridge standing beside his car. The doors and trunk were open, she said. When asked how she could be sure it was Grim, she smiled and said he was easy to spot, what with all his tattoos.

The autopsy of Cynthia Campbell was performed by Dr. Michael Berkland. Janice Johnson, an investigator with the Florida Department of Law Enforcement, along with Detective Davis, were in attendance. As Berkland began to peel off the sheets and plastic bags, a piece of green carpet fell out. Davis recognized the carpet—he'd seen a similar strip hanging on the rail of Grim's back porch.

Once the layers wrapping the remains were removed, investigators got a look at Campbell's body. It wasn't pretty. She'd been brutally beaten, possibly with a hammer. The medical examiner counted at least eighteen injuries to her face and head. In addition, there were eleven stab wounds to her chest, one penetrating the heart. Additional trauma included a broken left wrist and bruises on her arms. "Defensive wounds," Berkland said.

A fighter all her life, Campbell had obviously struggled hard against her assailant.

There were also postmortem injuries to Campbell's sex organs.

Investigator Johnson and a team of forensic specialists drove to Campbell's house. While searching for evidence, they found the lawyer's home to be neat and clean. There were no signs of a struggle.

Grim's residence was a different story. Proof of foul play was everywhere. Two damp mops were soaked in what appeared to be blood. Dried blood was found on the floor and cabinets in the kitchen. It was obvious that Grim had tried to clean the area but couldn't remove all the stains. Later DNA testing proved that this blood matched that of Cynthia Campbell.

A trash bag with two bloody fingerprints was found on top of the microwave. The prints were later matched to Grim. Inside the garbage pail, the detective located a bloody pillow case that had the same design patterns as the sheets pulled off Campbell's body.

Johnson found additional evidence, including blood-stained shorts and shoes, in the dining room and living room.

In fact, Grim's whole house was a gold mine of evidence. Campbell's broken eyeglasses, along with other incriminating items, were found in a cooler on the back porch. In addition, a coffee cup found on a kitchen counter had Campbell's fingerprints on it.

DNA testing later matched Campbell's blood found on a pair of cutoff jeans in Grim's house. A bloody steak knife located in the cooler yielded DNA matching both Campbell and Grim. According to court documents, a "hammer found in the same cooler also yielded genetic markers consistent with the victim, as did swabbings from the mops found in the kitchen, from the kitchen floor and from the box of trash bags found on top of the microwave." Stains from another pair of shorts and a shoe found in his living room sealed the case against the ex-con.

After eluding Detective Wiggen, Grim had fled the state.

Three days later, he was arrested in Oklahoma.

Cynthia Campbell was an unlikely victim. Neighbors said she was friendly and outgoing. She regularly attended neighborhood barbecues. Connie Kelley, the paralegal who typed for Campbell, stated that she "was a real sweet girl, funny. She was hilarious and had a good sense of humor."

Campbell began her career as a registered nurse. After suffering a debilitating shoulder injury on the job, she changed careers. She attended law school and fifteen months before her death, she was accepted into the bar. In addition to having her own law office in Pensacola, Cynthia worked for a Milton law firm whose specialty was medical malpractice cases. Campbell had a special knowledge of both medical and legal issues. Because of that, she was a rising star in the west Florida legal community.

The only connection between Grim and Campbell seemed to be that they were neighbors. Media reports that Campbell had handled the Grims' recent divorce turned out to be untrue. A second rumor was that she had been murdered by a home-builder whom she had sued. Although she did take the company to court over what she described as a "defective" home she'd bought, investigators determined that there was no connection between that incident and her death.

Her friends and co-workers were stunned by her death.

"I think it's a tragic thing," her friend, T.A. Leonard, said. "I still don't understand it. She had fought hard to get where she was. She worked hard for everything she got."

As investigators dug into Grim's background, disturbing parallels in this case and his previous crimes became clear.

In 1981, he was arrested in Jacksonville for committing an armed robbery.

A year later, while Grim was awaiting trial for that crime, a Pensacola woman reported that she was walking to work when Grim got out of his car and grabbed her. He attempted to choke her, but she was able to break away. Grim refused to give up—he chased and caught her. Dragging her to his car, he threatened to kill her. Thinking quickly, the woman told Grim that she'd dropped her purse on the ground and if he murdered her, it could be used as evidence against him. He got out to retrieve the purse, leaving his keys in the ignition. As soon as he exited, she jumped into the driver's seat and drove away.

On the same day, just a few blocks away, a resident saw a small, heavily-tattooed stranger inside his home. The man chased Grim away. Never one to be deterred by the law or by common sense, he walked next door and attacked a woman with a knife. When she screamed for her brother to come to her assistance, Grim still refused to leave. It was only after the woman's brother entered the room and rushed toward Grim that he fled.

According to court documents, "in yet another incident, a fourteen-year-old female student was accosted as she walked to class, by a man in jogging shorts who dragged her into a wooded area near the school. She screamed, attracting the attention of a security guard who chased the man away. The victim's earrings had been torn from her ears and she was cut on her hands and elbows during the attack."

Norman Mearle Grim was arrested for the crimes. Police found two handguns and ammunition stolen from a home that was a only block from all the attacks.

He was sentenced to twenty-five years in prison for various crimes including kidnapping, robbery, burglary, carrying a concealed weapon and battery with a deadly weapon.

He served only eight years.

After he was released, he relocated to Texas, where he was convicted of burglary and theft. He served two years in a Texas prison, then he was released on probation to Florida. Grim moved to Milton.

As investigators continued to dig into his past, they found that he'd been discharged from the Navy for "unspecified reasons." Family members would only say that he "got in trouble." Grim had also served time for charges that included domestic battery and drug offenses. According to a psychiatrist who examined him while he was incarcerated, his drugs of choice were marijuana and LSD. He also drank so much alcohol that he developed an immunity to it.

At the trial, the evidence was so overwhelming that the defense was reduced to trying to prove it was planted by the "real" murderer. Bloody fingerprints, matching DNA, items from Grim's house that were found on

Campbell's body and items that she owned, such as her own glasses, that were found in his home, told a different story.

The jury took little time convicting him.

In the sentencing phase (in which Grim refused to participate), the defense claimed that he'd been abused by his father during childhood, that he had an antisocial personality and that he had an impulse-control disorder.

Circuit Judge Kenneth Bell didn't buy it. On December 21, 2000, he sentenced Grim to death for a "senseless and brutal" crime.

Campbell's parents, Ralph and Dorothea, flew from Pittsburgh, her hometown, to attend the trial.

"The way I look at it is [that] he committed a capital crime and murdered Cindy," her father said in an interview with the *Pensacola News Journal* on December 22, 2000. "And according to the laws of Florida, the penalty is death."

As the sad-faced father left the courtroom to return home, he mused on the futility of it all.

"I have talked enough," Ralph Campbell said. "You can go back and forth with this now until doomsday, [but] it won't change a thing."

Norman Mearle Grim, who caused so much suffering in his life, has never shown any remorse at all for the unprovoked, brutal murder of Cynthia Campbell.

He currently sits on Florida's death row, awaiting the outcome of his appeals.

This is yet another case where the killer, Norman Mearle Grim, should have been locked up. Because of his criminal past, prior convictions and obvious hostility toward women, he should have served his full prison term. He didn't, however, and Cynthia Campbell was his final victim.

Chapter 13
Death Row Granny

"If you shoot me, we'll all die."
Helicopter pilot, replying to hijackers.

Exactly one week before Christmas day, a helicopter lifted off from the Keystone Heights Airport. It was a six-seater and its purported mission was to fly some passengers to Lake City to look at real estate.

The passengers couldn't have been any more different. One, a petite, graying blonde, identified herself as "Josie" and spoke with an English accent. As soon as she entered the airport lobby, she began complaining. They were already late, she said, and they needed to leave immediately. When she saw the helicopter, she didn't like the fact that it was yellow. And when she learned there would be two pilots, she demanded that one be left behind.

The other woman was a brunette, much taller than Josie with a nice figure and pretty features. She didn't give her name and she couldn't have been more than thirty. The younger woman remained silent as the pilot, John Patrick, helped her load a suitcase into the chopper. The carry-on was constructed of silver aluminum and taped shut with gray duct tape. It was heavy, maybe about forty to fifty pounds.

When Josie had called to make arrangements for the trip, she said there would be five passengers—the others were to be picked up at Live Oak.

It was 2:30 P.M. All that winter in 1999, the weather in Florida had been quite warm, but a front was moving in from the northwest and cooler temperatures were expected.

Almost immediately after they became airborne, Josie said, "I know we're late, but can we fly over the city of Starke?"

"No problem," Patrick said. "It's right on our way."

The headset he wore, the vibrations inside the cab and the woman's English accent made it difficult to communicate. It didn't bother him, though—he was used to transporting odd characters across the north-central part of the state.

But he wasn't prepared for what happened next.

Less than five minutes into the flight, the younger woman ripped Patrick's headset off. Before he could look back, he felt the cold steel barrel of a gun pressed against the back of his head.

"Do exactly as I say," the woman said.

"Okay."

"Do exactly as I say and you won't get hurt," she repeated.

He nodded.

"Fly to Raiford prison," the younger woman said. Union Correctional Institution had purposely been built far away from towns and cities. The prison housed the worst of Florida's prison inmates and was also home to the nearly four hundred prisoners on the state's death row. Many were notorious for their brutal crimes: Bobbie Joe Long, the "Gainesville Ripper" Danny Rolling and the child-rapist and murderer Mark Dean Schwab.

The pilot had no choice but to comply with the demands of the younger woman. He "squawked" transponder 7500, which is the international alert for a hijacking. However, because the helicopter was flying at only a few hundred feet, the tower was unable to pick up the warning.

The younger woman handed Patrick a clipboard. Attached was a hand-drawn map of the prison complete with an "X" that marked the spot where the women wanted to land.

"Keep your hands on the controls," the younger woman said. Then, she placed a new set of headphones over the pilot's ears. They were attached to a tape recorder and she turned it on.

"Can you hear that?" she asked.

The pilot nodded.

The audiotape had been made by the Englishwoman. She ordered the pilot to fly directly over the prison grounds, drop the suitcase at a designated location in the recreation area and fly back to the perimeter of the institution. After landing on the other side of the outer fence, they were to wait for five prisoners to break out. Then they would fly to Jacksonville.

Patrick probably thought, *What have I gotten myself into?*

In addition to the hijacking, he had another problem—clouds were building in front of him, the first signs of the anticipated cold front. In fact, the skies ahead were purple, and in the distance, he could see bolts of lightning. If they kept going, they would head straight into the storm.

"Go to Starke," the younger woman ordered.

"I don't know the exact location," Patrick replied, trying to stall.

"You've got a lot of experience," the woman said. "Go to Starke." She pushed the muzzle of the pistol against his head.

Tension was building inside the chopper. He could smell the cold sweat of fear on all of them. The thwump-thwump-thwump of the blades sounded like a death rattle.

"Look up ahead," Patrick said. "We'll never make it through that storm."

As he spoke, a savage burst of lightning flashed up ahead and a peel of thunder rocked the chopper. It seemed to shock some sense into the women.

"Turn around," Josie ordered. "Go back to Keystone Heights." There was panic in her voice.

Before they could change their minds, the pilot veered the chopper back the way he came.

The younger woman grabbed the clipboard out of his lap, ripped up the maps and she jerked the earphones off the pilot's head.

"They won't be out in the yard anyway, what with the storm and all," Josie said, her voice shaking.

The pilot breathed a sigh of relief. It had been twenty minutes of hell, but now it was over.

Ronald Clark, Jr., was raised in Jacksonville. His mother and father separated when she suddenly declared that she was a lesbian. His father had regularly abused drugs and Clark began using before he became a teenager.

He was an equal-opportunity user—prescription drugs, hard drugs, anything he could get was fair game. He often drank as many as two twelve-packs of beer in a day. To support himself, he worked odd jobs and stole from friends. As he grew older, he moved into an abandoned school bus that was parked behind his father's house. When his father was working, Clark routinely ripped off the old man's stash of dope.

In 1984, he was sentenced to two-and-a-half years in prison for child molestation.

A year after getting out, he applied for a job on a shrimp boat currently docked in Fernandina Beach. The captain of the "Bloody Mary," however, knew of his reputation and wanted someone more dependable. He decided to hire someone else.

The day before the boat was to go out to sea, Clark picked up Charles McElroy Carter, the man who'd been hired for the job he wanted. With several friends, they went out drinking. A few hours later, Clark drove to a remote area where everyone got out of the car to urinate.

As they stood in the darkness relieving themselves, Clark pulled a sawed-off shotgun out of the car and shot Carter in the chest. As his victim lay unconscious, Clark walked up and shot him in the face with a deer slug. Then he took eleven dollars and Carter's boots.

After threatening his companions with death if they didn't keep quiet, Clark went back to the shrimp boat. When Carter didn't show up, he was reluctantly hired. He worked for the two weeks the boat was out to sea, then never came back to work again.

It took nearly a year before one of the witnesses came forward and identified Clark as the murderer. By that time, he'd claimed his second victim.

On January 12, 1990, Ronald Clark and John Hatch were hitchhiking from Yulee to Jacksonville. Ron Willis, driving a black pickup truck, stopped and gave them a lift. Clark was carrying a pistol that his friend had stolen earlier in the week. He whispered to Hatch that he intended to steal the truck.

According to court documents, "Hatch had Willis stop the truck at a point past a food store...there were no lights in the area where he stopped. According to Hatch, Clark then got out of the truck and walked toward the back of the vehicle. At that point, Clark started shooting Willis as he was inside the truck. Clark shot seven or eight times."

Clark pushed Willis into the middle of the seat and climbed in under the steering wheel. Hatch piled into the passenger side. They drove to a remote location and dumped the body. Clark took a wallet and cowboy boots from the victim. The next day they went back to the scene carrying cinderblocks and rope. Binding the body, they dumped it into the water off Nassau County Sound Bridge.

Later that day, they parked outside a motel. By that time, Willis's wife was searching for her missing husband. When she drove by the motel and saw the truck, she called police.

Clark and Hatch quickly confessed, each blaming the other for the shooting. Hatch turned state's evidence and was sentenced to twenty-five years. Clark was given a death sentence. For the earlier murder of Charles Carter, he was sentenced to life in prison without parole.

While waiting on death row, Clark met an assortment of remorseless killers. Among them were those who, according to the Department of Corrections, would become involved in the escape attempt.

Konstantinos Fotopoulos was the son of a wealthy family who owned the popular boardwalk on Daytona Beach. One of his stated goals was to start a "Murder Club." He recruited his girlfriend, Diedre Hunt, and another friend, Kevin Ramsey. On the night of October 20, 1989, they drove to a remote area for target practice. Once there, Fotopoulos held Ramsey at gunpoint, while Hunt tied him to a tree. Fotopoulos then ordered Hunt to shoot Ramsey while he videotaped it. She shot the screaming, begging victim three times. When Ramsey didn't die, Fotopoulos finished him off with a single shot to the head.

Fotopoulos also wanted to kill his wife, so that he could collect on a $700,000 insurance policy. He and Hunt recruited a drifter named Bryan Chase to come into his home and shoot his wife. While she was sleeping, Chase crept up the stairs to the bedroom and shot her in the head. Fotopoulos then ran into the room and fired several rounds into Chase, killing him. Police investigating the "self-defense" shooting located the videotape of Hunt killing Ramsey. Fotopoulos's wife survived the attack, but he was convicted of first-degree murder and sentenced to death for the murder of Ramsey. Hunt was given life.

Thomas Anthony Wyatt was Wendy Calderon's pen pal boyfriend. In 1988, he and Michael Lovette escaped from a North Carolina prison. They made it to Vero Beach, where they stole a car. In the glove compartment, they found a .38-caliber handgun. While robbing a pizzeria, Wyatt shot and killed three employees. He also raped one of the females. Traveling west across the state to Tampa, he abducted a woman from the parking lot of a bar and raped and murdered her. DNA from both of the rape victims matched Wyatt and he was sentenced to death. Lovette ended up with eleven life sentences.

Leonardo Franqui and five others robbed a bank in North Miami. During the robbery, Franqui and two other cohorts shot a security guard.

He died on the scene and Franqui and the others were tried, convicted and sentenced to death.

Clarence Jones and two convicts escaped from a prison in Maryland. On July 7, 1988, Tallahassee police officers Ernest Ponce de Leon and Greg Armstrong were called to check out a suspicious car parked behind a laundromat. As the officers were running a computer check on the escapees, Jones opened fire. Two shots hit Ponce de Leon, killing him. Armstrong was wounded, but was able to return fire, hitting Jones. The cop killer was sentenced to death.

Every day for months, while in the recreation yard, Clark and the others planned their escape. Josie Clark became a pawn in a doomed scheme hatched by five desperate killers.

As they traveled south on U. S. 301, barreling through the speed traps of Lawtey and Waldo, Josie Clark must have wondered how her life had come to this strange nexus. The woman who was driving, Wendy Calderon, was almost a stranger to her. And yet together they'd attempted to spring their lovers from one of the most secure prisons in the country.

Josie Davenport had been born in Keighley, West Yorkshire. Before marrying, she worked in a solicitor's office. Josie and her husband moved to the Isle of Wight and opened two successful businesses. There they raised four sons, but after twenty-four years, her marriage ended. She was set adrift; forlorn, lonely and in need of human companionship.

After her divorce, Josie came to the United States to visit a friend. While in Virginia, she spotted an advertisement in a local magazine. Ronald Wayne Clark, Jr., an inmate at Union Correctional Institution in Florida, had placed the ad for a pen pal. His photograph portrayed a baby-faced young man with bulging biceps—it was obvious that he kept himself in great shape.

When she read about how he spent twenty-three lonely hours every day inside a six-by-nine foot cell, she cried. He was innocent of the robbery and murder for which he'd been convicted, he said. She was touched to the core by what she felt was his plight and knew she had to write this man who seemed as sad as she was.

Little did she know, Ronald Clark was a scam artist. At any given time, he was corresponding with at least a dozen women. He used his pen pal ads to obtain money, love and assistance in his numerous legal appeals.

When he received a letter from the Englishwoman who now lived in Virginia and read the flowery prose, he could sense an unfulfilled longing behind each line. Before he even finished, he knew he'd found someone to implement a plan he'd been formulating for months. Clark acted immediately, sending Josie Davenport a long letter designed to reel her into his trap.

"He paid me compliments," Josie later said. "He [sent me] jewelry and flowers and I was flattered. He made me feel like a queen. In that year, he'd given me more attention than any other man in my life."

For several months, Ronald Clark had been mulling over a scheme to do something no one had ever done. He was going to escape from Florida's death row. And he needed someone exactly like his soon-to-be-wife Josie to help him.

Clark's time was slowly ticking away. In 1991, he'd been convicted and sentenced to death for one murder and life in prison for a second. As his appeals were routinely rejected by the courts, his desperation grew. While executions were seemingly random—two or three a year in Florida—you never knew when your number might come up. And in the back of his mind, there was always the chance that the state could revert to a Texas-style system where they would begin to clean out death row.

For Josie, Clark's letters hit a soft spot. The death penalty had been abolished in England in the 1960s. Few in that country believed people should die for their crimes. Even for murder, most inmates served just a few years.

Ronnie insisted that he was innocent, and she believed him. He'd been the pawn of a prosecutor who used his case for political advancement. His accomplice, the man who'd actually committed the crime, had only gotten a sentence of twenty-five years and was already out on parole.

After a few months of writing her nearly every day, Ronnie told Josie he thought he was in love. He sent her bouquets of roses and jewelry. When he asked her to visit him, she drove twelve hours to the prison. She was stunned by how attractive he was. She stayed for three days. They spoke to each other through glass windows like teenaged lovebirds. When she left, she was smitten.

One year after she wrote her first letter to him, Josie and Ronald Wayne Clark, Jr., were married in the prison chapel.

"You think that pilot got our tag number?" Wendy Calderon asked.

They were driving her brother's car. It had North Carolina plates.

"I think he may have seen it," Clark answered.

"I don't think so," Calderon said.

The car rocketed through the one-light town of Hawthorne. Orange groves dotted the land and fruit stands sat on every corner.

"Slow down," Josie said. "It wouldn't pay to get pulled over now."

Calderon glared at her and sped up.

The car somehow made it all the way to Citra, another one-light town, without being stopped. Josie had been living there, working as a nanny to George Wall's two children. As soon as Josie saw her employer, she broke down. "I've done it now," she said, sobbing. "I tried to get them out with a helicopter."

Wall knew that Josie's husband was in prison. As the women related what had happened, he was appalled.

"How did you get involved in this when you've got kids?" he asked Josie.

"It seemed like a perfect plan," she said. He could only shake his head.

While Josie was upset and crying, Wall seemed rational and controlled. He noted that Wendy never expressed remorse or regret.

Nevertheless, the employer was frightened. The women had an arsenal in the car and could easily kill him in order to silence him. Wall ordered them to leave and never come back.

They quickly loaded up their possessions and drove off.
As soon as the car was out of sight, Wall called 911.

The tale helicopter pilot John Patrick told police was so outlandish
that, at first, they thought he was lying. It was only when they checked the
helicopter and found a broken headset and an empty clipboard that they
began to believe him.

He told investigators that the car driven by the suspects had fading
red paint. He'd even written down the license tag number. Police quickly
discovered that the car was registered to Wendy's brother.

The younger woman ordered him to help Josie with the suitcase once
they landed, he stated. As he did so, she rushed to the car and climbed into
the driver's seat. The pilot lugged the heavy suitcase over to the car and
placed it in the backseat. He told police that he just wanted them to leave
as quickly as possible. Josie kept apologizing, stating that she didn't wish to
hurt anyone. Before she got in the car, she hugged the pilot.

Since hijacking is a federal crime, the Clay County Sheriff's Office
contacted the Federal Bureau of Investigation. In addition, the Florida
Department of Law Enforcement and Department of Corrections were
briefed on the case.

Wendy Calderon was quickly identified as the driver of the car.

Within the hour, the Clay County Sheriff's Office received a call from
Josie's employer. He informed detectives that Josie Clark was the second
person who had participated in the hijacking and that it was her intent to
free her husband from death row.

Police agencies in surrounding counties were alerted to be on the lookout for the wanted car. Two hours later, the vehicle was stopped in St. John's
County, just south of Jacksonville. Calderon and Clark were arrested.

While Calderon would not speak with the cops and requested an
attorney, Josie opened up. She stated that her husband and another death row
inmate she knew only as "Kosta" had planned the hijack attempt. They'd used

emissaries to give her money to buy guns and had intimidated her when she attempted to back out. If she didn't go through with the plan, Josie said, they threatened to travel to England and kidnap her grandchildren. Some of Kosta's relatives and some Cubans were also involved, she said. Josie claimed that a Cuban inmate named "Frankie" was in on the plot as well.

Over an eight-month period, she was given between three and four thousand dollars to purchase weapons. Most had been bought at gun stores and pawn shops. The plan was to load the guns and wire cutters in a suitcase and drop it into the recreation yard at a time when Ronald Clark and his pals were scheduled to be outside.

Her husband and five friends would retrieve the suitcase and use the guns to kill any guards in the area. Then they would cut their way through the fence and run to the waiting helicopter. Once they were free, Josie and Ronnie planned to fly to England and live happily ever after.

Investigators shook their heads. The plot seemed more like something from a movie than real life.

The suitcase hadn't been found in the car. When investigators questioned her about it, Josie told them that she and Calderon had placed the valise next to a dumpster somewhere along U.S. Highway 19. She led police to a Moose Lodge near Palatka and there, in the back of the building, they located it.

Inside, encased in pillows and foam rubber, were two Russian-made SKS 7.62 mm rifles. They were fully loaded. Two bolt cutters were also in the suitcase.

Although the plan had failed, it was a close call. Officials didn't even want to think about what could have happened had the women been successful in dropping that suitcase inside the prison walls. Department of Corrections officials quickly met to try to figure out how to prevent an aircraft from flying over the prison.

Based on information given to them by Josie, investigators identified Ronald Clark, Thomas Wyatt, Clarence Jones, Konstantinos Fotopoulos and Leonardo Franqui as the inmates suspected of planning the escape. Between them, they'd been convicted of nine murders. All were hardcore, cutthroat thugs who would show no mercy if they got their hands on a cache of weapons. The press was having a field day. Here was a real-life "Thelma and Louise." It was all over the six o'clock news, cable television, newspapers and magazines. The headlines told the story: "Women hijack chopper for prison break." While few people had heard of Keystone Heights or Starke or Citra, that just heightened the mystery and made the case even more attractive.

In reality, Josie was in over her head from the moment she picked up a pen to write a hardened inmate. Ronald Clark had had his scam in place for several years. He'd become the self-styled "Death Row Poet," attracting some media attention. His writing was pure unadulterated doggerel—in fact, the poems were laughable. The last lines of an effort entitled, "My Final Journey," read:

> For I had no support from the US Court who assigned me
> Mr. Davis an incompetent attorney and that's why I'm off
> on my final journey.

Clark also fancied himself a death row reformer. He once went on a "hunger strike," calling for improvements such as air conditioning ("as we enter the hottest part of the year, underwashed bodies in overcrowded, airless areas without ventilation and circulation increase potential for violence and illness") and videotaped documentation of correctional officers when they used force to subdue rowdy inmates.

Investigators wondered how someone with no criminal record and no history of deviant behavior could have become involved with such a hardcore inmate. Author Sheila Isenberg interviewed more than two dozen "death row groupies" before writing the book *Women Who Love Men Who Kill*. "Most of these women have been abused in their earlier lives," she wrote, "by parents, fathers, first husbands or first boyfriends. So a relationship with a man behind bars is a safe relationship. The guy can't hurt them."

Unfortunately, Ronald Clark had spent a lifetime brutalizing people.

Josie was just another victim. As investigators interviewed her, they got a glimpse of how inmates can manipulate a naïve follower. After she and Ronnie married, Josie said, she moved to Florida to be near him. On visits, they would "joke about outrageous ways to break him out, but as far as I was concerned, they were just jokes."

She found out it wasn't a joke when a relative of Ronnie's showed up at her house carrying aerial photos of the prison yard. "She inferred [that] she knew where my family lived," Josie said, "and [stated] that if I didn't help Ronnie escape, they would be hurt."

During her visits to the prison, the other inmates involved in the plot tried to intimidate her. "If you don't help us escape," they told her, "we know where your granddaughter lives."

Then two "Cubans," complete with expensive suits and sunglasses, showed up at her door and handed her $500 to purchase guns for the escape. She did so, but "chickened out," sold the guns and flew back to England. But after three weeks, she missed Ronnie, so she came back to Florida.

As soon as she returned, relatives of the inmates began showing up at her home. Again, she was given money to purchase weapons. She did so once again, but repeated the process of returning to England. This time she stayed for three months. "I missed Ronnie," she said. "He'd called my son's house and said he was missing me and I stupidly convinced myself the trouble would have died down."

The love-struck wife returned for the third time. This time she'd reluctantly made up her mind to help out with the plan. Using money given to her by relatives of the inmates, she once again purchased guns, bolt cutters and a heavy-duty suitcase.

Earlier, Josie had been approached by Wendy Calderon, Thomas Wyatt's friend. Together, they carried out the plan.

Once they entered the helicopter, Josie was terrified. "When I saw [Wendy] threatening [the pilot]," she said, "I started crying and screaming at her. But she shouted at me to shut up. We got to three miles from the jail. The pilot was terrified and told us the weather was bad and it wasn't safe."

When they landed back in Keystone Heights, Josie was relieved that the ordeal was over. Gullible as she was, she later said, "I thought if I told everyone exactly what had happened, I could go home to my family."

However, Josie was charged with air piracy, a federal offense that carries up to twenty years with no possibility of parole. Even while she awaited trial, she thought she would be freed.

The inmates said to be involved in the escape attempt had long ago learned that the right to remain silent was their ticket to lesser sentences. None ever admitted to having any knowledge about an escape attempt. Those two "crazy women" must have come up with the plan themselves, they said, and no one in the joint knew anything about it. With no evidence, none of the suspected participants were ever charged.

Like a true sociopath, Ronnie let Josie take the fall.

She was tried in the United District Court for the Middle District of Florida. The evidence against her was overwhelming. She was convicted, but a judge sentenced her to the minimum of twelve years in prison instead of the maximum.

The Feds weren't happy with that jail term, however. They appealed and a higher court bumped the sentence up to the max—twenty years without parole.

She is currently serving her time in a federal prison in Connecticut. "It's awful here," she said. "One evening a week I attend Bible study. The other evenings I just stay in my room and read and pray."

Josie is attempting to work through prison formalities to divorce Ronald Clark.

"I know I've been a fool," she said. "But I was in love and I would have done anything for Ronnie. Now I know those men on Death Row will do anything to be free. I'm sure he saw me coming and saw me as his way out."

Wendy Calderon was sentenced to eleven years and three months for her participation in the crime. She is currently free on parole.

Ronald Clark continues his masquerade as the Death Row Poet as he awaits execution.

In Florida's prisons, inmates are allowed to place advertisements on the Internet and in magazines and newspapers. (Laws that have attempted to restrict inmates' freedom of speech have been negated by court decisions.) Most of the inmates are scammers in the extreme, yet their requests for companionship and money seem to appeal to some women (and men). So the con artists keep conning and sad ladies like Josie Clark keep falling for them. Unfortunately, in a few instances, these normally law-abiding citizens are sometimes talked into participating in criminal acts on behalf of their inmate husbands and boyfriends. It's not likely to change any time soon.

Chapter 14
The Diary

"How're we gonna do it?" Valessa asked.
"Let's use bleach," Adam said.

> Valessa Robinson and Adam Davis, conspiring to
> murder Valessa's mother.

L et's kill my mom," Valessa said rather casually. It seemed like quite an offhanded comment, as if three friends were chatting about a rock concert or a used car one of them planned to buy.

Fifteen-year-old Valessa Robinson was thin, almost waifish. If you could get past the baggy clothes and the ear, tongue and eyebrow piercings, she would have been a pretty girl. But her demeanor had "rebel" written all over her.

Adam Davis was her boyfriend. "Rattlesnake," as he liked to call himself, had just been released from prison on a burglary charge. At nineteen, he was into hard drugs and had been arrested numerous times. He was six feet tall and weighed about 140 pounds. He was proud of his many tattoos, especially the cross on his right arm which bore the initials, "KD." It was in memory of his father, who had been killed in a motorcycle accident.

Jon Whispel, also nineteen, was a follower. He didn't seem to realize that every time he hooked up with Adam, he wound up being arrested.

It was nearing midnight on Friday, June 26, 1998. The trio was eating burgers in a diner near Carrollwood Village subdivision in Tampa, Florida. Valessa's home was just a few blocks away.

As Whispel thought about Valessa's proposal, he was troubled. "How we gonna get away with this?" he asked.

It never occurred to him that there was something so monstrous about the proposal that he should run for his life. Or better yet, go to a pay phone and warn Valessa's mother that she might be in danger. At the time, it just seemed easier to go with the flow.

With lowered voices, the friends discussed how to kill Vicki Robinson. After rejecting several options, Adam decided that he would inject heroin into her body. Since Vicki wasn't a doper, he reasoned, the injection would cause a massive rush of narcotics into her system, stopping her heart. Cops would think she'd overdosed. That way none of the three would be blamed.

As they trooped out of the diner that evening, there seemed to be little rational thought behind their decision to murder Vicki Robinson.

But if there was a reason, the last entry in Valessa's diary gave some hint of it.

The teenager had kept a journal for years. Her final entry, penned three weeks before the murder, was revealing. It touched on her obsession of having a baby with Adam. And it described the rage she felt toward her mother.

"Dear Journal," she wrote. "I haven't written for a while, but there's been a good reason that if you haven't noticed the pages that were ripped out of my journal, you know now. The reason for that is because my mom read my journal and made copies of five pages. It really pisses me off that my mom would invade my privacy like that. I can't trust her now that she's done this. Before I trusted her for almost anything, but now I won't be able to trust her at all. [On] May 20th, me and Adam sat down and had a discussion about having a baby. He decided that since I'm still a minor and everything else that we should wait a year or more..."

The diary, hundreds of pages in all, told the sordid story of a wasted life. It described how Valessa sneaked out of her room at night to attend wild sex parties and detailed her experiments with marijuana, Extacy, LSD and other mind-altering drugs. The overriding theme of the last sections of the diary was her obsession with Adam. But most of all, it described the intense hatred she felt for her mother. (Parts of the diary were later published in the *St. Petersburg Times*.)

When Vicki Robinson opened that diary, it sealed her fate.

Vicki was a pretty divorcee struggling to raise two teenage daughters. Her eldest daughter, seventeen-year-old Michelle, was an honor student who'd given Vicki a few problems, but had grown out of her rebel stage.

But Valessa had begun her personal rebellion early. Her musical tastes evolved from gospel music to rockers like Bush and Bruce Springsteen. Lately, she'd been listening to alternative metal bands such as Marilyn Manson, Korn and Rage Against the Machine.

She lived in the twilight of a dark room, with a black strobe light in the ceiling. Valessa kept the door locked, partly to keep her mother from seeing the clutter. But the main reason was so she could sneak out at night. She'd been detained by police on several occasions for shoplifting, truancy and creating a disturbance at a local mall. On other occasions she'd run away from home, causing her mother to search for her all over Tampa. In a recent incident, the police were called to help find the missing girl. When they found Valessa with an adult who was supplying her with drugs, they arrested him. Officers lectured the teenage girl on the dangers of the street, but it did little good.

After yet another violent confrontation, Vicki had Valessa committed to a local mental health facility. Following a two-day evaluation, the troubled teenager was released.

Valessa's choice of friends was a constant worry for Vicki. They all seemed older than she and many were obviously drug users. Even worse, some had served time in prison. Vicki attempted to set limits by asking Valessa to bring her friends home so she could meet them. And she forbade Valessa to go out without her permission.

A devout Christian, Vicki attempted to teach positive values to her daughter. She enlisted her daughter in a private church school and took Valessa to worship services. While Valessa listened to punk and grunge music, Vicki liked gospel songs. She and her fiancé, Jim Englert, had met at a church function and made it a point to be present at the many Bible studies that their congregation sponsored.

Vicki was a successful real estate agent. She was attractive, a self-starter, a natural at sales and a compassionate friend. A few years before, she'd purchased a beautiful three-bedroom home on a cul-de-sac in the upscale Carrollwood subdivision.

Her one worry in life was Valessa.

By late May, Vicki suspected that Valessa was having sex. She decided to do something she hadn't done in years. While Valessa was at school, she opened her daughter's bedroom door. Plowing through the litter, she searched the room and found her daughter's journal. What she read shocked her to the core.

Valessa described the many sex acts she'd committed with numerous boys. According to her diary entries, she liked "doggie style" sex best. In pornographic detail, she described her feelings as she engaged in the practice. She also wrote about her drug use. "Yesterday," she wrote, "I tripped on acid for the first time. It was fun. Everything was funny and everything tickled." To Vicki, it seemed that Valessa's whole life was an unending search for self-destructive pleasures.

By then, Vicki had met Adam Davis, a parolee. Although he seemed nice enough when he was introduced to Vicki, she saw the lack of purpose in his life. The combination of Valessa's rebelliousness and Adam's lawbreaking proclivities was the final straw. Vicki realized she was in over her head.

After having Adam arrested for child abuse, because of his sexual dalliance with Valessa, a minor, Vicki vowed to get her daughter the help she needed. After Adam bonded out of jail, he immediately began seeing Valessa again. On June 26, Adam was due in court to face charges of having sex with a minor. Because of his previous record, he could very well have ended up doing hard time.

Vicki tore out several pages of the diary, made copies and took them to the staff of a nearby Christian boarding school. Though the $900 per month fee would strap her financially, Vicki was determined to save her daughter. In addition to academic studies and religious training, students were required to perform manual labor on the school farm. The term lasted eighteen months and the school boasted a high success rate in turning around the lives of wayward teens. Vicki signed Valessa up, but hadn't yet told her about it.

For the first time in months, Vicki felt she was taking positive action to help her daughter. On the night of June 26, 1998, she went to bed feeling good about the future.

The three friends moved out of the shadows and entered the house. They tiptoed to Valessa's room. They were angry, because they hadn't been able to find a source for the heroin they needed.

But at least they'd been able to score a syringe.

And Jon had a pocketknife with a four-inch blade. Actually, it belonged to Valessa, but he'd borrowed it. He liked to play with it. Tonight, as they discussed their latest failure, he opened the blade, shut it, then opened it again. Over and over. Every time he closed the blade, it clicked, driving Adam and Valessa crazy. After Rattlesnake glared at him, Jon put it in his pocket.

Adam suggested using bleach to kill Valessa's mother. When Jon looked skeptical, Rattlesnake said, "I seen it in a movie once. Bleach makes air bubbles and..." His voice trailed off as if no other explanation was needed.

"Let's do it!" Valessa said.

She walked into the kitchen and poured bleach into a glass. Then Adam loaded the syringe.

Jon sat on the bed smoking a cigarette while Adam and Valessa walked down the hall to Vicki's bedroom.

Holding the syringe, Valessa opened the door. They entered slowly and peered down at her sleeping mother. She was wearing a peach-colored nightgown. A night-light illuminated Vicki's skin, causing it to glow like phosphorous.

As they stood over her, Vicki suddenly awoke. Her movement startled Adam and Valessa. Then Vicki sat straight up. The intruders panicked and bolted out of the room. They raced back down the hall and re-entered Valessa's bedroom. Breathless, Adam shut the door and placed the syringe in the closet.

"What happened?" Jon asked.

"Bitch woke up," Adam said.

Almost immediately, there was a knock on the door.

Adam took a deep breath, then opened it.

Vicki looked past him and ordered Valessa to grab her sleeping bag and come into her room.

As she turned to walk back down the hall, Adam grabbed her. He jerked Vicki to him, placing her in a full-nelson. He later said he used a "sleeper" hold like he'd seen in a wrestling match on television.

It didn't work. Vicki struggled ferociously, dragging Adam down the hall.

They slammed into a wall, then fell onto the floor.

Jon and Valessa stood in the bedroom, pale and shaken. They listened as Vicki fought with Rattlesnake. Jon lit up another cigarette, nervously inhaling the rancid smoke deep into his lungs.

"I need the syringe!" Adam yelled.

Valessa raced out of the bedroom. She found Adam in the kitchen on top of her mother. He was choking her, but Vicki was fighting back. Valessa jumped onto Vicki, locking her legs around her mother's ankles.

"Where's the needle?" Adam demanded to know.

"I dunno."

"Damn!"

Adam jumped up and raced toward the bedroom. "Hold the bitch!" he yelled back at Valessa.

He found the syringe, then rushed back to the kitchen.

Valessa was still fighting her mother, trying to hold her on the floor as Vicki attempted to rise.

Adam fell on Vicki and stabbed the needle into her neck. She saw it coming and screamed, "What's that?"

Jon heard the struggle. From the bedroom he could see arms and legs flailing. Sensing the desperate fight, he took Valessa's knife from his pocket, opened it and ran into the kitchen. He handed it to Adam. Later he was asked why he did it. "To this day, I don't know," he said. "And I don't think I'll ever know." Jon ran back into Valessa's bedroom and cowered there as Adam and Valessa continued their attack on Vicki.

Adam plunged the short blade into Vicki's neck. She groaned, then began fighting with a fierceness none of them had seen before. Rattlesnake responded by cursing her and slashing her face, her hands, her throat. After ten minutes, Vicki's strength ebbed. Now Adam was able to stab her without opposition.

Finally, she lay in a bloody heap, motionless.

Breathing heavily, Adam and Valessa walked back into the bedroom. Valessa, staring at the blood on Adam's clothes, said, "Baby, you better wash your hands."

Rattlesnake walked into the bathroom and cleaned up while Valessa and Jon sat on the bed inhaling cigarettes. The only sound was the faucet running. Then it shut off and Adam joined them.

In the darkness, they probably thought about what they'd done. Except for Jon, there was no regret. In fact, Valessa and Adam were angry that Vicki had struggled for her life.

But they soon brightened up. The realization surged through them like electricity—now they were free! They'd have wheels, money, food, drugs. And, unlike Valessa's mother, they didn't have to work for it.

Then, from somewhere far away they heard a low moan.

Rattlesnake started.

Jon and Valessa stared at the door, gape-mouthed.

In the kitchen, Vicki Robinson was sobbing.

"Bitch won't die," Adam said.

He took the knife and went back to finish her off.

When investigators entered the residence, they found little to indicate that a bloody struggle had ensued. But the strange disappearance was so unlike Vicki that TPD threw all it had into the investigation.

The day after the murder, Jim called the Tampa Police Department. Vicki had missed several appointments, he said, and her van was missing. And she had vanished. It was totally out of character, the concerned fiancé said. Vicki wouldn't just disappear. He asked if an officer could go to check out her house.

When police located the rap sheets of Adam and Jon, the two immediately became suspects. Since Valessa was also missing, cops wondered whether she was a victim or a fugitive. The trio had disappeared, along with Vicki and her minivan.

Later that day, someone began using Vicki's credit cards. Investigators contacted the credit union and administrators agreed to limit the amount that could be withdrawn to $100 per day.

The card was now being used every day, allowing cops to track the fugitives. They were moving west, resting at truck stops, eating fast food, sometimes staying at low-rent motels. Perry, Florida. Crestview, Florida. Loxley, Alabama. Gulfport, Mississippi. The killers passed through Louisiana and into Texas. Seven days later, at 3:45 A.M., Pecos County Sheriff Bruce Wilson got a call from the Texas Rangers. He was informed that two fugitives on a murder warrant from Florida might be heading into his jurisdiction. According to the Rangers, a third person, a female juvenile, may also be in the van. Wilson strapped on his .45-caliber semiautomatic pistol and called Deputy Larry Jackson. The two picked up a police cruiser and drove to Fort Stockton. There, in the median beneath an overpass, they waited.

Suddenly a teal-green minivan with Florida tags drove by them. Jackson, an expert marksman, rode shotgun as the sheriff pulled out behind the van. They followed long enough to run the license plate and found that it had been stolen. After observing a male and female in the front and a second male in the rear, Sheriff Wilson turned on his lights and activated the siren.

The van darted ahead, picking up speed until it was going more than 100 miles per hour. An attempt by highway patrol officers to use tire spikes failed and the van increased speed until the sheriff clocked it going more than 130 miles per hour. The few travelers on the interstate were sent scampering off the road by the fleeing van.

Sheriff Wilson had been involved in many pursuits and easily kept up with the van. As they neared the Fort Stockton exit, he decided it was time to stop the fugitives. He nodded to Jackson, then pulled alongside the speeding vehicle.

Jackson had a 16-shot, .40-caliber glock semiautomatic handgun. He leaned out of the window, took aim and fired.

WHOOOSH! The left rear tire went flat.

The van kept going.

Jackson fired again, knocking out the right rear tire. The flat tires spun dust and sparks at the pursuing car.

Above it all, Wilson and Jackson heard the blare of Korn emanating from the car stereo.

Jackson fired again. And again. One of the front tires exploded. Still the van kept going. By now, several state troopers and Pecos County deputies had joined the chase in a convoy of flashing lights and wailing sirens.

Just before it reached the Fort Stockton exit, the van careened off the pavement and spun down an embankment. Wilson braked the cruiser and pulled up a few feet behind the van. But then it turned and came straight back at them. The vehicle looked lopsided as it hurtled toward them with only one good tire. Jackson stepped out of the cruiser, aimed and fired again. His bullet took out the last tire. The driver still wouldn't stop.

Jackson moved into position so that he had a clear shot at the driver, but he wanted to give the suspect one last chance to surrender. He aimed, fired low and heard the bullet thud into the driver's door.

Finally, reluctantly, the vehicle ground to a halt.

Jackson rushed the driver. "Get out!" he yelled as he jerked open the door. But Rattlesnake swung his fist at the deputy. Jackson slammed his gun against Adam's head, then dragged him from the car.

Sheriff Wilson and other lawmen rushed up to help.

While several officers subdued Rattlesnake, others ordered Valessa and Jon out of the van. They meekly complied.

Within minutes, all three fugitives were lying in the Texas dust, hand-cuffed, each facing his or her own future alone.

Jon Whispel was the only one of the three who showed any remorse. He quickly told investigators what had happened.

After the murder, he said, they wrapped Vicki's body in trash bags and dumped her into a plastic garbage can. Then the three loaded her in the van along with shovels and a hoe. They dragged her to a wooded area behind Whispel's mother's house. After a half-hearted attempt to bury Vicki, they covered her body with palm fronds and left her among a grove of trees.

"Where is she located?" the investigator asked.

Jon drew a map and Texas authorities faxed a copy to Tampa officials.

Valessa was interviewed next.

"Before I stabbed her, I had to pin her down," she said.

"How was your mother dressed?"

"In her nightgown."

"How was she dressed when she was placed in the garbage can?"

"In her nightgown," Valessa said.

The Texas interrogators were amazed at her lack of emotion. Her responses were matter-of-fact, as if murdering her mother was as natural as the rising and setting of the sun.

Adam blamed the killing on LSD. He took all the blame, stating that Valessa had nothing to do with it.

When asked what they'd done with the body, he confirmed that they'd bought bags of cement from a local hardware store and had planned to encase the corpse in the cement and dump it in a canal. He'd seen that in a horror flick, he said. (To investigators it seemed that all of Adam's plans came from television or the movies.) They changed their minds when they were unable to get the cement mix to harden.

Their next plan was to dig a grave and bury the body. However, after digging for a few minutes, they became tired and decided to simply place the corpse of Vicki Robinson in a wooded area.

Adam also drew a map showing where Vicki's body was dumped.

Tampa cops were on the phone getting minute-by-minute reports of the confessions. Once they learned where the body was concealed, they converged on the spot.

The trash can was in a forest near a cattle ranch. Surrounded by oak trees, wild palms and an occasional sweet gum, the can was indeed covered by palm fronds. When they opened the lid, the first thing investigators saw was the bloody nightgown. At the bottom of the can, Vicki Robinson's hair was caked in blood. Her face had been slashed so many times that it was unrecognizable.

One of the detectives, who had a teenage daughter, turned away and made the sign of the cross. Later he stated that it was as much an entreaty to keep evil from his door as it was a prayer.

Within hours, Tampa police Lieutenant John Margicano and Detective James Iverson were in Texas. The three fugitives repeated their confessions to the Tampa investigators. This time, their statements were taped, thereby sealing the fate of the murderers.

Jon Whispel, whom authorities believed was the least culpable in Vicki's murder, turned state's evidence. He pled guilty to second-degree murder and received twenty-five years in prison. For the reduced charges, he agreed to testify against Adam Davis and Valessa.

There was little doubt about the outcome of Rattlesnake's trial. He was convicted of first-degree murder, grand theft and theft of an automobile. By a seven-to-five vote, the jury recommended that he be put to death. A judge concurred and sentenced him to die.

Valessa's trial presented more of a problem to prosecutors. To begin with, she was a minor, only fifteen, when the murders were committed. Although she was tried as an adult, the sympathy factor was always present.

The second problem prosecutors faced was Valessa's statement in the first interview with Texas cops in which the teenager confessed to stabbing her mother. Police didn't believe that Valessa had used the knife on her mother, although they knew she was the instigator and had helped Rattlesnake hold down the struggling woman. After telling Texas cops that she alone had murdered her mother, Valessa recanted her confession and claimed Adam had been the lone attacker. On the flight to Texas, she asserted that she was an unwilling hostage.

Valessa's attorneys were convinced of her innocence and promised a fight-to-the-finish battle for acquittal. At their own expense, they bought stylish clothes for the teen and had her hair made up in a subtle fritz style. Each day she came to court dressed in plaid skirts, soft blouses, bobby socks and penny loafers. Her piercings were gone and she looked nothing like the acid freak she once had been—now she was a innocent-looking schoolgirl whom her attorneys always referred to as "this child."

Despite overwhelming physical evidence and the testimony of Whispel, Valessa's attorneys refused to give an inch. They tried to paint her as the pawn of an evil boyfriend whose nickname was "Rattlesnake." The defense team contended that Valessa had been abused by Adam and was terrified of him. He alone was responsible, they said. He alone planned the murder, and he alone carried it out.

When the jury retired, the prosecution knew the decision was seriously in doubt. Although they had presented a logical progression of the crime implicating Valessa as the instigator and an active participant, they knew the teen's attorneys had won the battle of emotions. The question to be answered had been framed by the defense: Could it be that this sweet-looking schoolgirl murdered her own mother?

Valessa could have been found guilty of first-degree murder, second-degree murder, third-degree murder or manslaughter. Or she could have been acquitted.

The jury deliberated for days. At times they were on the verge of being unable to reach a verdict. But finally, after nearly two weeks, they announced that they had come to a conclusion in the case. Valessa was convicted of third-degree murder, escaping a sentence of life in prison.

The judge gave her the maximum, twenty years, with the possibility of parole after serving 85 percent of her sentence. Many family members were disturbed at what they felt was a lenient sentence.

Others thought Valessa should have been acquitted. Her biological father, Chuck, directed his anger at his former wife, stating that Vicki was too easy on her daughter.

Many who heard his comments thought the remarks sounded like sour grapes. Where had *he* been? they asked. Once, when Valessa had gone to St. Louis to visit him, they said, he'd sent her back home after two days because she was so unmanageable.

The debate over the verdict raged back and forth among the public. One Internet blog speculated that the O. J. Simpson jury had retired to Florida. Some blamed Vicki. One writer even went so far as to compare her dealings with her daughter with Munchausen's syndrome by proxy.

Valessa is currently incarcerated in Florida State Prison for Women at Lowell. She is scheduled to be released in 2016, unless she is paroled earlier.

Raising teenagers has always been difficult. However, in modern society, with its emphasis on sex, drugs and having a perpetual party, it can be even more difficult. When a mom with traditional values clashes with a punk-oriented daughter, the sparks can set off an explosion of violence. Many Florida cities have enclaves of teens who have little ambition except to get high on drugs and have sex. Most will grow out of their rebellion, but some, like Valessa Robinson, will end up committing vicious crimes.

Chapter 15
The Dark Forest

"I only hurt people when I have to."

Loran K. Cole, threatening his kidnapped victim.

Prisoner Web pages began appearing on the Internet in the late 1990s. Sponsored by organizations such as the Canadian Coalition Against the Death Penalty and ALIVE, the pages gave convicted murderers a forum to expound on their cases and advance positive images of themselves. While one could still view creepy-looking mug shots on some department of corrections Web sites, these pages presented a different look—cozy photos of inmates holding kittens or posing as wounded innocents.

These sites were slow to catch the attention of the public. That changed when child murderess Susan Smith of South Carolina produced a Web page that announced she was "sensitive, caring and kind-hearted." A storm of negative publicity caused her to withdraw the page. Soon the notoriety of prisoner Web pages rivaled that of murder memorabilia: the collecting of letters, artwork and other personal items of infamous criminals.

Prisoner Web pages can have a devastating effect on the families of the victims of the incarcerated's heinous crimes.

Twenty-four-year-old Sayeh Rivazfar was searching the Internet when she stumbled onto Raymond Wike's Web page. Her terrified mind spiraled back to the summer's night when Wike abducted eight-year-old Sayeh and her younger sister Sara from their Pace, Florida, bedroom. He drove them to a rural area and forced Sayeh to lie on the trunk of his car while he raped her. Then he cut Sara's throat, killing her. Wike taunted Sayeh, telling her to say her prayers. As she mumbled the Lord's Prayer he slashed her throat and repeatedly stabbed her.

Miraculously, Sayeh survived. She wandered through the woods until she found a highway where a passerby picked her up and called police. The evidence against Wike was overwhelming. He was captured, tried, convicted and sentenced to death.

Fifteen years later, Sayeh, now working as a law enforcement officer in New York, stated that she became physically ill when she discovered Wike's Web page. Seen petting a dog, he described himself as "caring and easy going" and stated that he was a victim of a miscarriage of justice.

"It is very disturbing," Sayeh said. "It makes me think the criminal now has more rights than the victim. I have no words for this. It is disgusting. The lies!"

Once prisoner Web pages began to appear on the Internet, victims' families took the issue to state legislatures, where laws were passed banning the pages. The courts, however, ruled such laws were a violation of the inmate's right to free speech as well as a violation of the rights of the organization sponsoring the Web page.

On some Web sites, the convicted killers ask readers to correspond with them. Debra Buchanan, spokesperson for Florida's Department of Corrections, speaks of the dangers of writing to death row inmates. "I caution people to be careful," she said, "because while there are some legitimate pen pal requests, it's often an appeal for money. They [inmates] are looking for people to continue preying upon."

Those involved in the anti-death penalty movement state that prisoners should be able to show a "human" side of themselves. Besides, they may actually be innocent of the offenses of which they were convicted, and the Web pages give them a format to help prove their innocence.

While Charlene Hall, Vice President of the criminal justice reform organization Justice for All, agrees that prisoners have as much of a right to use of the Internet as anyone, she suggests doing research on the cases before taking the word of a convicted murderer.

"If they can kill," she said. "They can lie."

On a February 18, 1994, afternoon, a blue convertible arrived at the main entrance of Ocala National Forest Road. The car, driven by eighteen-year-old John Edwards, was followed by a gray car operated by his twenty-two-year-old sister, Pam.

John began setting up camp while Pam visited the restrooms. When she returned, Pam noted the lack of amenities. "This is about the ultimate in roughing it," she said to John.

They both laughed. "It's only for two nights," he replied.

As John was securing the ropes of their tent to a stake, a stranger walked up. He was short, stocky and had long hair and a beard. He wore camou-flage trousers and a blue and black-checkered jacket. Introducing himself as "Kevin," the stranger told the siblings that he and his brother were camping nearby. Then he offered to help John gather firewood.

Pam was annoyed. She'd planned to spend the weekend being alone with John. They intended to hike together and photograph some of the huge alligators known to inhabit the Forest. The last thing she wanted to do that Friday afternoon was to play hostess to a smelly stranger who chattered incessantly.

John Edwards was a freshman honor student at Florida State University in Tallahassee. He was already taking courses that would enable him to obtain a degree in chemical engineering. Friendly and likable, John had been received into a fraternity. A star baseball player in high school, he'd recently tried out for the venerable Seminole baseball squad and had successfully made the team.

John had been anticipating the weekend with his sister for weeks, since he'd seen very little of her the past three years. The family was scattered all over the globe—John and Pam's parents were civilian educators on a military base in Okinawa, Japan. Although John and Pam both lived in Florida, their schedules were such that they rarely saw each other.

After spending an hour with them, "Kevin" finally left.

Pam cooked some potatoes and carrots over the campfire. As they ate, she and John began catching up on family business. Because of her love of children, Pam, also a college student, was majoring in elementary education. She had an affinity for the outdoors, but she told John, tongue-in-cheek, that she was reconsidering her love of nature because of this trip. They laughed again.

By now, a full moon had risen. As they laughed at stories of their childhood in Japan, Pam felt they were redeveloping the closeness they'd been missing. With the aroma of the dying fire filling their nostrils, they were at peace.

At 8:25, Kevin appeared out of the darkness, startling Pam. A man he introduced as his brother "Chris" followed him. Chris carried a heavy bat-sized walking stick. As they talked around the fire, Kevin informed them that he had a wife and children. (This was one of many lies he told them, though John and Pam had no reason to disbelieve him.) His wife was upset, he said, because he was spending a couple of weeks camping without his kids.

After an hour, Kevin began urging the siblings to go with them to take night pictures of some giant "crocodiles" which he claimed occupied a nearby waterhole. Pam knew there were no crocodiles in the Ocala National Forest, so she assumed he meant alligators. Pam had spent a rigorous day studying, driving to Ocala, then helping set up the campsite. She told them that she was too tired to go, but John seemed eager to photograph the "crocodiles." Pam eventually relented.

The Ocala National Forest, called simply the Forest by locals, was established as a national woodland in 1908. The topography consists of thousands of acres of highlands, coastal lowlands, prairies, springs, lakes and ponds. Towering palms, large oaks, cypress and scrubby sand pines are indigenous to the forest. In the fall, hunters routinely bag quail, dove and other small game. Black bear and deer roam the backwoods and locals still claim to occasionally spot a nearly-extinct Florida panther. Nearby, Rodman Reservoir has long been considered one of the best bass fishing lakes in the country.

Locals generally avoid the most remote sections of the Forest, because of the people who have been known to inhabit it. Potheads, drunks, fugitives and other undesirables live in tents or makeshift camps.

Visitors John and Pam Edwards didn't know that Kevin and Chris fit each of these categories. Because of their "wanted" status, they didn't even use their real names.

At about 10:00 P.M. the four began walking in single file. Kevin was in the lead, Pam walked second and John was third. Chris, who followed up the rear, carried the walking stick on his shoulder. Kevin, ever talkative, wondered aloud what would happen if the column were to be attacked by a bear. Then he answered his own question. "The third one in line always gets it," he said, roaring with laughter.

Pam didn't think it was funny. All she wanted was to return to the camp and go to sleep.

After forty-five minutes of wandering through the dark forest, Pam realized there was no alligator waterhole. After she expressed her doubts, Kevin and Chris decided to "take a piss" and stepped behind a tree.

When they emerged, Kevin grabbed Pam and threw her to the ground. He hit her several times with his fist to subdue her, then handcuffed his victim.

About twenty feet behind, Chris was having a much tougher time. At six feet three inches, John Edwards was whipcord slim and in excellent shape.

As Kevin was attacking Pam, Chris swung the walking stick at John, striking a blow that glanced off John's head. But John was too fast and too strong for his attacker. He grabbed the stick and ripped it from Chris's hands. Then he reluctantly proceeded to beat his assailant about the head and shoulders. Chris tried to run, but John caught him. Chris fell to the ground, moaning and begging for mercy. John, who had never been in a serious fight in his life, relented.

He turned and ran to help his sister. Idealistic and inexperienced in the ways of criminals, John lacked a killer instinct. In his haste to get to his sister. John made a fatal mistake: He dropped the walking stick as he ran.

Pam was lying with her hands tied behind her back. Kevin had backed off and John knelt beside her.

Suddenly, Kevin jumped on his back. Chris, meanwhile, got to his feet. He was still moaning as he picked up the stick and ran to the scene of the scuffle. Using the stick like a baseball bat, Chris struck a resounding blow to the back of John's head.

John crumpled to the ground, knocked senseless. As he lay helpless, Kevin tied his hands with a shoelace he'd been carrying in his pocket. Then he placed the siblings side by side, facedown on the ground.

Immobilized, with ants swarming over their bodies and stinging them, John awoke. Groggy, he turned toward Pam. "I'm sorry," he whispered.

"Why are you doing this?" Pam asked Kevin.

Panting hard, Kevin stated that he needed their cars. Then he went through their pockets, taking their personal property, including their jewelry. The loot included a twenty-dollar bill, Pam's matching gold rope bracelet and necklace, John's gold rope chain and his gold ring. He even took a coupon for snack food from the pocket of Pam's sweatpants.

Kevin instructed Chris to take Pam up the trail to the men's campsite, then dragged John off the path into a clump of palmetto bushes.

"Why the hell did you hurt my brother?" he asked, his rage building. When he received no answer, he struck John solidly across the head with the walking stick. Several more blows rained down onto the helpless victim until the ground was dark and bloody.

From the tent, Pam heard "gagging" sounds. When Kevin returned a few minutes later, she asked him if her brother was all right.

"I guess he's vomiting," Kevin replied. "Maybe he's having trouble with his dinner."

She noticed Kevin and Chris snickering.

Finally, Kevin said, "You're gonna have to sleep between the two of us."

Pam's heart sank. "Are you going to do anything to me?" she asked.

"Any damn thing I want to," Kevin answered. "How old are you?"

"Twenty-one."

"Well," Kevin drawled, "It ain't like I'm getting a virgin." He laughed again.

After disrobing her, Chris pulled Pam into the tent while Kevin went back to "check" on John. A short while later, Pam heard more moaning and a gurgling sound.

When Kevin returned, Pam asked him about her brother. Kevin informed her that John's head was hurt about as badly as his brother's. "He'll definitely pitch again," her abductor said.

The light in the tent was generated by a yellow plastic flashlight. Pam watched in terrified disbelief as Kevin unbuttoned his trousers. She crossed her knees, prepared to resist. But when Kevin told her he would go back up the trail and kill John, she complied.

At first light, Kevin announced that he intended to go check on John. When he returned, he told Pam that her brother was fine. Then he stated that he was going out to buy some marijuana. He told Chris to pack up.

Chris, still whining about his "broken" hand, began shoving items into a backpack. Pam considered pushing past him and fleeing. But she reasoned that even if she could get away, Kevin would kill John when he returned. She decided to wait it out.

Several minutes later, Kevin came back into the tent. He seemed pleased with himself.

"Scored some weed," he said.

Chris eagerly accepted a joint.

They lit up, then Kevin offered Pam a joint. At first she refused, but she noticed Kevin was getting angry. Because of her concerns for her brother, she accepted the pot and pretended to smoke it.

To her horror, Kevin raped her again. Then he asked Chris if he wanted "some." Chris refused and seemed uncomfortable with the situation.

Kevin ordered Pam to put her clothes back on. She gladly complied, then the three left camp. They headed across the prairie in a direction unfamiliar to Pam. Kevin forced her to carry a camera bag and a backpack. After they traveled about a mile, Kevin led them into a grove of pine trees.

There he took a ball of twine out of his pocket and wrapped it around Pam's ankles. Then he made her lean face-first against a pine tree where he used a second roll to tie her to the tree. Using roofing tacks and the blunt side of a hatchet, Kevin nailed the twine to the tree. He then tied her hands behind her back.

Pam guessed that it was about 1:30 Saturday afternoon when her assailants left.

She waited a few minutes, then began struggling against her bonds. Although the twine was thin, she couldn't believe its strength. She began yelling for help, but no one heard. It would be about two o'clock the following morning before she pulled one arm free and began to remove the twine. In that night of horror, Pam imagined poisonous snakes crawling on John or alligators making a feast of her helpless brother.

Once she freed herself, Pam lay exhausted at the base of the tree. She was afraid to move. If her assailants returned and found her gone, they might backtrack and kill John.

After hours of indecision, Pam crawled to her feet and began to walk the mile back toward the spot she thought John would be found. Briars cut her skin and her feet sank into the mud as she trudged along. Mosquitoes feasted on her flesh and she was terrified of alligators, but still she hunted for trails that she might recognize. Try as she might, however, she couldn't find John.

Finally, she gave up and walked back to a road she'd crossed in her search.

Tad Frunkus, camping with his family, had driven to a convenience store about twenty miles away. As he was coming back, he was amazed to see a girl staggering along the road. Tad slowed and she waved him over. Opening the passenger door, he motioned her inside.

"I need to call the police," she said. As they roared back to the convenience store, Pam Edwards spilled out her story to this kind stranger.

Tad was stunned. He and his family had been camping just a hundred yards away.

Pam's nightmarish ordeal triggered a vivid memory in his mind. The day before he'd been searching for firewood when he came upon a large mound of branches, palm fronds and pine cones. He later testified that the mound looked like a "blind" built so that no one could find it. Behind the blind, he'd seen a two-person pup tent and two unfriendly strangers.

"[One of the men] actually bared his teeth at me," Tad later said. "They acted like I was trespassing. They gave me a weird feeling."

The convenience store was located near Altoona, in Lake County. Since the crime had taken place in Marion County, Pam was escorted by Lake County deputies to Munroe Regional Medical Center in Ocala.

Marion County Sheriff's Department Detective Bill Sowder took the call. He taped a statement from Pam, gently encouraging her to remember as many details as possible. Her wounds were photographed—these included a deep gash on her head and ligature marks on her wrists and legs.

Then Sowder drove Pam back to the crime scene. On the way, she gave him a detailed description of her attackers.

The detective and victim turned onto Forest Road 86, then turned again on 86-F. Lake and Marion County deputies had already set up a perimeter around the crime scene.

As they drove, Pam spotted her car. It had been backed into a wooded area beside her old campsite. The vehicle was promptly impounded.

Pam pointed out the campsite to Sowder, then showed him where the assailants had camped. There, Sowder came across a backpack, a pair of boots, some twine and a long arrow shaft meant to spear fish. But lawmen couldn't find John's blue car and discovered the tag missing from Pam's vehicle. Sowder put out an updated BOLO (be on the lookout), transmitted by Lake County deputies.

A deputy drove Pam back to the hospital where she underwent a rape examination. Afterwards, she called her mother in Japan. Sobbing, Pam described the horrifying ordeal. Her parents immediately booked a flight to Ocala to be with their daughter and search for John.

Serological testing revealed the presence of semen inside Pam, as well as on her panties and sweatpants. Fibers consistent with a blue and black-checkered shirt were found in pubic hair combings.

At about 2 P.M., Detective Sowder received a call from Detective Jim Wisniewski. John's body had been located. Wisniewski stated that he'd been walking down a trail when he saw an area where the ground and leaves had been disturbed. He heard bottle-flies buzzing, then he saw a circle of blood with dirt sprinkled over it. On a nearby trail, Wisniewski came across more blood. Following the blood trail for about 100 feet, he found John's body.

The teenager lay facedown under a mound of pine needles, sand and freshly-cut palm fronds. He was wearing a sweatshirt and jeans and his hands were clasped in a fetal position. His left wrist had a shoestring tied around it and a shoestring was partially wrapped around the right wrist.

As investigators combed the area for additional evidence, John's body was taken to the morgue.

John Tilley, a forensic artist, met with Pam about five o'clock that Sunday afternoon. Based on descriptions she gave him, Tilley completed sketches of the suspects. These sketches were released to the media.

About an hour later, Marion County Sheriff's Department investigators Thomas Bibb and Carmen DeFalco met with Pam. She recalled that one of the suspects had a chipped tooth and wore an earring. Tilley made another sketch adding this information. The sketches were sent to all local law enforcement agencies and published in local newspapers the next day.

Three days later, forensic pathologist Dr. Janet Pillow performed an autopsy on the body of John Edwards. John was six feet three inches tall and weighed 175 pounds. Dirt was found in his mouth. His throat had been cut, making a single incision across his neck going through the muscles into the airway.

In addition to scores of lesser injuries all over John's body, his skull had been fractured. The fracture extended from the base of the skull to the bone that sits on top of the left eyeball. Dr. Pillow concluded that John had received at least three potentially-lethal blows to his head by an object that had a blunt surface.

Dr. Pillow would later testify in court that John had died in the early morning hours on Saturday. She also stated that the teenager had been alive when all of his wounds were inflicted. After hours of torture, he finally succumbed when his assailant slit his throat. The cause of death was listed as air hunger (the inability to breathe). Dr. Pillow had seen few murders as brutal as this one.

The Marion County Forensic Unit was promptly dispatched back to the Hopkins Prairie death site for yet another search. It didn't take long for a crime scene technician to locate an oak club near the area where John's body had been discovered. The stick was about four feet long and as thick as a baseball bat. It was later identified in court as the "walking stick" that Chris had carried.

Ken Ergle had been a law enforcement officer his entire working life. When he faced reporters on Saturday morning, he opined that his deputies would solve the case within twenty-four hours. He told the press that the case was falling into place and the perpetrators would soon be arrested.

By Sunday evening, he wasn't so sure.

While there seemed to be plenty of evidence, his investigators had been unable to put names on the assailants.

Bob Banker was a clerk at an auto parts store in Ocala. As he left to go home at 4:30 Saturday afternoon, he saw a blue car in the parking lot. A handwritten note on a jagged piece of cardboard was affixed to the dash. The note read: "We'll be back for our car later. It broke down."

Later that evening an Ocala Police Department patrolman spotted the car and notified the sheriff's department. It was towed to the county jail where it was searched and analyzed by a forensic team. Investigators discovered numerous personal items belonging to John and Pam as well as a fingerprint belonging to an individual identified as William Paul. A background check revealed that Paul was wanted in Osceola County for violation of probation.

On her way to work Monday morning, a delivery driver for the auto parts store, Molly Feathers, was listening to a local country music station. During a news report, she heard that the car had been found. She also heard a description of the two men who had murdered the camper.

She began loading her delivery truck and saw two men cutting through an alley behind the store. This wasn't uncommon, since the Salvation Army Center of Hope was only a couple of blocks away. Vagrants often used the alley as a shortcut, but the description from the radio clicked in.

The driver looked again. Both men wore camouflage clothing. One had a goatee and the other wore an oversized brass belt buckle with the inscription "KC" on it. Molly waited until they were out of sight, then sprinted for the door.

"Call the law," she shouted as she entered the store. "I just saw those two wanted men."

Banker reached for the phone while his co-worker relayed the descriptions of the men. After police failed to respond as quickly as she thought they should, the driver returned to her truck. Cops or no cops, she had deliveries to make. But she wondered as she drove her route whether the men she'd seen had been captured.

They hadn't. Molly saw them again on her way back to the store.

Now they were walking down Magnolia Avenue as if they didn't have a care in the world. She was so sure it was the fugitives that she whipped her truck around and went looking for a police officer.

She quickly flagged down the unmarked unit carrying detectives Bibb and DeFalco. (In Marion County, unmarked police vehicles are instantly recognizable due to their plain black-wall tires and the police antennas mounted on the trunk.) These investigators had exhausted their leads and were cruising around in the area where the blue car had been located.

Molly explained her suspicions to the detectives and told them where the men were located.

Bibb burnt rubber as he headed toward Magnolia. Moments later, the cops came to the railroad tracks that cut through the heart of Ocala. A train was passing and the mechanical arms were down at the crossing. As they slowed, Bibb and DeFalco spotted the suspects just inside the barrier, evidently waiting for the train to pass. Both men wore camouflage hats and jackets. One was wearing brown moccasins with leggings.

Bibb and DeFalco exited the car, drew their weapons and ran toward the two men.

"Police!" DeFalco shouted. "On your faces!"

The men raised their hands and slowly sank to the ground. DeFalco sensed that they had both been arrested before—they knew exactly how to act to prevent a physical confrontation.

The manhunt was over.

As the suspects were transported to the Marion County Jail, dozens of reporters milled outside. Also waiting were friends of John Edwards, who had driven down from Tallahassee to show support for Pam and her parents.

Lou Ciaccia, a fraternity brother of John's, said he was a friendly, likable person and a brilliant student.

"It's very sad," he said. "He had a lot of friends and was very popular. He really had it all ahead of him."

He surmised John's genial manner may have contributed to his death.

"He was a very upbeat, very outgoing guy," Lou mentioned. "Probably it wouldn't have happened if he weren't so nice to people."

Inside the interrogation rooms, detectives were trying to figure out who the assailants were.

"Chris" was the first to break. His name was William Christopher Paul, he said. A resident of Chattanooga, Tennessee, Paul was a thief and a chronic user of marijuana. Beginning at age thirteen, he'd spent time in virtually every juvenile institution in the Volunteer State. He admitted that he was an accessory to the murder and rapes. He blamed his accomplice, Loran K. Cole, also known as "Kevin," as the main perpetrator.

About fifteen minutes after Paul made his limited admission—in a room across the hallway—Cole told investigators his name and admitted that he'd been an accessory to the crimes. Not surprisingly, he blamed his partner as being the instigator.

Later that evening, Pam Edwards was called to the jail to view a lineup. She immediately picked out Loran Cole as the man who called himself "Kevin" and raped her twice. She was also adamant that he was the only one of the two who had the opportunity to murder her brother.

Early Monday morning, state's attorney Brad King met with his senior assistants. He appointed John Moore to be in charge of the prosecution. As Moore began preparing his case, he pulled up Cole's rap sheet. This included an extensive record of theft, burglary and dealing in stolen property, but he'd spent just two years and nine months in Florida prisons and jails. He also had a record in Ohio that included three theft-related charges in 1986 and 1987. Most recently, Cole had been sentenced to spend five years and six months in prison for dealing in stolen property. He'd been sentenced in 1992 but was released on June 15, 1993, after serving just one year and four months of that sentence. At the time of his arrest, Cole had warrants out for his arrest from Florida and Ohio.

William Paul accepted a plea bargain on July 14, 1995. He agreed to serve a life sentence with the possibility of parole if he would testify truthfully in the proceedings against Loran Cole.

The trial of Loran Cole began as scheduled with Circuit Court Judge William Swigert presiding. The state planned to seek the death penalty for the brutal murder.

Don Gleason, Cole's attorney, told the jury that evidence would show that his client was guilty of "some crimes," but that did not mean he murdered John Edwards.

To contradict that statement, Pam Edwards, now attending college in Colorado, was called to the witness stand. *St. Petersburg Times* crime reporter Victoria White wrote: "Over several hours, in a strong, clear voice that rarely broke with emotion, she spoke of how Cole and his companion, William C. Paul, first gained their trust with offers of help with their campfire, guidance through the woods and casual conversation, then jumped them suddenly on the moonlit night."

Pam hadn't wanted to go on the walk in the woods that Friday evening with two men they had just met. But she relented after her brother said with a big smile, "Oh, come on."

When they had been immobilized on the ground, John told her he was sorry for coaxing her to go on the hike. By morning, her only sibling was dead, his throat slashed. She testified that she remained captive through Saturday evening, then her abductors tied her to a tree.

At one point, Pam testified, she heard children setting up a camp nearby. Cole told her that "things would get ugly" if she called for help. Pam told jurors that she began to cry then. "I'm going to be a teacher," she said. "I love children."

During the cross-examination, Gleason asked her just a few straight-forward questions, leaving uncontested her identification of Loran K. Cole as both her kidnapper and rapist.

While she did not actually see Cole murder her brother, she explained that he had slipped off several times to "check" on John in the woods. Prosecutors theorized that it was on one such visit that Cole had killed John.

Don Gleason tried to suggest that Paul also had been alone in the woods with John. But on re-direct questioning, Pam stated that Paul's time alone with her brother was no more than a minute.

The defense was broken by Pam's testimony. The prosecution didn't even need Paul's testimony and he was never called.

After only seven hours of deliberation, the jury reached a verdict. Loran K. Cole was found guilty of two counts each of sexual battery while armed, robbery while armed and kidnapping while armed. They also found Cole guilty of first-degree murder. In separate proceedings, the jury unanimously recommended the death penalty.

Judge Swigert concurred and on December 20, 1995, Cole was sentenced to death.

While William Paul serves his sentence in one of Florida's maximum security prisons, Loran Cole sits on death row in Raiford.

Loran Cole created a Web page in 2000 on a site sponsored by the European Council Against the Death Penalty. The page, which has stayed on the Internet for years, is entitled: "A theologian awaits his execution." With this resource, he continues to deny his guilt.

In an "essay" about his case, Cole writes, "The theologian Loran Cole shall be executed by the state of Florida. Loran was innocently sentenced to death."

Charlene Hall, vice-president of the pro-death penalty site Justice for All, said, "It can be a horrible, shocking moment when they [victims' families] find a Web page dedicated to their loved one's killer, full of lies."

On his Web page, Cole describes himself as a high school graduate with a 4.0 grade point average. (According to available records, he dropped out of school in the tenth grade.) He also claims to have two bachelor's degrees, a paralegal certificate and claims to be working toward his doctorate in theology. He never mentions his many felony convictions prior to the murder.

Cole would have the reader believe that he was merely an unwilling witness to a brutal killing. "Should it be possible," he writes, "that you can be hold [sic] responsible for the offense of another person?"

He continues, "Imagine you're on the way in a car with your buddy, he says, 'Stop at that shop, I need something to smoke.' You stay in your car and cannot see what's happening in the shop. Your buddy comes back as if nothing did happen. Four blocks later the car is stopped by the police. It emphasizes that your buddy robbed the shop. He's going to be arrested and you, too—as an accomplice, though you didn't notice the robbery. You did nothing, but you're going to jail and get accused and condemned for a robbery of whom you don't know anything."

As Cole's appeals wound through the courts, semantics became twisted and the truth murky. In one hearing, Cole's new lawyer, Leslie Scalley, attempted to lay the blame for the murder on William Paul. "If you can't believe Pam Edwards's testimony that she didn't have sex with Mr. Paul," she asked, "how can you believe beyond a reasonable doubt that Mr. Paul did not have an opportunity to kill John Edwards?"

It didn't go unnoticed by the court that a brutal rape had become, in the mind of the defense, the equivalent of "having sex." The court ruled resoundingly, once again, in favor of the prosecution and against Loran Cole.

In fact, the convicted murderer has lost every appeal his lawyers have ever filed. The legal machinery, it seems, rumbles slowly and fitfully toward the extinction of Loran Cole.

What happens when young, naïve teenagers meet hardened criminals in the jungle? It's almost like a storyline from a movie. In this chapter, rape, murder and savage brutality played itself out in a remote area of the Ocala National Forest. For many years, the Forest had been attracting dopers and fugitives and yet the Forest Service had not dealt with the problems effectively. An innocent brother and sister suffered the consequences. It wasn't until many years later that the park rangers attempted (with limited success) to crack down on crime in the Forest. In the meantime, many hunters, fishermen, trail-walkers and nature-lovers have abandoned the Forest. The tragic crimes that continue to take place there must be stopped.

Part Three
A Poison Needle or the Chair?

Introduction

Even before it became a state, Florida was executing killers. The first execution took place in 1827 when the territory of Florida hanged a soldier named Benjamin Donica. Though the details of his crime are lost to time, records indicate that he committed a murder in Escambia County. Four additional executions followed before the mosquito-infested swamplands of America's southern peninsula became a state in 1845.

In the years that followed, the death penalty was meted out for crimes such as aiding a runaway slave, rape and accessory to murder. There were 117 hangings and 223 electrocutions. As of 2009, twenty convicted murderers have died by way of lethal injection.

Two, or maybe three, women (the number varies depending on which list is checked) have been executed in the state. Judias "Judy" Buenoano and Aileen Wuornos have had books written about their murderous lives. But it is also reported that before the Civil War, a slave named Celia was hanged for murdering her owner, Jacob Bryan, with a hoe.

A strange case in Key West ended on the gallows in 1897. A black man named Sylvanus Johnson was accused of raping a white woman. Mrs. Maggie Atwell nearly died from the assault and horrific beating that followed. A group of white men threatened to lynch Johnson, but were stopped by the sheriff and a group of armed black men. A race war nearly followed. William Gardner, a white man who had nothing to do with the affair, was shot and killed by a group of blacks. The mayor of Key West asked for the local militia and "national troops" to quell the violence. Johnson was then put on trial and admitted the assault. Incredulously, he seemed stunned when he was convicted. He exclaimed to the judge: "If God Almighty was a negro and had to be tried in Key West today, he would be hung!" The judge reminded him that he had admitted his own guilt. While awaiting his appeals, the sheriff further enraged white residents by taking the rapist on a drive around the city. After stopping at Leon's Saloon and drinking for two hours, the sheriff took the prisoner to his mother's house so she could tell her son goodbye. Sylvanus Johnson was strung up on September 13, 1897.

In 1910, Clevie Tedder, a thirteen-year-old girl, was riding her bicycle to school in Deland when Irving Hanchett, a fifteen-year-old parolee from the Connecticut State School for Boys, attacked her. It was one of the most brutal murders on record. "A bicycle which the girl was riding," reported the *Atlanta Constitution*, "was found 100 yards from where her body was discovered, indicating the assailant had struggled with her for this distance after knocking her from her wheel. In the body of the girl sixty-two knife wounds were counted. She was literally cut to pieces." In addition, she had been savagely beaten. Shoe prints and ripped clothing strewn along the trail indicated that Clevie had fought to the very end. Hanchett was quickly tracked down, and it was only due to quick thinking on the part of the local sheriff that he wasn't lynched then and there. At trial, Hanchett said he murdered the girl because she refused his advances. Though only fifteen, the killer was hanged.

On several occasions, the state executed four prisoners in one day. For example, an article in *The Evening Independent* in Massillon, Ohio, reported that on March 23, 1942, "four convicted slayers were put to death within fifty-eight minutes in Florida's electric chair today. The men, in the order in which they went to the chair, were: Worth Roberson, convicted of killing Mrs. Annice Roberts in Gilchrist County in 1937; Angie Michael Ciangetti, sentenced for the hammer slaying of Mrs. Anna K. Henson at Daytona Beach in 1940; Jecy Crawford, Negro, who stabbed Bronson Sweat to death in Jacksonville in 1939 and Walter Roberson, Negro, convicted of killing his wife with an axe in Dixie County."

In 1972, the United States Supreme Court ruled that capital punishment was unconstitutional. The death sentences of ninety-five convicted murderers were commuted. Just four years later, the justices reversed the decision and reinstated the ultimate penalty. This ushered in the "modern era" of executions. The first inmate in Florida to be executed after reinstatement was a drifter and petty crook named John Spenkelink who had been convicted of killing his traveling companion.

The story of how Florida's electric chair was replaced with lethal injection is told in chapter 16, "Son of Sparky."

The first Florida inmate to succumb to "Old Sharpie," as the needle came to be called, was a career robber named Terry Melvin Sims. On December 29, 1977, Sims and an accomplice entered the Longwood Village Pharmacy in Longwood intending to rob it. At the same time, a uniformed off duty deputy named George Pfeil walked into the store to pick up a prescription for his wife. When Sims saw the cop, he fired twice. Pfeil was mortally wounded, but pulled his gun and shot Sims in the hip. After more than twenty years of appeals, on February 23, 2000, Sims was strapped onto Florida's new gurney and peacefully drifted into a never-ending sleep.

Since 1990, Florida has averaged about two executions per year. During this time, the United States Supreme Court has further restricted who can

264 *Introduction*

be executed. The mentally retarded, persons under the age of eighteen and rapists (unless they murder someone while committing their crime) can no longer be put to death.

Like hanging, then electrocution, lethal injection is now under attack.

On June 8, 2000, as Bennie Demps was being strapped onto the gurney, he spoke to the onlookers. "They butchered me back there," he said. "I was in a lot of pain. They cut me in the groin. They cut me in the leg. I was bleeding profusely. This is not an execution, it is murder."

In 1971, while Demps and his companion were trying to crack open a stolen safe in an orange grove near Leesburg, a real estate agent drove up carrying a couple who were looking to buy property. The duo shot them, killing Nicholas and Celia Puhlick.

Demps had his death sentence commuted to life in prison during the brief period in which the death penalty was ruled unconstitutional.

Demps, unmindful of his good fortune, joined a group of inmates called "Perjury Incorporated." Their stated purpose was to rid the prison of "snitches." On September 7, 1976, he and several other inmates stabbed Alfred Sturgis to death. That's how Demps came to face the needle, which he said tortured him. Since he'd committed three atrocious murders, most Floridians didn't much care that he suffered for a few minutes before being put to sleep.

The future of capital punishment in Florida is in question. The majority of the justices of the Florida Supreme Court seem to view the death penalty negatively. If it weren't for the fact that the state's residents are overwhelmingly and fervently in favor of meting out death to murderers, the statute might already have been struck down.

Chapter 16
Son of Sparky

"Look, Allen, I think we could clear the whole matter up if you'd come downtown for an interview."
"Sure, I got nothing to hide. Let's get this over with."

> Detective Charles Kessinger, questioning suspect Allen Lee
> Davis about evidence in relation to a triple homicide.

When Old Sparky, Florida's seventy-six-year-old electric chair, had developed a penchant for fire and smoke, it was unceremoniously dumped. A new chair, rebuilt partly from the wood, leather and buckles of the ancient one, took its place. It was called Son of Sparky.

It sat for weeks, then months, unused and waiting, until seven o'clock on the morning of July 8, 1999.

That's when the door of the execution chamber opened and a wheelchair-bound prisoner was pushed into the room by four prison guards.

Allen Lee Davis, like Son of Sparky, had a nickname: Tiny. It was like calling a bald-headed guy "Curly." Davis weighed in at 349 pounds, just one less than the limit the electric chair could hold. Underneath a prison-issued white button-down shirt, his belly rolled with flabby layers of fat. The cellulite from Davis's thighs threatened to burst through his navy blue shorts. His swollen feet were shoeless, covered only by white medical stockings.

Davis's head had been shaved and glistened with gel. His face was fish-belly white and his eyes darted here and there. As he was wheeled toward the electric chair, the prisoners' lips quivered. Veins in his neck bulged out. There would be no bravado at this execution. A Texas prisoner facing the chair once said, "It's a good day to die. I walked in here like a man and I'm leaving here like a man." Not so with Allen Lee Davis.

In an adjacent room, twenty people had gathered to watch the convicted robber, child molester, burglar, thief and multiple murderer die. There was John Weiler, husband and father of the victims; a sister of victim Nancy Weiler; Ginny Brown-Waite, a state senator; John Sugg, an anti-death penalty activist and member of the American Civil Liberties Union of Florida; a couple of cops and some newspaper reporters. Peering into the death chamber through a panel of spotless glass, each was transfixed with his or her own thoughts.

The four guards grasped Davis's arms and attempted to pull him out of the wheelchair. He didn't budge. His hands trembled and he shook his head.

The second time they tried, the guards were more forceful.

They hoisted him into the chair, but he barely fit. His chest pounded and vibrated against his shirt as he wheezed.

During the sixteen years he'd spent in his cell at Florida State Prison in Starke, Davis had bloated up like a putrefying carcass. He superseded the bland prison menu by ordering a constant stream of chili dogs and candy bars and root beer from the prison canteen.

Over the years, Davis's regimen of "rest and ingest" caused him to develop hypertension, osteoarthritis, asthma and diabetes. He could barely hold his coffee cup due to shaking, and he gradually became deaf. Only fifty-four, doctors said that he had arteries of someone twice his age.

At 7:08, the guards strapped Davis's arms to the chair. Two leather belts were buckled tightly around his stomach. A metal conductor was attached to his right leg, about halfway between his ankles and knee.

The witnesses watched in silence as the guards strapped a heavy leather mask onto the lower part of Davis's face. Then they placed a black veiled hood similar to a welder's helmet over his eyes. Inside the hood was a one-size-fits-all round metal conductor. It was supposed to fit snugly around the head, but Davis's skull was too big. When the guards forced it, he roared once. Then, a moment later, he bellowed in pain again.

The seconds were ticking down.

At 7:09, the warden, standing in the background, asked Davis if he had any final words. Almost imperceptibly, he shook his head.

Suddenly, there was a popping noise. Davis jerked forward, like he'd been hit with a defibrillator. The searing smell of flesh enveloped the room.

His chest heaved. He was slammed with another jolt. Then another. Finally, he slumped in the chair, motionless.

Moments later, a trickle of blood began streaming down the mask, dripping onto Davis's chest. In an article entitled, "A Florida Execution," published on the American Civil Liberties Union of Florida Web site, activist Sugg described what he saw: "The power hit [Davis], he lurched against the straps. Then the gruesome part began. Blood blossomed on his shirt front, growing to about the size of a large saucer. There was more blood around his collar."

Several spectators gasped. Others sat pale and shaken. Some witnesses claimed that Davis was still breathing, even after the three jolts.

"[The execution] wasn't nice," said John Weiler. "I didn't expect it to be nice. I would have liked it to be a lot more painful. It was nowhere near the pain he inflicted on his victims."

Two previous executions in the state's original electric chair had brought howls of protest from around the world, but Florida officials blithely ignored the obvious problems with Old Sparky. Many viewed the chair like a once-kindly uncle who had developed dementia and turned mean: Just nurse the contraption along and maybe the problems will go away.

They didn't go away and Son of Sparky was supposed to correct them.

After the Tiny Davis fiasco, Floridians could no longer ignore their demented uncle.

On October 27, 1924, Frank Johnson, convicted of murdering a Jacksonville railroad engineer during a robbery, was the first person to die in Florida's new electric chair. Before his electrocution, local sheriffs had presided over the hanging of those sentenced to death.

Florida's chair, built by a cabinet shop in Jacksonville and electrified by none other than George Westinghouse, soon became known as Old Sparky. Although death in the chair could be gruesome at times, it was considered more humane than hanging.

One of the most infamous murderers ever executed in Florida was Guiseppe Zangara, convicted of shooting Chicago mayor Anton Cermak in Miami. While on stage with Franklin Delano Roosevelt during a political rally, the mayor stood in the background. Zangara, a disaffected anarchist, was in the crowd waiting for his chance to assassinate the hated president. However, as he raised his pistol, a bystander saw it and grabbed the shooter's hand just before he fired. Zangara missed Roosevelt, but scored a clean shot on the unlucky Cermak.

On March 20, 1933, ten days after being convicted of the murder, Zangara was led to the chair. His last words, directed toward a prison chaplain, were: "Get to hell out of here, you son of a bitch. I go sit down all by myself. Viva Italia. Goodbye to all poor people everywhere. Lousy capitalists. No picture? No one here to take my picture? All capitalists, lousy bunch of crooks. Go ahead. Push the button." Zangara seemed more upset about not having cameras to record his final exit than the actual execution itself.

A few years later, on December 11, 1936, the *Bradford County Telegraph* in Lake City published a semi-facetious article about two convicted murderers facing execution just before Christmas. "Can you imagine such a gay old fellow as Santa Claus, bringing you a black bordered death warrant eleven days before Christmas?"

In 1955, Samuel Hornbeck was electrocuted even though he didn't actually kill anyone. A longtime criminal with rap sheets in seven states, Hornbeck and Myron Goldman attempted to rob a tavern on the outskirts of Jacksonville. As they ran out to their getaway car, they were surprised by police. In a running gun battle, Jacksonville police officer Thomas A. Robinson was killed. Goldman, who shot Robinson, was also killed in the shootout, and Hornbeck was captured. Since Florida law makes all participants equally guilty if someone is murdered during the commission of a crime, Hornbeck's long career as a thief, burglar, robber and quasi-murderer came to an ignominious end in the wide-open arms of Old Sparky.

During its long, eventful life, it jolted the final breaths from 266 men and one woman. Black widow serial killer Judy Buenoano was unlucky enough to draw a ticket for the chair while Aileen Wuornos won the death row lottery: lethal injection.

Possibly the most reviled murderer in the history of the Sunshine State was serial killer Ted Bundy. On a raw, rainy day in February of 1978, twelve-year-old schoolgirl Kimberly Leach disappeared from Lake City Junior High School. Two months later, her body was found facedown in a hog trough in Suwannee County, about thirty-five miles away. Her throat had been slashed, her genitals mutilated and semen was found on her panties. Evidence pointed to Bundy as the killer and he was convicted and sentenced to death. In a separate trial, he was also convicted of murdering Lisa Levy and Margaret Bowman in the horrific Chi Omega sorority attacks in Tallahassee. (The total number of Bundy's victims was at least thirty-five—he was deathly afraid of being electrocuted and attempted to barter information about the locations of some of his victims for more time.)

On January 24, 1989, Bundy was strapped into Old Sparky. Two minutes later, he was dead. Radio stations across the state celebrated with the sounds of frying pans sizzling. Partiers outside the prison overwhelmed the few anti-death penalty opponents, chanting, "Fry, Bundy, fry."

By 1990, many states were moving away from the electric chair as a means of execution. But Florida doggedly stuck to its heritage. Then, on May 4, a prisoner named Jesse Tafero was strapped into the chair. He'd previously been convicted of numerous crimes, including rape, robbery and burglary. But that day he was scheduled to die for murdering Florida Highway Patrolman Phillip Black and a visiting Royal Canadian Mounted Policeman named Donald Irwin. During a routine traffic check, Tafero pulled a pistol and gunned down the two officers.

As the executioner pulled the switch, the prisoner's head erupted in flames. A witness to the execution, Ellen McGarrahan, described the scene in *Slate*: "The flames are nearly a foot high, they arc out from underneath the black leather hood; there is smoke, the huge buzzing sound of the electricity...There's ash falling on Tafero's shirt and he's nodding his head, he's heaving his chest in and out..." After three slugs of the current, Tafero finally slumped forward, dead.

By 1997, all but four states had switched to lethal injection. But not Florida; they still remained true to Sparky.

On March 24, Pedro Medina, released from a Cuban mental hospital and shipped to Florida in the notorious Mariel boatlift, was executed for murdering an Orlando schoolteacher. Blue and orange flames shot up out of his death mask and smoke filled the chamber. Michael Minerva, Medina's attorney, said, "It was brutal, terrible. It was a burning alive, literally."

Florida Attorney General Bob Butterworth had a different take on the execution. While speaking to reporters, he said, "People who wish to commit murder—they better not do it in the state of Florida, because we have a problem with our electric chair."

The new chair had been conceived for one purpose: to execute a behemoth named Allen Lee Davis. Old Sparky had too many miles on it. It was broken down and creaky and officials felt it wouldn't support Davis's weight.

There was another reason, according to McGarrahan. "The guards were worried that if the chair broke apart during an electrocution," she wrote, "the thick, black, high-voltage wires screwed to the inmate might rip loose and electrocute everybody in the room."

After a consultant was hired and recommended that the chair be replaced, officials took a replica of Old Sparky from the prison museum and patched it together with components from the *real* Old Sparky.

Thus, Son of Sparky was born.

"Bloody death in the chair," screamed one headline from a July 19, 1999, article in the *Miami Herald*, after Davis's execution. "Witnesses said the blood appeared to come from Davis's chest," the article read, promulgating a myth that exists to this day. (An autopsy as well as photographs taken immediately after the electrocution revealed that the blood was from a nosebleed. The bleeding was caused by blood-thinning medications taken by the obese inmate.)

The writer of the *Miami Herald* article didn't quote John Weiler, who had held a news conference immediately following the execution.

"Davis didn't show an ounce of remorse!" he exclaimed.

Once, many years before, the anguished husband and father had said, "My personal life, career and all my dreams, including my home, are all gone. It is cruel and unusual punishment [for] the victims living and dead to know that this animal still breathes." The grieving husband was good for many quotes, had the media wanted them. But because he refused to join the politically correct bandwagon, he was ignored by most writers for the mainstream media.

The ACLU even went so far as to criticize Weiler himself. Anti-death penalty advocate John Sugg wrote: "Weiler...said that 'God approves' of the people of Florida killing Davis. At that, I am troubled. Whenever a state usurps God's prerogatives of meting out life and death, we're on desperately dangerous ground."

John Koch, a reporter for the Florida Radio Network, said, "This execution of Tiny Davis was not bloodless. The man obviously suffered."

"Florida's record of executions," claimed ACLU Executive Director Howard Simon, "and the Legislature's obsession with electrocution as the method of execution, has been barbaric."

Weiler responded by calling the murders of his wife and children "barbaric."

He had a point. Had those who complained about the brutality of the execution been at the crime scene and witnessed the murders of Davis's victims, they may have been less inclined to criticize capital punishment.

On and on it went. "Florida's Messy Executions Put the Electric Chair on Trial," roared a headline from an anti-death penalty article in the *New York Times*. The article of nearly two thousand words couldn't find the decency to even mention the names of the victims and treated John Weiler as if he was invisible. The reporter did, however, quote several anti-death penalty writers and criminologists who professed that execution of murderers was not a deterrent.

Amnesty International, which not only is opposed to execution but also to life sentences, released the following quote: "Blood poured from the chest and mouth of convicted killer Allen Lee Davis..."

Truth seemed to no longer matter in the debate.

After Davis's execution, there were few pro-death penalty articles. One stands out. Bob Greene, editorialist for the *Chicago Tribune* and formerly opposed to the death penalty, wrote: "There was quite a bit of blood in the Weiler home after Davis killed the mother and her two children. Considerably more blood than inadvertently appeared on Davis' shirt during the execution....And now Allen Lee Davis is dead. Evidently his death was a somewhat unpleasant experience for him. There are a lot of things in this world for the public to worry about. Davis' discomfort is not necessarily one of them."

The *Florida Times-Union*, located in Jacksonville where the crimes occurred, published an article on July 9, 1999, entitled,"Justice is done." It raised an interesting question:"A protester outside the prison carried a sign asking, 'Why do we kill people who kill people to show that killing people is wrong?' The answer: We don't. Rational people know it is wrong to kill. Killers are executed to make certain they do not kill again."

Within days of Davis's botched execution, the case made its way from the court of public opinion to the Florida Supreme Court. And a series of photographs released by one of the justices would crash the court's Web site and help turn the tide in the much-contentious debate.

After the bloody electrocution of Allen Lee Davis, attorneys for Thomas Provenzano, the next prisoner on the state's list to be executed, filed an emergency appeal with the Florida Supreme Court.

On January 10, 1984, Provenzano had walked into the Orange County Courthouse for a hearing on a disorderly conduct charge. He'd come prepared. Two handguns and a semiautomatic rifle were sewn into his clothes. His mission was to murder the two police officers who had arrested him.

As bailiff William Wilkerson began to search him, Provenzano pulled out a handgun and began firing. Wilkerson, shot in the face, was killed on the spot, while security guards Harry Dalton and Mark Parker were severely wounded. Dalton was paralyzed and died seven years later from complications caused by the shooting. Parker was also paralyzed from the shoulders down. The two officers he'd planned to kill were in another room and escaped the carnage.

There was no doubt about Provenzano's guilt, only his mental state. His attorneys tried to use the "not guilty by reason of insanity" defense. It failed miserably for one reason—he really wasn't crazy. Provenzano was convicted and sentenced to death. He later took to calling himself "Jesus Christ" in hopes of getting his sentence overturned, but the courts consistently ruled that he was legally sane.

Provenzano was scheduled to become the forty-fourth inmate to be electrocuted since the reinstatement of the death penalty in 1976. After Davis's bloody death, the Florida Supreme Court delayed the killer's execution in order to rule on whether the electric chair was constitutional.

On August 3, 1999, after hearing from dozens of witnesses who had viewed not only Davis's execution, but also the previous executions of Judy Buenoano, Daniel Remeta, Leo Jones and serial murderer Gerald Stano, the court ruled that "Florida's electric chair as it exists in its present condition does not constitute cruel or unusual punishment, and therefore, is not unconstitutional."

However, the dissenting opinion written by Justice Leander Shaw vibrated with anger and indignation toward a government that would allow the "torture" of a condemned man.

"The execution of Allen Lee Davis," Shaw wrote, "...differed from prior executions in that here, Department of Corrections officials took post-execution color photos of Davis before he was removed from the electric chair. (Several of the photos are appended to this dissenting opinion.) These photos, when combined with eyewitness accounts, provide a vivid picture of a violent scene..."

Three photographs were published. They'd been taken seconds after the current was switched off. One was a side shot of Davis slumped in the chair—a puddle of blood stained his shirt. The second photo showed his face and the bloody mask. His white shirt had been unbuttoned, showing smears of blood staining his chest and stomach. The third picture was another close-up of his face—an image of agony that belied the argument that Davis felt no pain.

When the photos appeared on the Web site of the Supreme Court, they were viewed by millions. The reaction was predictable. Europeans concluded that Floridians were brutal, uncouth assassins. More than one visitor to the Web site posted one word: "Barbarians." Many Americans agreed. The majority of Floridians, however, felt that the unremorseful killer got exactly what he deserved.

Those three photos were to be Thomas Provenzano's ticket to a much easier death. As his appeals surged toward the district court of appeals, it looked as if the scheduled executions in Florida would be held up for months, maybe years, while the Federal courts debated whether the electric chair constituted "cruel and unusual punishment." To make sure there were no lengthy delays in the process, the Florida legislature reluctantly passed a bill adding lethal injection to the state's methods of execution.

Inmates now had two choices—Son of Sparky or Old Sharpie, as the needle was now called. Many breathed a huge sigh of relief. Only a masochist, it was felt, would choose electrocution over lethal injection.

Provenzano was not a masochist. He chose Old Sharpie. On June 21, 2000, he was strapped onto a gurney and stuck with a needle. For murdering one man and paralyzing two more, he went to sleep forever.

Allen Lee Davis was born in Millinockett, Maine, on July 20, 1944. His mother, Sandra, was sixteen and his father, Nathan, was one year younger. They married shortly after she became pregnant.

The Davis clan had little money. Allen, called Bud, initially lived with his grandmother. "When Bud was a baby," a relative said, "he sometimes had convulsions. He could hardly breathe and would choke and shake all over." Since the family couldn't afford a doctor, they hired the services of a mid-wife. Her remedy was to cool the child down with water.

Davis's parents had two more sons. They separated shortly after their third son was born. Nathan joined the Navy and made it a career. Since he was at sea during most of his career, he rarely saw his kids. Yet the Navy sent Sandra a small "child support" allotment each month.

Millinocket had a population of about 5,000 people. For most of the year, subfreezing temperatures enveloped the area. Davis grew up on the wrong side of the tracks, in "The Pines." At one time, fifteen relatives lived in a small house with Davis's parents, including Allen and his two brothers. They cut their own wood to heat the house. There was no running water or inside bathrooms. The home was "as cold inside as it was outside," said one relative close to the family.

After she had separated from her husband, Sandra moved with her sons to nearby Skunk Hollow. There she rented a rat-infested, wallpaper shack with no heat. When Davis was nine, Sandra divorced his father and married Kenneth Douglas. Things didn't get any better. The family moved again, this time down the road to Medway. Since neither parent worked, they qualified for food stamps to supplement the meager allotment sent by the Navy.

Allen Davis was large and heavy for his age and had trouble making friends. He also stuttered.

As he grew older, he began getting in trouble. In 1961, he was convicted of child molestation in Bangor, Maine. He was sentenced to six months to three years in prison for fondling an eleven-year-old girl.

Unfortunately, his large, extended family blamed his criminal activities on everyone except Davis, helping to enable his illegal behavior that would end with the deaths of three innocent victims. The police "had it in for him," relatives claimed. His father was abusive. His stepfather was a brutal drunk who treated his children like slaves. The kids at school picked on Davis. The poverty he grew up in was responsible for his antisocial behavior. Family members claimed he was easily led and therefore not responsible for his acts.

They even blamed his victims. For instance, when he was arrested for child molestation, relatives claimed that Davis "had never forced himself on a child if the child did not resist or complain."

In 1963, after being released from prison, Davis went to Maryland to live with his natural father. Two years later, a drunken Davis crashed Nathan's car and the two friends who were with him were killed. After he fully recovered from his injuries, Davis was convicted of involuntary manslaughter. He served a brief sentence in a federal prison for this offense.

Davis entered Spring Grove State Hospital near Baltimore a year later for "treatment of his abnormal attraction to young children." Hospital records indicate that Davis "knew something was wrong with him but he does not know how to help himself." He reported to staff that "if [the children] don't say anything...he continues...and most of the time...the children seem willing."

Like many pedophiles, throughout his life Davis continued to maintain that his young victims "wanted" to have sex with him.

In 1969, Davis's natural father and stepmother moved to Jacksonville, Florida, and Davis moved there to be close to them. He worked at several jobs but never stayed employed for long. He was fired from one job after he became angry and destroyed an expensive machine on purpose. He worked for a while at his father's successful construction company, but didn't last there, either. He was laid off from his last job as well.

Shortly before committing a robbery that would once again send him to prison, Davis was caught staking out a residence with a revolver and stocking mask. His plan, he admitted, was to commit an armed home invasion robbery. He also robbed an oil company employee at gunpoint, but was never charged with that crime.

On October 6, 1973, Davis and a friend robbed a businessman who was making a deposit at a bank automatic teller machine. Davis plead guilty to the armed robbery and was sentenced to fifteen years in prison.

In 1979, he was released on parole.

Almost exactly three years later, while still under state supervision, Davis committed one of the most heinous crimes in Jacksonville history.

When Jacksonville Sheriff's Office Homicide Detective Charles Kessinger entered the Weiler home, he found a gruesome scene.

It was Wednesday, May 12, 1982.

The next-door neighbor of the Weilers, who lived in Jacksonville's exclusive subdivision, had called the sheriff's office asking the dispatcher to send a deputy for a "welfare check" on the family. (Jacksonville was the largest incorporated city in the world—in the 1960s, Duval County had been consolidated into the city proper and the Jacksonville Sheriff's Office served the entire county.) John, the husband of Nancy and father of nine-year-old Kristy and five-year-old Kathy, had been trying to call his family for several hours, the neighbor said. He was in Pittsburgh on business and had been unable to get anyone to answer the phone. He'd finally called the neighbor and asked her to check on his family. After receiving no answer to her repeated knocks on the door of the Weiler residence, she called police.

Two deputies arrived and entered the home through an unlocked door. They came on a scene out of a horror movie. Three blood-soaked bodies lay in separate rooms. After checking to see if an intruder was hiding in the house, they backed out and called the Homicide Unit.

Kessinger cautiously entered the house, careful not to disturb evidence. Almost immediately, he saw a child lying motionless on the living room floor. She looked to be five or six years old and was facedown. Her arms were outspread—it looked as if she'd been trying to swim out of a massive puddle of blood that surrounded her. Because of her bloody clothing, Kessinger was unable to see where her wounds were located. The child's face had numerous abrasions on it, but most of the bleeding seemed to come from her back.

She was dead.

He looked around. A table was knocked over and a child's sneakers lay several feet apart near the fireplace. *Had she been trying to get away*, Kessinger may have wondered, *and literally run out of her shoes?*

He continued moving through the house. There were three bedrooms. The first was empty.

In the second room, another young girl lay dead. Face up on the bed, she was older than the child in the living room, although Kessinger couldn't guess her age. She was wearing leotards and a black blouse. (Kessinger later learned that she'd just returned home from a dance recital before she was murdered.) Surrounding her were the remnants of childhood. Stuffed teddy bears. Dolls. Wall posters of rock stars. A bookbag lay beside the bed. The sheets the girl reclined on were stained blood-red.

This time the detective could instantly see what had caused her death.

One bullet had torn through her blouse and entered her chest. A second round had shattered her face. Her arms were pinned behind her back. Kessinger bent down and saw the wisp of a nylon cord inching out from beneath the child. It was obvious that her hands had been tied behind her back.

The killer had rummaged through the room. Drawers were open and items had been knocked off a nightstand.

Something wasn't right about the scene. The first thought that popped into the detective's mind was to check out sex offenders in the area.

As he moved slowly about the house, a team of forensic specialists stood in the background. They'd been made aware that they were about to investigate one of the most brutal mass murders in the history of the city. There would be lots of media attention. They had to get it right.

Kessinger stepped into the master bedroom.

Yet another body lay on the floor at the foot of the bed. The bloody scene was a replay of the previous murders. The face had been pulverized and the only way the detective could tell that the victim was a female was because she wore a gown and had long hair.

Kessinger stepped carefully around the body. He peered into the bathroom and stopped in his tracks. The tub was half-full of water. He deduced that the woman had been taking a bath before she was attacked.

Had she heard the gunshots? Had she heard her children scream? Did she instinctively realize that something was amiss and rush out to check on her children only to be confronted by a killer?

A question kept gnawing at Kessinger. All three victims had had their faces mutilated. Why?

As the detective maneuvered past the body to return to the living room, something caught his eye. A broken piece of wood, maybe two inches long and an inch wide, lay on the floor near the victim's head. It had some kind of design or logo on it. As he walked out of the house, he called the evidence to the attention of the forensics crew.

Kessinger's next stop was to speak with the next-door neighbor who'd called 911. John Weiler was a good friend, she said. He was an engineer and had recently been transferred back to the company's main plant in Pittsburgh. He didn't want to pull his children out of school in the middle of the year, the neighbor said, so he was temporarily commuting back and forth. In June, the family planned to join him up north.

"He seemed very much in love with his wife and adored his children," the neighbor said.

Nancy Weiler was a stay-at-home mom. Much of her time was devoted to helping out in the school her children were attending. In fact, Nancy was the secretary of the Parent-Teacher Association of her children's middle school.

Kristy would have turned ten tomorrow, the neighbor said, and she planned to have a birthday party at home after school. All the kids were supposed to arrive dressed up like disco dancers. Kristy was a beautiful child and as smart as she was pretty. Even at nine, her goal was to become a nuclear engineer.

Katherine, called Kathy, was five. She was as smart and as pretty as Kristy, but she wasn't as outgoing as her older sister.

"Do you know of any enemies the family might have?" Kessinger asked the neighbor, who was still reeling from the events that transpired.

The neighbor seemed puzzled by the question, as if the thought hadn't crossed her mind. She shook her head. "Beautiful family," she said. "They have it all."

It was late in the afternoon when Kessinger walked to the house on the other side of the Weiler residence. The home was on prime property, backed up to a canal that fronted the Intracoastal Waterway. A black, oversized pickup truck sat in the driveway.

Allen Lee Davis's father answered the door.

Nathan and his wife had been bowling last night, he explained, and had returned home about ten o'clock. Kessinger noticed that he seemed reserved. His wife barely spoke. The Weilers seemed to be nice enough, the man said, but their paths didn't cross much.

"Do you have any idea who might have broken into the Weiler home?" Kessinger asked.

Nathan shook his head.

Just then, Allen Lee Davis walked into the room. He was huge, at least 300 pounds. Nathan introduced him as his son, "Bud."

"Bud was the last to see them alive," his father said.

"How do you know?"

Davis spoke for the first time. He stuttered and was difficult to understand, but he seemed eager to talk.

"Those two girls asked me to come over and fix their bathroom door," Davis said. "But when I got there, I found out somebody else had done it."

"What happened then?"

"I left. That was the last I seen them."

"Did you see Mrs. Weiler?"

"Yeah," Davis said. "I spoke with her for a minute. She told me the job was already done. Then I came back over here and got in my truck and went back home."

His father was listening to the conversation.

"I know this looks bad," Nathan said. "But a gun I had is missing."

"How do you know?" Kessinger asked.

"Well, it was on the top of the refrigerator when we left home last night. Now it's gone."

Kessinger, Davis and Nathan walked into the kitchen.

Nathan took an ad off a nearby shelf and handed it to the detective.

"It looked just like that," he said. The gun in the advert was a .357 Magnum Ruger Blackhawk revolver.

"How did it go missing?" Kessinger asked. "Did anybody break in?"

Nathan shook his head and stated that he'd bought the gun about ten years earlier. He'd recently gotten a notice from the manufacturer asking that he return it for a safety recall. Davis's father was planning to send it back and placed it on the refrigerator. Nathan handed Kessinger a box of ammunition he'd bought when he got the gun.

"Does anybody else have a key to your house?"

"My son, Bud," he said, looking over at Davis. "He was over here last night while we were gone. He called me and asked if I was going to be home. I told him we were going bowling, but it would be all right for him to come over."

"One other thing," Nathan said. "I only keep five bullets in it. Even though it's a six-shooter, it's safer that way."

Kessinger turned to Davis. "Did you know the Weiler family?" he asked.

Davis shook his head.

"You never met them?" Kessinger asked.

"Not before last night."

"Why would they ask you to fix their bathroom door if you didn't know them?"

Davis shrugged.

"Did you take your father's gun?"

Davis hesitated again, then said, "No."

"Would you mind if we take a look in your truck?"

"No problem," Davis said.

A member of the forensics team, which was still in the Weiler house, was called outside. She conducted a brief scan of the truck.

"Look at this," she said, pointing to a length of nylon rope. "Looks just like what Kristy was tied with."

She bagged the rope and added it to other evidence that had been found in the Weiler home. Behind the seat, she saw a shirt—it was stained with a red substance that looked like blood. She took that as well.

"I know it doesn't look good," Davis blurted, after watching the quick perusal of his truck.

Kessinger didn't want to jump to conclusions, but he figured he had a good suspect. Davis had admitted being in the suspect's home at about the time the family was murdered. The rope certainly looked like a match to the one used to tie the child's hands.

Kessinger looked out on the road and saw several news vans parked in front of the Weiler home.

Davis agreed to go downtown for questioning.

In the afternoon, Dr. Bonaficio Floro, Duval County medical examiner, came to the Weiler residence to oversee the removal of the bodies.

"When Floro left the house yesterday afternoon," an article from the May 13, 1982, *Jacksonville Times-Union* read, "he wiped tears from his eyes and brushed aside reporters' questions until he had made a preliminary examination. He was visibly shaken."

Later, Floro told reporters that he got emotional, because he was the father of a twelve-year-old girl and two younger boys. "You get emotional for anybody who had kids that died," he said. "They're so innocent. They did not know what was going on."

In the autopsy, Floro concluded that Nancy Weiler had died of "blunt trauma" to the head, face and neck. She'd been struck at least twenty-five times with a blunt object. Her skull was fractured in several places and her face had been beaten so severely that she was unrecognizable. She was three months pregnant and the child had died from lack of oxygen.

Kristy had died of gunshot wounds. She'd been shot in the "upper left chest area" and in the face. Floro stated that either would have killed her.

Kathy had been shot in the lower back and bled to death. She'd been beaten about the face, possibly with the gun, but those injuries were not life-threatening.

Night had fallen when Davis and Detective Kessinger arrived at the station. Lieutenant Derry Dedmon was assigned to polygraph Davis.

When asked if he had murdered Nancy, Kristy and Kathy Weiler, Dedmon said that the machine indicated Davis was lying.

After the examination, Davis looked worried. Finally, he stood up and said, "I flunked it, didn't I?"

Dedmon nodded.

Davis was arrested immediately and charged with the three murders.

The search of the Weiler home and questioning of friends and neighbors of Davis had turned up a wealth of evidence.

Most telling were pieces of a gun found near Nancy's body. "These pieces," a court document read, "included a medallion with a Ruger Blackhawk trademark, pieces of a wooden grip handle, pieces of a trigger guard and a main spring set, all of which were consistent with having come from a Ruger Blackhawk revolver." Although the gun was never found, the pieces exactly matched the same kind missing from atop his father's fridge.

Detectives concluded that Davis had beaten Nancy with the gun and, during the horrific assault, broke the handle and trigger guard.

The bullets found in the victims' bodies matched the make and manufacturer of Nathan's gun.

In addition, a length of nylon cord taken from Davis's pickup was "fracture matched" to the rope that was used to tie Kristy's hands. Mary Henson, a microanalyst for the Florida Department of Law Enforcement, later testified that "the rope around Kristy's hands had been cut from the rope found in Davis' truck." Because it was nylon, the pieces fit together perfectly like those of a jigsaw puzzle.

Three neighbors said that around nine o'clock they noticed Davis walking up the road about a block from the Weiler residence. All three had recognized him because of his massive size. One neighbor said he had a gun.

Detectives interviewed a friend of Davis's. He stated that at about 6:30 that afternoon, Davis had called him. He was out of a job, he said, and wanted to commit a burglary. The friend drove Davis to his father's house and returned home.

At about 9:00, Davis called and asked his friend to pick him up. He parked about a block from Davis's father's house and Davis walked to him. Davis was carrying three paper sacks; one had a 35 mm camera in it. Davis said he'd committed a burglary to get money.

John Weiler had returned home and had gone through the house where his family died. He identified several missing items, including jewelry and a 35 mm camera. The distraught father went to stay with friends.

Investigators continued to interview Davis. After a while, he finally admitted to taking the revolver off his father's refrigerator. He stated that he "might have" taken it with him to the Weiler home. He remembered "quarreling" with Nancy Weiler. She was yelling and screaming at him and he was backing away.

But he said he couldn't remember what happened after that.

He continued to insist that he'd gone to the house to repair the door. Prosecutors would later argue that it made no sense for Nancy Weiler to send her children next door to ask a complete stranger to come into her house when the work had already been done by a neighbor she knew.

Although DNA testing was not available in 1982, blood typing was well-known to investigators. Court documents later revealed the findings of the serologist.

"Blood on the defendant's boots could not have been his own (or Kathy's or Kristy's), but was consistent with having come from Nancy Weiler (it matched by type and two enzymes) and also approximately 2.4

percent of the total population," the document revealed. "Blood on the defendant's shirt could not have been his (or Kathy's or Kristy's), but was consistent with having come from Nancy Weiler (matching by type and four enzymes) and also approximately .86 percent of the population (less than one in a hundred)..."

As investigators continued to interview Davis, the local media grabbed onto the case and ran. In fact, in Davis's later appeals, the defense would claim that because pretrial publicity was prejudicial, the verdict should have been dismissed.

One of the news items the defense objected to was published by the *Jacksonville Journal* on May 13. The headline read: "Explaining girl's slaying a tough job for teacher."

"Kristina," the article read, "who was called Kristy, was a bouncy, 'cheerleader type' who enjoyed doing handicrafts with her mother... She had been selected by her classmates as the March 'supercitizen'... Yesterday would have been her tenth birthday. She had planned a birthday party at her home after school and her class was taking a field trip to the zoo."

Another *Jacksonville Journal* article was entitled "Alligator impedes probe." The article described searchers in the canal behind the Davis's house who were unable to continue to look for the missing gun because of a group of huge, aggressive alligators. Police were fearful "not that another suspect might be at large, but that relatives or friends of Allen Lee Davis, the thirty-seven-year-old shipyard welder charged with the triple slayings, could try to prevent investigators from discovering evidence."

Davis's father, who had cooperated with the police, surely was furious.

John Weiler was also enraged. His whole world was crumbling. And for what? A few hundred dollars worth of jewelry and a camera? Nancy would have given Davis that to spare the lives of her kids. The barbaric nature of the murders ate at him. Even if the rest of the world was against him, he would spend his life making sure that Allen Lee Davis was executed for his horrific crimes.

The trial opened on February 1, 1983, before Circuit Judge Major B. Harding. Davis was charged with three counts of first-degree murder.

Since Davis admitted to being in the Weiler home, but not to the murders, prosecutors used circumstantial evidence to buttress their case.

It was believed that Davis broke into the home for two primary purposes. The first was to burglarize the home and take items he could sell, and the second was to molest Kristy Weiler, whom he'd seen during his many visits to his father's house.

As he entered the home, Davis saw Kristy (who'd returned home almost simultaneously) and held her at gunpoint, forcing her into her bedroom. He tied her hands behind her back, then tried to molest her. However, the frightened girl screamed. Davis panicked and shot her, first in the chest, then in the face.

He now realized that he had to get rid of everyone in the house. He spotted five-year-old Kathy, who had heard the commotion and gunshots, fleeing through the living room toward the front door. Davis fired three rounds. One hit her in the back. She fell, but continued to moan and claw at the carpet. Davis thought he had one bullet left in the gun, since he had used five. He decided to save that round for his next victim, so he beat the dying child in the face with the pistol until she stopped moving.

By this time, Nancy Weiler had heard the gunshots and jumped out of the bathtub. As she raced toward her bedroom door to try to protect her children, she was met by Davis. He pointed the gun at her and pulled the trigger, but there were no bullets left in the pistol. Davis then began beating the defenseless woman about the face. He hit her at least twenty-five times, cracking her skull in several places and breaking the gun.

After killing the occupants of the house, Davis rummaged through each room, taking three bags full of items he could quickly sell, including jewelry and the expensive camera.

On the way out, he may have dumped the gun in the canal, or he may have kept it and gotten rid of it later.

Davis called his friend to come pick him up. They met a block away from the Davis's house so witnesses wouldn't see the truck in his dad's yard.

The defense attempted to get the case thrown out because of massive pretrial publicity. When that failed, they used the insanity defense.

Three days later, the jury convicted Davis of the three counts of murder. A month later, he was sentenced to die.

Fast-forward sixteen years.

Allen Lee Davis was executed.

Even before he was forced into the electric chair, his victims were largely forgotten.

As the cold-blooded monster roared his way to extinction, his own suffering became the focus of the courts, the media and the public.

Nancy, Kristy and Kathy Weiler deserved better.

So did John Weiler.

A substantial majority of Floridians believe in the death penalty. Serial killers such as Ted Bundy, Danny Rolling and Aileen Wuornos have paid the ultimate price for their heinous crimes. Lesser known child-sex murderers who have been executed (Mark Dean Schwab, Aubrey Dennis Adams, Jr., Arthur Frederick Goode, Richard Henyard, etc.) make it difficult for even the most avid anti-death advocate to argue successfully with the average Florida citizen. But the trend of the courts is to abolish the death penalty. Several botched executions, such as the one described in this chapter, and the release of innocent persons from death row, have given ammunition to those who oppose executions. For better or worse, the death penalty is probably on its last legs.

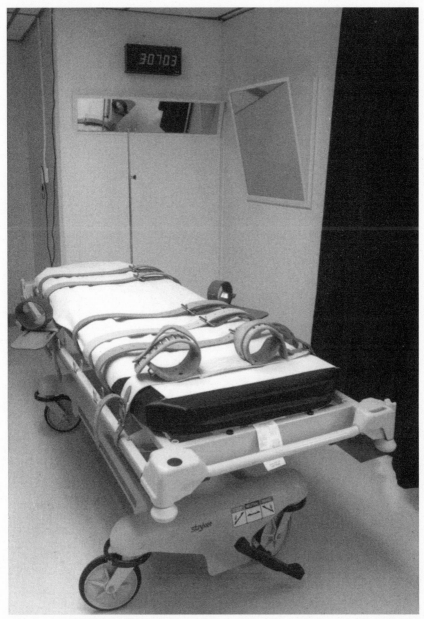

Florida's lethal injection gurney, where "Old Sharpie" sends death row inmates to their final resting place.

Conclusion

A skinny ponytailed stranger began breaking into the homes of women in New Smyrna Beach in 2001. Some were young, others as old as eighty-nine. Nicknamed the "Naked Tickler" by the media, he wore a ski mask but no clothing. He caressed his sleeping victims' feet until they awoke—then the intruder fled the scene, holding his hands over his genitals. He was never caught. It's thought that the Tickler victimized at least twelve women before disappearing back into the shadows.

Florida seems to have more than its share of such weird crimes. In another instance, astronaut Lisa Nowak drove non-stop from Houston, Texas, to Orlando to confront a hated rival for the hand of a fellow space traveler whom she loved. According to news accounts, Nowak wore a diaper so she wouldn't have to stop. This bizarre incident had Floridians shaking their heads.

Hundreds of thousands of new residents move to the Sunshine State each year. Combined with the twenty million who already call Florida home and the fifty million or so tourists who arrive annually, people can sometimes feel like trapped mice.

With so many individuals in one place, a small percentage are going to be deranged. Some of these individuals will commit strange crimes such as those mentioned above.

Most of us who call Florida home go about our daily lives, rarely thinking about the murderers who walk among us. Unless some unusual crime grabs the headlines, we like to make "water fountain talk" about our favorite sports team or maybe the latest hurricane or wildfires or any of the many ecological disasters that regularly afflict the state. (For instance, with our constantly surging population, how long will our water hold out?)

Traditional values, in our opinions, have deteriorated. Those cultural beliefs were once the glue that held society together. Some of today's youth have no moral compass to ground their behavior. Florida seems to be a hotbed for teens who torture and murder the homeless—the usually mild weather that brings transients to our state may inadvertently put them in danger.

Three Broward County teenagers snuck up on a homeless man sleeping on a park bench. Using baseball bats, seventeen-year-old Thomas Daugherty and nineteen-year-olds William Ammons and Brian Hooksbegan began beating forty-five-year-old Morris Gaynor. By the time they were done, they'd broken his nose, fractured five ribs and crushed his skull. He died a few hours later. The year was 2006. A previous attack by the same group of teens on another homeless man had been captured on video and its viciousness stunned even seasoned cops.

Daugherty, the ringleader, received life in prison. He came from a highly dysfunctional home. His mother admitted on the stand that he began smoking marijuana at age eleven. His father wasn't around and he grew up with little guidance.

Florida's state-of-the-art transportation system facilitates those who commit illegal acts. The state has two major interstates (I-75 and I-10) that crisscross the state. In addition to the Florida Turnpike, a toll road that traverses the entire east coast, thousands of other modern freeways spider-web the state. This mobility makes fleeing from a crime easy.

All-night convenience stores and restaurants are easy targets. On July 22, 2008, a murder was caught on videotape near I-10 north of Lake City. Linda Raulerson was closing a food store at 9:00 P.M. when a man entered through the front door. Without provocation, he stepped up to the counter and shot her. Although wounded, Raulerson complied with the gunman's demands and handed him the cash. But even that failed to appease him and he fired again. She died alone behind the counter of the store she'd owned for many years.

The entire robbery took only a few seconds. It was recorded on an audio/video monitor. After gunning down Raulerson, the robber sprinted outside, got into a white car and drove away. The case, which remains unsolved, illustrates the mobility of Florida criminals. Stymied law enforcement officials theorized that the killer may have pulled off the interstate and committed a "quickie" robbery, maybe for gas money. Within minutes, he could have been miles away.

As we've discussed, Florida is a body dumper's paradise. On the night of January 23, 1971, a group of drug smugglers planned to meet a shrimp boat off Sandy Creek in the Gulf of Mexico. The ship was loaded with tons of marijuana from Colombia. Walter Gale Steinhorst was guarding the only road into the isolated area where the drop-off was to be made.

Suddenly, a pickup truck drove up. Steinhorst was amazed to see two men and two teenage girls in the truck. He was even more amazed to find out that he knew one of the men. (Cops never determined why the four were there—many thought it was for a rendezvous, others thought they'd gotten wind of the drug transfer and wanted to watch.)

Steinhorst immediately shot and killed Harold Sims, the man he recognized. Afterwards, he held Douglas Hood, Sandra McAdams and Sheila McAdams captive until the drop was made. Then the smugglers made a decision to execute the unlucky trio.

It didn't take them long to figure out where to dump the bodies. In Florida's Panhandle, sinkholes can be hundreds of feet deep. The four bodies were wired to cinderblocks and dumped in a "bottomless" sinkhole in Taylor County, miles away from Sandy Creek.

About a year later, a scuba diver stumbled onto one of the corpses and the sordid scheme was busted. (Even so, only Steinhorst and one cohort were convicted of murder because the FBI, which had set up the whole operation as a sting, did not cooperate with local police.)

Swamps teeming with man-eating alligators. Sinkholes that drop deep into the earth. Long-winding rivers and creeks barely known to man. Vast stretches of overgrown forests that even hunters and fishermen shy away from. Florida is the perfect place to get rid of a corpse.

Even though a few Florida murderers have been convicted without a body, the lack of remains makes the job of prosecutors much more difficult.

Eccentric people and bizarre plots: who knows what strange case is unfolding at this very moment in Florida?

Acknowledgments

These are the acknowledgments of Robert A. Waters:

Without New Horizon Press and Editor-in-Chief Dr. Joan S. Dunphy, this book would not have been possible. Thank you so much. Justin Gross, Editor-Publicist, and Ron Hart, Production Editor, also deserve praise.

If it weren't for my wife, Marilyn, I'd have never made it this far in life or as an author. As Barney Fife would say, "You're the cats."

My son and daughter, Sim and LeAnn, who have always supported their dad and his weird obsession with writing. Thanks.

My brother Zack, Civil War historian and author in his own right, has always encouraged me to the fullest.

A special thank you to my aunt Mary Beth Williamson, who researched "The Tattoo Man" and obtained information for me.

Two Internet friends and authors, Laura James from Michigan and Gary Boynton from Washington, edited the first draft of my original proposal as well as several chapters. Your suggestions paid off.

Thanks to Pastor Rod Myers of the Sarasota Central Church of Christ for his insights into the Carlie Brucia case and for the photographs of Carlie's Memorial Garden.

Fran, Dot and Glenn Moore have been special friends for many years now. I love y'all.

Finally, throughout the years, Central Church of Christ in Ocala, Florida, has been a place of hope and refuge for me and my family. A huge thank you to my fellow travelers in faith.

Resources

If you would like to donate or volunteer your services to these worthwhile foundations and organizations, please use this contact information.

Amanda Brown Foundation
5810 Dayton Street
Zephyrhills, FL 33542
http://www.amandabrownfoundation.org/
The Amanda Brown Foundation was formed to educate others about the dangers of child abductions and to provide families with resources, information and comfort during a crisis.

Carlie's Crusade Foundation
http://www.carliescrusade.org/
Provides parents and guardians with information about sex offender laws and also teaches children self-preservation/self-defense skills to help better defend themselves against abductions.

Defenders Motorcycle Club, Inc.
P.O. Box 10764
Naples, FL 34101-0764
http://www.defendersmc.org/
(Darla Lathrem Fallen Heroes Event)
A fraternal motorcycle club for active and retired law enforcement, emergency serv-ices, military and public safety professionals. The Defenders Motorcycle Club assists in raising money for families of local law enforcement officers, military per-sonal and firefighters.

National Center for Missing & Exploited Children
Charles B. Wang International Children's Building
699 Prince Street
Alexandria, Virginia 22314-3175
1-800-THE-LOST (1-800-843-5678)
http://www.missingkids.com/
The National Center for Missing & Exploited Children's mission is to help pre-vent child abduction and sexual exploitation, help find missing children and assist victims of child abduction and sexual exploitation, their families and the profession-als who serve them.

The Officer Down Memorial Page, Inc.
http://www.odmp.org/
Dedicated to honoring America's fallen law enforcement heroes. It is with great honor that the ODMP pays a lasting tribute to these officers by preserving their memories within its pages.

Vicki Robinson Foundation
P.O. Box 262691
Tampa, FL 33685-2691
http://vickirobinson.com/
Goal is to provide valuable information on residential treatment centers, counseling, religious programs, support groups, community service and other organizations helping troubled children and parents with troubled children.

Jimmy Ryce Center for Victims of Predatory Abduction
www.jimmyryce.org
Aims to increase public awareness of sexual predators and predatory abductions, as well as providing American Kennel Club (AKC) bloodhounds free to law enforcement to find abducted and lost children.

Thunder Beach Motorcycle Rally
PO Box 18259
Panama City Beach, FL
32417-8259
http://www.thunderbeachproductions.com/
(Kevin Kight Memorial Parade)
Assists in organizing/arranging charity events used to support families of law enforcement officers who have been killed or injured.

Bibliography

Adam Davis *v.* The State of Florida, No. SC00-313 (2003).

Allen Lee Davis *v.* The State of Florida, No. 76,640 (1982).

"Alligator Impedes Probe." *Jacksonville Journal,* May 18, 1982.

Allison, Karen. "Original Florida is Alive and Well in Redland."
http://fundandsun.com. (Accessed April 16, 2009).
http://fundandsun.com/1tocf/nat/red/redland.html

"Bonaficio Floro Wipes Tears." *Jacksonville Times-Union,* May 13, 1982.

Bragg, Rick. "Florida's Executions Put the Electric Chair on Trial." *New York Times,* November 18, 1999.

Buckley, Cara. "Farming's Uncertain Future – The Battle for the Redlands." *Miami Herald,* August 19, 2002.

Carlton, Sue, Thomas French and Anne Hull. "The Great Divide." *St. Petersburg Times,* April 9, 2000.

—. "Mad Love." *St. Petersburg Times,* April 10, 2000.

—. "The Lost Boy." *St. Petersburg Times,* April 14, 2000.

Carter, W. Horace. *Nature's Masterpiece at Homosassa.* Tabor City, NC: Atlantic Publishing Co., 1981.

Clark, Lesley. "Blood Death in the Chair." *Miami Herald,* July 9, 1999.

Cox, Mike. *The Confessions of Henry Lee Lucas.* Pocket Books, 1991.

Doig, Matthew. "Judges Didn't See '97 Report on Smith." *Sarasota Herald Tribune,* February 14, 2004.

Dwight T. Eaglin *v.* The State of Florida, No. SC06-760 (2003).

"Explaining Girl's Slaying a Tough Job for Teacher." *Jacksonville Journal,* May 13, 1982.

Florida Department of Law Enforcement Investigative Report Case #OR-20-0069 (2008).

"Florida Execution of 350 Pound Inmate Turns Bloody." *Miami Herald,* July 9, 1999.

Florida Supreme Court Loran Cole *v.* State of Florida, No. 87, 337. (1994).

Gerhard Hojan *v.* State of Florida, No. SC05-1687 (2003).

Greene, Bob. "Who Weeps for the Weiler Family?" *Chicago Tribune,* July 14, 1999.

Grimme, Don. "Night Workers May be Putting Their Lives on the Line for Their Jobs." *South Florida Sun Sentinel,* March 14, 2002.

Jame Bailey *v.* State of Florida, No. SC07-748 (2005).

Jimmy Mickel *v.* State of Florida, No. 4D04-1482 (2003).

Joseph Smith *v.* State of Florida, SC06-9747 (2004).

Juan Carlos Chavez *v.* The State of Florida, SC94586 (1996).

"Justice is Done." *Florida Times-Union,* July 9, 1999.

Kamiya, Gail. "Childhood's End." *Salon,* March 10, 2001.

Karsh, David. "Complete Interview with Dwight Eaglin." Waterman Broadcasting Co.(NBC2), March 8, 2006.

King, Brad. "The Case Against Charging Couey's Housemates." *St. Petersburg Times,* June 26, 2005.

McGarrahan, Ellen. "Florida Juice." *Slate,* July 22, 1999.

McCaslin, Daryl. "Media Advisory of Completion of Operational Review and Investigation." Florida Department of Corrections, January 20, 2004.

Orange County Sheriff's Office Supplemental Report Case #08-074777 (2008).

Ridley, Jim. "The Mysterious, Mundane Magic of Waffle House." *Nashville Scene*, August 11, 1997.

Robey, Sarina. Lee County Sheriff's Office, CFS #02-221418 (2002).

Robey, Steven. Lee County Sheriff's Office, CFS #02-221418 (2002).

Ryce, Claudine. "A Hug from Jimmy." *The Magazine of Stetson University* vol. 16, no. 1 (1997).

Sarasota County Sheriff's Office Case #04-9497 (2004).

State of Florida *v.* John Evander Couey, 2005-CF-298 (2006).

State of Florida *v.* Lionel Tate, 99-14401CF10A (2001).

Stephenson, Crocker. "Ex-guard Among 16 Charged in Gang Probe." *Milwaukee Journal Sentinel*, October 2, 2008.

Sugg, John. "A Florida Execution." *American Civil Liberties Union of Florida*, July 12, 1999.
http://www.aclufl.org/body_executionarticle799.html

Supreme Court *v.* Ronald Wayne Clark, SC 77, 156. (1990).

Walsh, John. "Adam Walsh Case Closed." http://www.amw.com. December 17, 2008.
http://www.amw.com/features/feature_story_detail.cfm?id=3078

—. *Tears of Rage*. New York: Pocket Books, 1997.

Waters, Robert A. "Interview with Drew Kesse." http://www.kidnapping-murderandmayhem.blogspot.com. August 12, 2008.
http://kidnappingmurderandmayhem.blogspot.com/search?updated-max=2008-09-09T06%3A15%3A00-07%3A00&max-results=29

White, Victoria. "Victim Tells of Kidnap, Rape, Fetal Ordeal." *St. Petersburg Times*, September 28, 1995.

Willie Seth Crain, Jr. *v.* State of Florida, SC00-661 (1999).